MARKET REPORT SERIES

OIL 2017
Analysis and Forecasts to 2022

Check out the new and improved *Oil Market Report* website!

The IEA has redesigned and improved its online *Oil Market Report* (*OMR*), making it easier for subscribers and non-subscribers to get important information from the site.

The *OMR* site — https://www.iea.org/oilmarketreport/ — now offers more powerful search options and a fully indexed archive of reports going back to 1990. The improved *OMR* also features interactive graphics as part of each monthly issue.

First published in 1983, the *OMR* provides the IEA view of the state of the international oil market, with projections for oil supply and demand 6 to 18 months ahead. For more information on subscribing to the *OMR*, please visit https://www.iea.org/oilmarketreport/subscription/.

INTERNATIONAL ENERGY AGENCY

The International Energy Agency (IEA), an autonomous agency, was established in November 1974. Its primary mandate was – and is – two-fold: to promote energy security amongst its member countries through collective response to physical disruptions in oil supply, and provide authoritative research and analysis on ways to ensure reliable, affordable and clean energy for its 29 member countries and beyond. The IEA carries out a comprehensive programme of energy co-operation among its member countries, each of which is obliged to hold oil stocks equivalent to 90 days of its net imports. The Agency's aims include the following objectives:

- Secure member countries' access to reliable and ample supplies of all forms of energy; in particular, through maintaining effective emergency response capabilities in case of oil supply disruptions.

- Promote sustainable energy policies that spur economic growth and environmental protection in a global context – particularly in terms of reducing greenhouse-gas emissions that contribute to climate change.

- Improve transparency of international markets through collection and analysis of energy data.

- Support global collaboration on energy technology to secure future energy supplies and mitigate their environmental impact, including through improved energy efficiency and development and deployment of low-carbon technologies.

- Find solutions to global energy challenges through engagement and dialogue with non-member countries, industry, international organisations and other stakeholders.

IEA member countries:
Australia
Austria
Belgium
Canada
Czech Republic
Denmark
Estonia
Finland
France
Germany
Greece
Hungary
Ireland
Italy
Japan
Korea
Luxembourg
Netherlands
New Zealand
Norway
Poland
Portugal
Slovak Republic
Spain
Sweden
Switzerland
Turkey
United Kingdom
United States

The European Commission also participates in the work of the IEA.

© OECD/IEA, 2017
International Energy Agency
Website: *www.iea.org*

Please note that this publication is subject to specific restrictions that limit its use and distribution. The terms and conditions are available online at *www.iea.org/t&c/*

FOREWORD

We present the findings of this year's report, which we have renamed the Market Report Series: Oil 2017 (formerly the *Medium-Term Oil Market Report*), in a very different market context than we saw a year ago, when surging OPEC production levels and stocks climbing ever upward contributed to prices falling to around USD 30 per barrel. Indeed today, the oil market is dramatically different as we return to formal market management by OPEC and leading non-OPEC producers and prices appear to have stabilised close to USD 55/bbl. This change is a reminder not only of the continued central importance of oil in global energy markets, but also why the IEA's continued emphasis on secure energy supplies remains so essential.

While the output reduction agreement takes shape, there is a broad debate on how quickly stocks will draw and when the market will rebalance. Another uncertainty is to what degree US light tight oil (LTO) and production from other non-OPEC countries will come bounding back, driven by higher oil prices and reduced production costs. Output levels are already edging up and look poised to rise over the course of this year. And the potential for new policies in the US that support further development have already boosted optimism in the oil patch there, though it will take some time for this to translate into new barrels.

While the US oil industry is seeing a revival, the dramatic declines in global oil industry investment over the last two years, and only modest signs of recovery in 2017, mean that it is far from clear that enough projects will enter the pipeline in the next few years to avoid a potentially tight market by 2020 and with it, the possibility of a price spike.

On the demand side, we see less uncertainty: growth will continue, driven mainly by Asia. India overtakes China as the main driver of demand growth, as was foreseen by the IEA some time ago. And while there has been much discussion and debate about a peak in oil demand, we see no such peak in sight. Thus, we will need to see more upstream oil investment and we will need to see it soon.

Given the many uncertainties on the production side and the expectation of sustained demand growth, many are predicting greater volatility in the oil market which generally has negative consequences for both consumers and producers. It is my hope that this report will provide clear insights on the next five years in the international oil market and that it will provide a constructive contribution to the debate. And in the meantime, the IEA will continue to watch the market, monitor developments and call for adequate investment to ensure secure energy supplies.

Dr. Fatih Birol
Executive Director
International Energy Agency

ACKNOWLEDGEMENTS

This publication was prepared by the Oil Industry and Markets Division (OIMD) of the International Energy Agency (IEA). Its main authors are, Toril Bosoni, Olivier Lejeune, Peg Mackey, Matthew Parry, Alfredo Peral, Kristine Petrosyan and Xiwei Emma Zhou. Nestor Abraham provided essential research and statistical support. Deven Mooneesawmy provided editorial assistance. Neil Atkinson, head of OIMD, edited the Report. Keisuke Sadamori, director of the IEA's Directorate of Energy Markets and Security, provided guidance.

Other IEA colleagues provided important contributions including Ali al-Saffar, Alessandro Blasi, Tyler Bryant, Emmanouil Christinakis, Davide D'Ambrosio, Kate Dourian, Marc Antoine Eyl-Mazzega, Nathan Frisbee, Marine Gorner, Tim Gould, Joerg Husar, Costanza Jacazio, Pharoah Le Feuvre, Cuauhtemoc Lopez-Bassols, Christophe McGlade, Pawel Olejarnik, Erica Robin, Sacha Scheffer, Renske Schuitmaker, Samuel Thomas, and Laszlo Varro.

The IEA Communications and Information Office provided production assistance and launch support. Particular thanks to Rebecca Gaghen and her team; Muriel Custodio, Adrien Chorlet, Astrid Dumond, Christopher Gully, Jad Mouawad, Bertrand Sadin, Rob Stone and Therese Walsh.

For questions and comments, please contact the Oil Industry and Markets Division.
For contact information, please see https://www.iea.org/oilmarketreport/contacts/

TABLE OF CONTENTS

Foreword 3

Acknowledgements 4

Table of Contents 5

Executive Summary 11

1. Demand 15

Highlights 15

Summary 16

OECD Demand 23
    Americas 24
    Europe 26
    Asia Oceania 27

Non-OECD Demand 28
    Africa 28
    Asia (non-OECD) 30
    Europe (non-OECD) 32
    Former Soviet Union (FSU) 33
    Latin America 34
    Middle East 36

2. Supply 39

Highlights 39

Trends in global oil supply 40

Non-OPEC supply overview 43
    United States 45
    Canada 49
    Mexico 53
    Brazil 54
    Other Latin America 56
    North Sea 57
    Australia 58
    People's Republic of China 59
    Other Asia 60
    Russia 61
    Kazakhstan 62
    Azerbaijan 62
    Africa 63
    OPEC 64

OPEC gas liquids supply 78

Biofuel supply 79
    Ethanol markets regional outlook 80

Table of Contents

    Biodiesel markets regional outlook 82

3. Refining and trade 85

Highlights 85

Overview 86

Refining sector outlook 87

Regional developments in refining 90
    North America 90
    Europe 91
    Former Soviet Union 91
    Middle East 92
    Africa 93
    People's Republic of China 93
    India 95
    Other Asia 95
    Latin America 96

Crude oil trade 96

Product trade 100
    LPG/ethane 100
    Gasoline/naphtha 101
    Diesel/kerosene 102
    Fuel oil 103
    Physical flows: implications for shipping 103

Developments in marine bunkers 104
    Switch to low sulphur fuel oil 105
    Switch to diesel 106
    On-board scrubbers 108
    Switch to alternative fuels 109

Conclusion 109

4. Trends in global oil storage 111

Highlights 111

Global overview 112
    OECD Americas 115
    OECD Europe 120
    OECD Asia Oceania 122
    Non-OECD Asia 124
    Middle East 127
    Africa 128
    Former Soviet Union 129
    Latin America 129

5. TABLES 133

LIST OF FIGURES

Figure ES.1 Global oil market balance 12
Figure 1.1 Global composition of total oil demand, 2014-22 17
Figure 1.2 Adjusted corporate average fuel efficiency for light-duty vehicles in the US 18
Figure 1.3 Global oil demand and savings from vehicle fuel economy standards (left) and 19
Figure 1.4 Average annual fleet-wide efficiency improvement of new passenger 20
Figure 1.5 Share of global energy consumption in LDVs and medium- and heavy- 21
Figure 1.6 Product specific breakdown of global oil demand, 2014-22 21
Figure 1.7 Global electric vehicle fleet 22
Figure 1.8 Relative evolutions of OECD and non-OECD oil demand, 2002-22 23
Figure 1.9 OECD Americas: oil demand, 2014-22 24
Figure 1.10 United States oil demand, 2014-22 25
Figure 1.11 Slowing pace of dieselisation 26
Figure 1.12 OECD Europe oil demand, 2010-22 27
Figure 1.13 Per capita European oil demand, 2016 and 2022 27
Figure 1.14 Japanese oil demand, 2010-22 28
Figure 1.15 Per capita oil demand, Africa, Europe and the US, 2016 and 2022 29
Figure 1.16 African oil demand, 2002-22 29
Figure 1.17 Chinese oil demand, 2010-22 30
Figure 1.18 Indian oil demand, 2010-22 31
Figure 1.19 Non-OECD Asia (excluding China) oil demand, 2002-22 32
Figure 1 20 Russian oil demand, 2010-22 34
Figure 1.21 Brazilian oil demand, 2010-22 35
Figure 1.22 Saudi Arabian oil demand, 2010-22 36
Figure 1.23 UAE oil demand, 2010-22 37
Figure 1.24 IRAN oil demand, 2010-22 37
Figure 2.1 Global liquids capacity growth 40
Figure 2.2 Global capacity growth 2016-22 40
Figure 2.3 Upstream investment and IEA global cost index 42
Figure 2.4 Selected sources of non-OPEC supply changes, 2016-22 43
Figure 2.5 Supply from non-OPEC top five sources of growth vs others 44
Figure 2.6 Annual increase from non-OPEC top five sources of growth vs. others 44
Figure 2.7 US total oil production 45
Figure 2.8 US oil output growth by type 45
Figure 2.9 Average oil well performance by US Shale play 46
Figure 2.10 Oil production per rig 46
Figure 2.11 US rig count vs oil price 46
Figure 2.12 US light tight oil production 46
Figure 2.13 US light tight oil production sensitivities 47
Figure 2.14 Estimated US ethane rejection 49
Figure 2.15 US LPG exports 49
Figure 2.16 Canada total oil production 50
Figure 2.17 Canada annual supply growth 50
Figure 2.18 US crude receipts from Canada 52
Figure 2.19 Crude oil prices 52

Table of Contents

Figure 2.20 Mexico total oil production 53
Figure 2.21 Brazil total oil production 54
Figure 2.22 Colombia total oil production 56
Figure 2.23 Norway oil production 58
Figure 2.24 UK oil production 58
Figure 2.25 China oil production 59
Figure 2.26 China 2016 annual output change 59
Figure 2.27 Chinese oversea investment 60
Figure 2.28 Russia total oil production 61
Figure 2.29 Russia y-o-y supply growth 2015-22 61
Figure 2.30 Average production costs (incl. taxes) of key producers in 2015 62
Figure 2.31 Evolution of production drilling rates in Russia, 2013-2016E 62
Figure 2.32 Low-cost Middle East drives growth 64
Figure 2.33 OPEC's cash crunch 65
Figure 2.34 Iraq leads growth 67
Figure 2.35 Iran rebuilds 68
Figure 2.36 UAE posts solid growth 70
Figure 2.37 Saudi sustains capacity 73
Figure 2.38 Angola, Nigeria struggle 75
Figure 2.39 Global biofuels production and growth 2016-22 80
Figure 3.1   Crude prices supported refinery margins in 2015 and constrained them in 2016 86
Figure 3.2   Refined product oversupply in 2014-15 resulted in refining slowdown in 2016 86
Figure 3.3   Annual refinery throughput changes 87
Figure 3.4   Global liquid fuels supply structure in 2016 88
Figure 3.5   Global refinery capacity net additions by region 89
Figure 3.6   Unused distillation capacity by region 89
Figure 3.7   Russian refinery intake annual growth 92
Figure 3.8   Middle East refining capacity changes 92
Figure 3.9   African developments by subcontinent 93
Figure 3.10 Developments in Chinese refining 94
Figure 3.11 Top five net importers of crude oil 96
Figure 3.12 Changes in net crude oil exports 98
Figure 3.13 Geographical structure of US imports 99
Figure 3.14 East of Suez crude oil balances 99
Figure 3.15 Tonnage requirements for oil products, 2016 vs 2022 104
Figure 3.16 Sulphur content in straight-run products 105
Figure 3.17 How refiners meet final oil product demand 106
Figure 3.18 Crude oil and diesel market drivers 107
Figure 3.19 Scrubber payback periods 109
Figure 3.20 Oil bunker fuel structure 110
Figure 4.1   Planned storage capacity growth by region and country 111
Figure 4.2   OECD oil stock falls since July 2016 112
Figure 4.3   OECD oil stocks vs North Sea Dated price 113
Figure 4.4   Mexico's industry product stocks 115
Figure 4.5   US tank storage capacity growth by PADD 116
Figure 4.6   Storage capacity under construction, expansion and planned in Canada, US 117

Figure 4.7 Mexico's net oil exports 118
Figure 4.8 Storage capacity under construction, expansion and planned in OECD Europe................ 122
Figure 4.9 Storage capacity under construction, expansion and planned in OECD Asia Oceania 123
Figure 4.10 China's implied crude stock change vs Dubai oil price... 124
Figure 4.11 Storage capacity under construction, expansion and planned in non OECD Asia 127
Figure 4.12 Storage capacity under construction, expansion and planned in the Middle East......... 128
Figure 4.13 Crude, product exports from five Middle East countries 130
Figure 4.14 Differentials to Dated Brent 132
Figure 4.15 BFOE, Troll crude loadings (left), Crude imports into Rotterdam (right) 132

LIST OF MAPS

Map 1.1 Global oil demand growth, by region, 2004-22 16
Map 2.1 Canada oil infrastructure 51
Map 2.2 Iran's oil and gas fields 69
Map 2.3 Libya's oil infrastructure... 71
Map 2.4 Nigeria's oil infrastructure 76
Map 3.1 Regional crude oil balances in 2016 and 2022 (mb/d)... 97
Map 3.2 Regional LPG/ethane balances in 2016 and 2022 (kb/d).. 101
Map 3.3 Regional gasoline/naphtha balances in 2016 and 2022 (kb/d)...................................... 102
Map 3.4 Regional gasoil/kerosene balances in 2016 and 2022 (kb/d) 102
Map 3.5 Regional fuel oil balances in 2016 and 2022 (kb/d) 103
Map 4.1: Mexico's oil infrastructure 119

LIST OF TABLES

Table 1.1 Global oil product demand (mb/d).. 15
Table 1.2 Global GDP growth forecast 16
Table 1.3 Asian oil demand; total (kb/d), per capita (b/d) 31
Table 1.4 Non-OECD European oil demand, kb/d 32
Table 1.5 Oil demand growth (kb/d) in the major economies of the former Soviet Union 34
Table 1.6 Latin American oil demand (kb/d) 35
Table 1.7 Middle Eastern oil demand (kb/d).. 36
Table 2.1 Selected company spending and production plans 41
Table 2.2 Non-OPEC supply (mb/d)... 44
Table 2.3 Estimated sustainable OPEC crude production capacity (mb/d)................................. 65
Table 2.4 Estimated OPEC condensate and NGL production (kb/d) 79
Table 3.1 Total oil demand and call on refineries 88
Table 3.2 Regional developments in refining capacity and throughput 90
Table 3.3 To scrub or to refine – comparative economics 108
Table 4.1 Storage capacity under construction, expansion and planned globally (mb) 113
Table 4.2 The 10 largest tank farms under construction/expansion globally 114
Table 4.3 The 10 largest planned storage additions in the US and Canada (mb) 117
Table 4.4 The 10 largest planned storage additions in OECD Europe (mb) 120

Table 4.5 Storage capacity under construction, expansion and planned in Europe (mb) 121
Table 4.6 The 10 largest planned storage additions in OECD Asia Oceania (mb) 123
Table 4.7 China's Strategic Petroleum Reserve 125
Table 4.8 India's Strategic Petroleum Reserve 126

LIST OF BOXES

Box 1.1 Efficiency policies curb demand growth 17
Box 1.2 Rapid gains in electric vehicle stock forecast but with only muted impact on global 22
Box 1.3 Emissions concerns impact dieselisation 25
Box 1.4 Jet fuel demand continues to fly 33
Box 2.1 Upstream investment sees modest increase in 2017, but costs rise too 41
Box 2.2 If the price is right 47
Box 2.3 New outlets spur US NGL supply boom 48
Box 2.4 Canadian producers eye export expansion, rail use to rise 50
Box 2.5 China slows pace on overseas oil investment 60
Box 2.6 OPEC takes charge 65
Box 2.7 Iran bounces back 68
Box 2.8 Libya's fragile recovery 71
Box 3.1 Lock, stock and 15 million extra barrels 89
Box 3.2 Security of oil supply: implications for Asian importers 99
Box 3.3 Will French dentists come to the rescue of the global shipping industry? 107
Box 4.1 Mexico energy liberalisation to boost private oil storage 118
Box 4.2 Oil price benchmarks move with the times 130

EXECUTIVE SUMMARY

In last year's Report, we noted that we were living through the first essentially free market in oil seen in modern times. A year later however, market management is back. The great experiment that started at the end of 2014 with OPEC's historic decision to pursue a market share strategy has ended and we are now coming to terms with the most comprehensive output reduction agreement seen since 2008.

The agreement, and its potential implications forms the backdrop of this year's five-year oil-market forecast, now called Market Report Series: Oil 2017 (formerly the *Medium-Term Oil Market Report*). We obviously can't say how long it will last because of the complex inter-action between judgements of oil market fundamentals and political factors that lie behind the deal. But we do know that the decision by OPEC and eleven non-OPEC producers to cut production for the first six months of 2017 has led to an increase in oil prices. Until the agreement was struck prices threatened to return to the levels seen in early 2016 when Brent crude oil traded for a time below USD 30/bbl. A repeat of such low prices would have been unwelcome for all oil producers whether they were involved in the agreement or not, although clearly it would have provided a shot in the arm for consumers.

The fall in oil prices upended the budget assumptions of all the producers, not just national companies entrusted with social and political obligations at home, but also their peers in the private sector. For OPEC countries, export revenues slumped to an estimated USD 450 billion in 2016, down from USD 1.2 trillion in 2012, causing major budgetary strains and in some cases making difficult political situations even worse.

Global oil and gas upstream investment fell by 25% in 2015 and by another 26% in 2016, affecting the major oil companies and smaller independents alike. In 2017 there are modest signs of recovery led by higher investment in the US light tight oil region. Alongside falling prices, costs have dropped significantly: we estimate that global upstream costs declined by 15% in 2015 and 17% in 2016. For their part, US light tight oil (LTO) producers saw even more striking cost reductions of 30% in 2015 and 22% in 2016. This also gives a clear indication that many are capable of positioning themselves to raise production in a lower price environment.

Another period of falling prices could have further pushed back critical investment decisions, and threatened the production recovery needed in the second half of our forecast. As it stands, when investment does recover, it will serve an industry that is far leaner and fitter than it ever was and that will be able to deliver more with less.

While the ultimate success or failure of the production agreement cannot be judged for some time, it is evident that the output cuts, totalling 1.8 mb/d if fully implemented, are taking place just as production from the non-OPEC sector as a whole, led by the US, is actually recovering – after falling in 2016 for the first time since 2008 – and when stocks of crude oil and products are at record highs. This scenario of ample supply, even as output cuts are implemented, explains the very flat crude-oil price futures curve on which our five-year forecast is based.

The price outlook is not static, of course, and towards the end of the period there is relatively little liquidity to aid price discovery. But what it does tell us is that investors do not expect oil supply to fall short of demand, even though the investment climate remains poor. We have examined worldwide projects and assessed the likelihood of their completion. Our analysis suggests that, unless additional projects are given the green light soon, towards the end of our forecast horizon we will be in a 104 mb/d market and the call on OPEC crude and stock change rises from 32.2 mb/d in 2016 to 35.8 mb/d in 2022. With the group forecast to add 1.95 mb/d to production capacity in this period, this implies that available spare production capacity will fall below 2 mb/d.

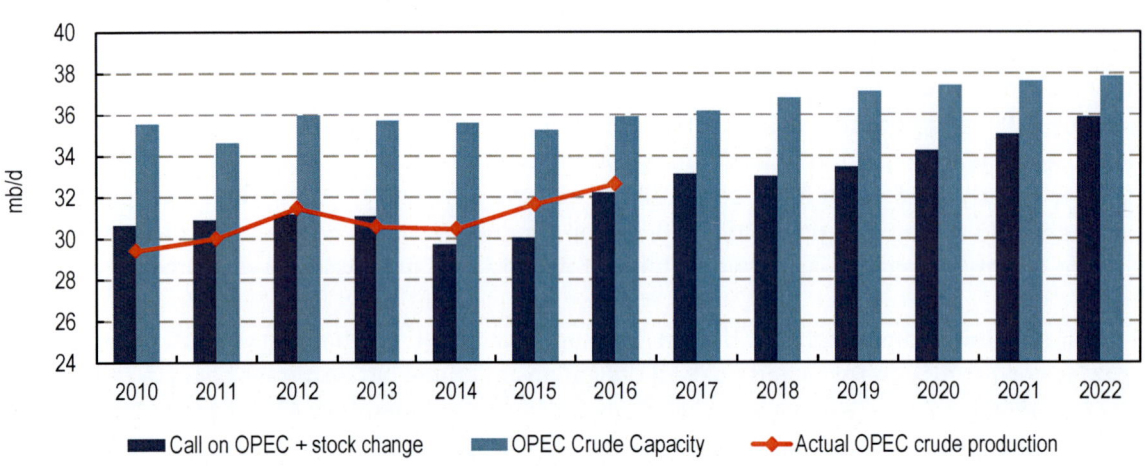

Figure ES.1 Global oil market balance

This suggests that the oil market will tighten and price expectations will rise. As today's overhang of surplus stocks is eroded, the main issue is whether or not investment recovers, and whether governments and companies take the current confidence that there is a floor under oil prices due to production management and bring forward new projects. If they do, then we can add to the known projects list for OPEC and non-OPEC countries, and concerns about a low spare capacity cushion will ease, and the current futures curve will prove to be resilient. If not, then new projects will not be brought forward and the curve will take a turn upwards, though we cannot be sure how sharply prices might rise.

Looking in more detail at the demand side of the balance, the recent tendency has been for numbers to be revised upwards. This is partly due to changes to historical data that raise the baseline for our forecasts as well as colder-than-expected northern hemisphere winters and other unforeseen events. But the dramatic fall in crude oil prices from the average of USD 100/bbl that prevailed in 2011-2014 to the average of USD 50/bbl in 2015-2016 clearly had a major impact on demand growth. We have emphasised the impact on producers of low prices, but they have clearly been a huge boost to consumers of oil.

In 2015, demand grew by 2.0 mb/d, the biggest year-on-year growth since the exceptional post-financial crisis recovery year of 2010, which was followed with very robust growth of 1.6 mb/d in 2016, including unexpected growth in the mature OECD markets partly due to colder than normal winter weather and higher demand from industrial fuel users. Our outlook for demand in this report is little changed from the one we published a year ago: global oil demand is expected to grow on average by 1.2 mb/d each year to 2022.

This net global figure contains OECD demand falling by an average 0.2 mb/d per year due to long term trends in fuel efficiency standards – discussed in detail in the demand section of the report – and changing demographics. In the non-OECD countries, there is still plenty of growth potential and we expect an upside of 1.4 mb/d each year to 2022. India, particularly, is gradually becoming the focus of attention as Chinese demand growth slows. Twenty years of strong demand growth in China, fuelled by rapid industrialisation and infrastructure spending, is giving way to a slower pace as the Chinese economy moves towards a services and consumer-led structure. In the five years to 2016, Chinese demand grew by 4.8% a year, compared with growth of 5.5% in the five-year period ending in 2011. For the period to 2022, China's demand will grow at an average annual rate of 2.4%.

Indian per capita oil consumption is just 1.2 barrels per year today, and the number is expected to reach 1.5 barrels per year by 2022. This compares to China's 3 barrels per capita per year today, a figure expected to be 2.5 by 2022. Although a direct comparison between India and China does not take into account societal and economic differences, the overall point is valid; there is clearly still plenty of growth to come from India. Indeed, that is also probably true for transportation fuels in many other developing economies, as more families move up the income scale and buy their first car. In our forecast period, this will almost certainly be gasoline-fuelled. While the much-discussed growth in the electric vehicles fleet is a very important longer term issue for oil demand, by 2022 we estimate that only limited volumes of global transport fuel demand will be lost to EVs from conventional fuels.

This Oil 2017 market report also looks at the implications of tighter vehicle efficiency standards now being applied to trucks for transport fuel demand. Even though big savings will be achieved over time, within our five-year outlook it is a question of merely slowing the rate of growth, rather than seeing a major change to the pattern of demand. The change in marine fuel specifications due to take place in 2020, another issue affecting transport fuels growth, is also analysed in some detail in this report. Although there are considerable uncertainties around the implementation of the International Maritime Organisation's regulations, we estimate that 0.2 mb/d of fuel consumption will be lost to the specification change and to LNG. For all these reasons, the much-discussed peak for oil demand remains some years into the future.

With oil demand growth expected to be steady, there are many issues on the supply side that shape our forecast. Perhaps the most relevant, because it is going on right now, is the pace at which LTO producers in the United States are able to turn the big increase in drilling activity we have seen in recent months into sustainable production growth. We believe that by the end of 2017, LTO production will be approximately 500 kb/d higher than a year earlier. Even in a world where oil prices do not move sustainably above USD 60/bbl, LTO production will continue to grow through 2022, adding 1.4 mb/d over the period, reflecting the enormous cost savings and efficiency improvements that have been made in what remains to a certain extent an experimental sector of the oil industry. If oil prices were to rise sharply to, say, USD 80/bbl our sensitivity analysis suggests that LTO production could rise by as much as 3 mb/d by 2022. The other countries that are expected to see their production increase significantly in our forecast period are Brazil, Canada and Kazakhstan, which will see their cumulative output rising 2.2 mb/d by 2022, reaping the rewards of investment decisions taken before oil prices declined. Total non-OPEC supplies are expected to rise 3.3 mb/d over the period.

We must acknowledge the discussion of a return to nuclear-related sanctions against Iran. At the time of writing there is no clarity on this issue and our forecast makes no assumption of change to the current arrangements. Another factor that might impact our outlook in the later years is the so-called Border Adjustment Tax that might be introduced in the US. At the time of writing however, there is little detail available on this issue and we have made no provision for it in our forecast. Likewise, we do not make any change to our numbers concerning whether the 2025 US target for a 54.5 miles per gallon fuel efficiency target might be rolled back.

Elsewhere in OPEC countries, how the situations in Libya, Nigeria and Venezuela will develop in the period to 2022 is hard to predict. Libya's situation is the most intractable but our working assumption is that production capacity there will increase modestly. For Nigeria and Venezuela, we have made very little change to our expectations of sustainable production capacity. In any event, the bulk of the growth will come from the major producers in the Middle East, who will contribute an estimated 1.79 mb/d to the total growth in OPEC production capacity of 1.95 mb/d. Production capacity is one thing; actual production is something else and the return of output management makes this part of the market balance harder to forecast.

Having taken into account the outlook for oil demand and supply, an interesting message that emerges is the changing pattern of global trade flows. In our forecast period, net export flows from OPEC countries – incorporating growth from the main Middle East producers but declines from elsewhere - will increase by 0.5 mb/d. This is significantly less than the forecast incremental growth in export potential from Brazil and Canada of approximately 1.6 mb/d. The Middle East producers, traditionally amongst the leading suppliers to growing Asian markets, cannot alone meet the growth in Asia's crude import requirement which will rise from 21 mb/d in 2016 to 25 mb/d in 2022 due to growth in demand and the decline in regional production. The East of Suez crude oil balance will fall further into deficit.

Evolving trade flows highlight the need for additional storage capacity. Over the past two years, a global supply overhang created trading and storage opportunities, particularly in non-OECD countries, where rising demand and import requirements have led to a build-up of strategic and commercial reserves. In this Report, for the first time, we provide an in-depth review of global storage developments to highlight where investments are being made.

In presenting our latest oil market analysis and forecast in Oil 2017, we are emphasising an important message: more investment is needed in oil production capacity to avoid the risk of a sharp increase in oil prices towards the end of our outlook period. The oil market today seems remarkably sanguine about this issue, but this feeling might not persist for too long before the realisation dawns that unwelcome price pressures might lie ahead.

1. DEMAND

Highlights

- **Global oil demand growth will average 1.2 mb/d, or 1.2% per annum, in 2016-22, equivalent to a net gain of 7.3 mb/d.** The forecast is roughly three-tenths of a percentage point below the growth seen in 2010-16.

- **From an average of 96.6 mb/d in 2016, global oil product demand will rise to 103.8 mb/d by 2022**, and it will break through the totemic level of 100 mb/d in 2019.

- **Underpinning this solid forecast is accelerating global economic growth.** According to the International Monetary Fund (IMF) GDP will grow at an average rate of 3.7% in 2017-22, with an accelerating trend through to the end of the decade, compared to the decelerating growth seen in 2014 to 2016.

- **On the flipside, forecasts of demand growth will be constrained by assumed improvements in vehicle fuel efficiencies and ongoing structural changes in the Chinese economy**, where the focus has already started to shift to domestic consumer demand and away from an oil-intensive, heavy manufacturing/export driven base. A continuation of this trend is foreseen through 2022.

- **The transport and petrochemical sectors account for the majority of the forecast growth,** at just under one-half and just over one-third of global demand growth, respectively, 2016-22.

- **Non-OECD countries account for all the growth forecast to 2022.** A modest net decline is seen in the OECD area due to slower economic growth and higher assumed vehicle efficiency improvements. Non-OECD oil demand rises by 8.5 mb/d, while OECD demand contracts by a net 1.2 mb/d over the forecast period. By 2022, non-OECD demand will be 28% larger than in the OECD.

- **Tightening marine emissions legislation shakes up bunker fuel demand from 2020.** With the International Maritime Organisation (IMO) confirming its proposed January 2020 start-up for the global limitation on marine sulphur oxide emissions, to 0.5% from its current 3.5% threshold, significant changes in the makeup of marine demand are anticipated. Although scrubbers can be retrofitted to vessels, allowing high-sulphur fuel oil to be used, adoption rates are likely to be restrained by the close proximity of the 2020 deadline. Hence, a combination of switching to marine diesel, blended products, low-sulphur fuel oil and/or liquefied natural gas (LNG) will be seen, along with some use of high-sulphur fuel oil.

Table 1.1 Global oil product demand (mb/d)

	2015	2016	2017	2018	2019	2020	2021	2022
OECD	46.4	46.7	46.8	46.6	46.4	46.2	45.9	45.5
Non-OECD	48.6	49.8	51.2	52.6	54.1	55.5	56.9	58.3
Total	**95.0**	**96.6**	**98.0**	**99.3**	**100.5**	**101.7**	**102.8**	**103.8**

DEMAND

Summary

The transport and petrochemical sectors will support relatively robust global oil product demand growth of 1.2% per annum in 2016-22; equivalent to a net gain of 7.3 mb/d. From 96.6 mb/d in 2016, global demand will rise to 103.8 mb/d by 2022, breaching the 100 mb/d threshold on the way in 2019. Growth will be on average three-tenths of a percentage point below the previous comparable time period, 2010-16, as efficiency gains, ongoing structural changes in the Chinese economy and fuel switching largely offset the impetus of accelerating global economic growth.

Table 1.2 Global GDP growth forecast

	OMR 2017, based on IMF January 2017	IMF October 2016	OMR 2016, based on IMF January 2016
2017	3.4%	3.4%	3.6%
2018	3.6%	3.6%	3.7%
2019	3.7%	3.7%	3.9%
2020	3.7%	3.7%	4.0%
2021	3.8%	3.8%	4.0%

Source: International Monetary Fund, *World Economic Outlook*.

Our GDP growth assumptions are derived from the IMF's October 2016 *World Economic Outlook*, partially updated in January 2017. This shows global growth averaging 3.7% in 2017-22, two-tenths of a percentage point higher than the previous six-year period and sharply up on 2016 when global economic growth was estimated at 3.1%. Furthermore, the IMF outlines a broadly accelerating economic growth forecast, in complete contrast to recent years. Our oil demand outlook is thus underpinned by a stronger macroeconomic environment.

Map 1.1 Global oil demand growth, by region, 2004-22

Despite this support, the IMF's October and January projections for global economic growth have

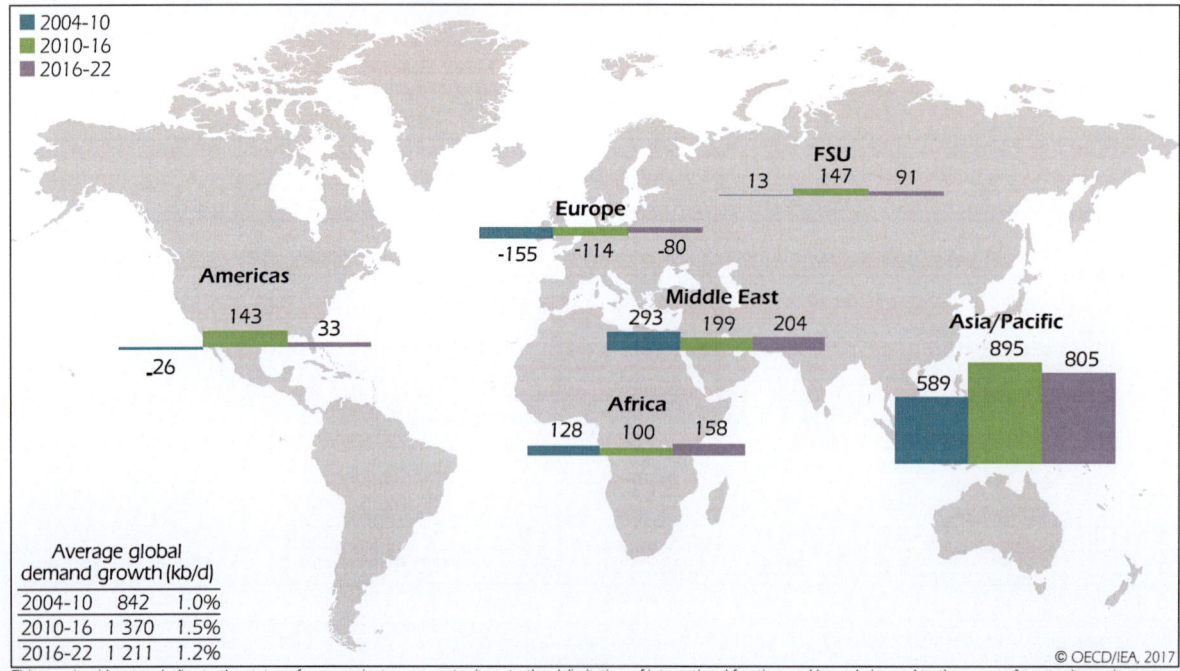

16   OIL MARKET REPORT 2017

been curbed by roughly two-tenths of a percentage point compared to those used in last year's *Report* (Table 1.2). Global economic growth is still forecast to be higher each year, post-2016, but lower than previously forecast. Any negative impact upon the oil demand forecast is, however, curbed by lower underlying oil price assumptions.

Among the major countries and regions of the world that contribute most to the weaker global economic outlook, compared to last year's *Report*, are India, France, Germany and the IMF's 'Middle East, North Africa, Afghanistan and Pakistan' regional grouping. Notable upgrades include the UK, Japan, People's Republic of China (hereafter referred to as China) and Russia.

This year's *Report* includes a significant number of important historical data revisions, adding approximately 0.5 mb/d to the 2015 baseline global demand estimate. The majority of the additions are seen in the US, Middle East and China, the latter largely due to revisions to refinery and import data.

Non-OECD economies are forecast to contribute a net 8.5 mb/d of oil demand growth in 2016 to 2022, while OECD countries overall decline by 1.2 mb/d. By 2022, non-OECD economies account for 56% of global demand.

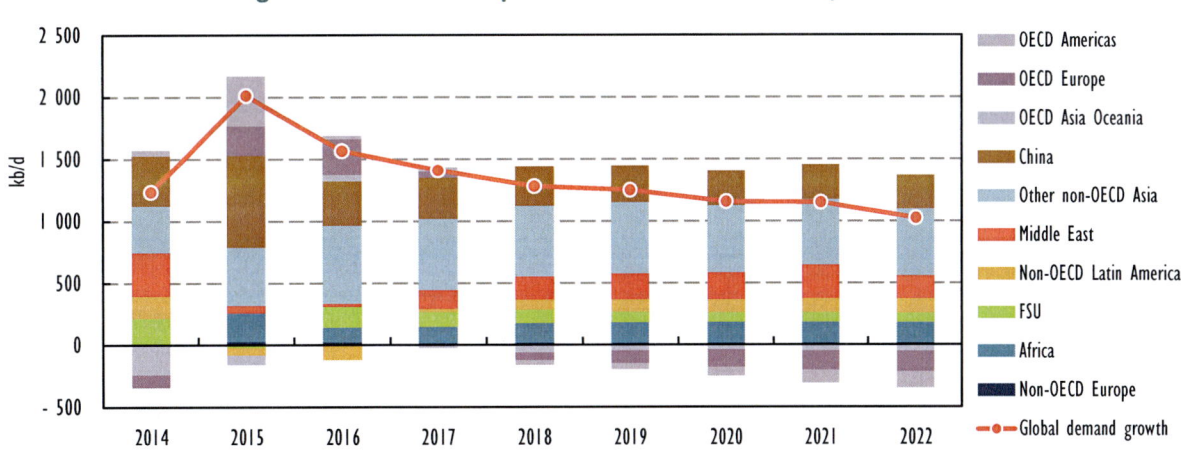

Figure 1.1 Global composition of total oil demand, 2014-22

Along with the trend towards more efficient oil use, two other factors that will curtail growth are the emerging structural shift that is occurring in the Chinese economy and the switching of demand from oil to natural gas and electricity. As China increasingly moves away from its reliance on heavy manufacturing and exports, oil intensity will fall and demand growth will ease.

> **Box 1.1 Efficiency policies curb demand growth**
>
> The world is becoming a more efficient consumer of oil due to a combination of high prices, when the price of Brent crude oil averaged more than USD 100/bbl in the period 2011-14, and active government policies. Mandatory fuel economy standards now cover roughly three-quarters of demand would have been 2.3 mb/d higher in 2014 than was the case (Energy Efficiency Market Report 2016).

Box 1.1 Efficiency policies curb demand growth (continued)

global passenger vehicle sales and are having a significant impact on consumption. Without these standards, global

The strong link between efficiency policies and outcomes can be seen with particular clarity in the US, where corporate average fuel economy (CAFE) standards effectively raised fuel economy by 39% as far back as between 1975 and 1985 (Figure 1.2). The period between 1985 and 2005 was, however, one of relative policy inactivity in the US and the fuel economy of the passenger fleet worsened, as bigger and more powerful vehicles increased their market share. Note that CAFE standards do not regulate the efficiency of specific models; instead, manufacturers must comply with a minimum average efficiency of all vehicles sold in a given year. CAFE standards thus give manufacturers flexibility to sell high and low efficiency vehicles while still achieving average improvements over the fleet of new vehicles purchased by consumers.

Figure 1.2 Adjusted corporate average fuel efficiency for light-duty vehicles in the US (litres/100 km)

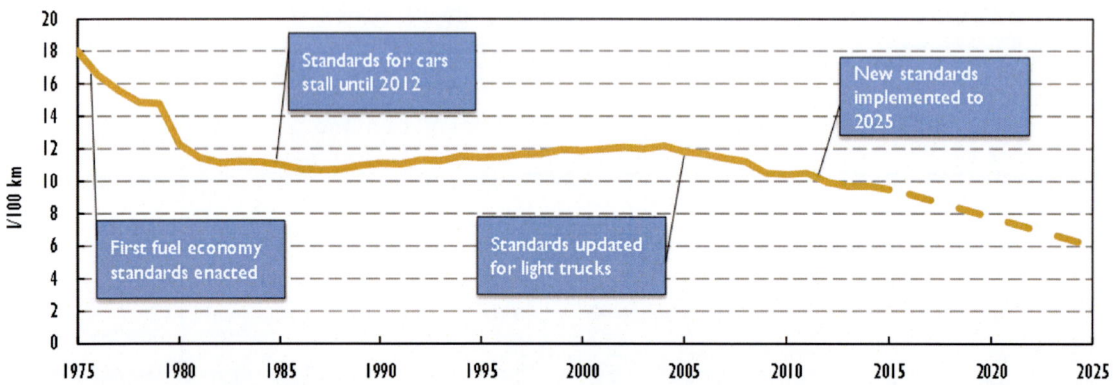

Standards for light-duty trucks in the United States were updated in 2005, and in 2012 the government implemented a comprehensive new regime that is set to run until 2025; it aims to improve the fuel economy of light-duty trucks by a further 34% between 2016 and 2025. Preliminary estimates for 2016 suggest that fuel economy gains continue to be made under the CAFE standards, despite lower gasoline prices.

Both the global coverage and strength of passenger vehicle efficiency standards are expanding. In 2015, 52% of all energy consumed by passenger vehicles was regulated by standards – up from 38% in 2000. China, the only non-OECD country to fully implement fuel economy standards, as of 2015, transitioned its vehicle standards to a corporate average approach in 2012. The efficiency of the Chinese light-duty vehicle fleet improved by an average 2.2% between 2013 and 2015 – a marked acceleration over the 0.3% improvement seen between 2005 and 2013. Japan has increased the minimum performance of its vehicle standards by more than any other country, improving efficiency by 27% since 2000 (International Council on Clean Transportation (ICCT)), 2015). If every major vehicle market had followed Japan's lead and improved their standards at the same rate, oil demand would have been a further 2 mb/d lower in 2015 (Figure 1.3). In other words, if the best-in-class efficiency standards on passenger vehicles were adopted around the world in 2005, the reduction in oil consumption would have jumped to 4.3 mb/d in 2015, which was equivalent to the total oil product demand of Canada and Mexico.

Box 1.1 Efficiency policies curb demand growth (continued)

Figure 1.3 Global oil demand and savings from vehicle fuel economy standards (left) and the additional savings potential of best in class standards in 2015 (right)

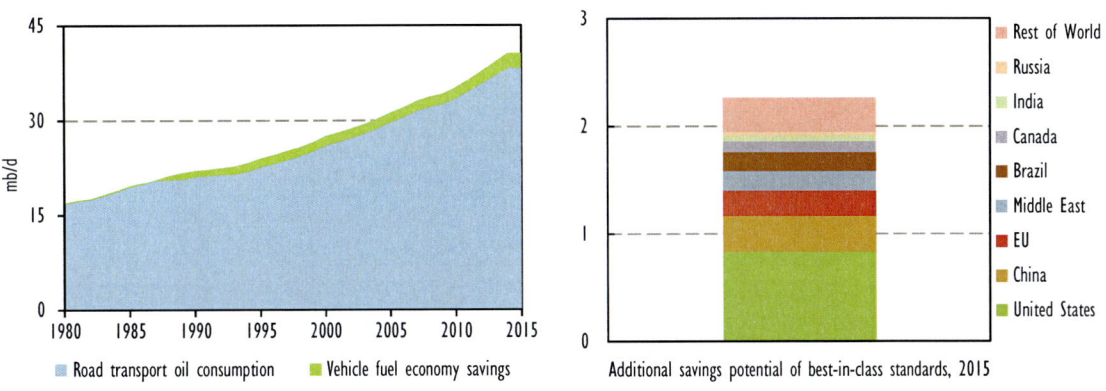

After reviewing existing standards, the United States Environmental Protection Agency (EPA) concluded that the fuel economy levels mandated by the standards to 2025 are technically feasible and cost-effective. The EPA subsequently finalised the rules for automakers in late 2016. Should these standards remain unchanged by the new administration, vehicle efficiency would increase by an additional 34% by 2025. India will start implementing standards for new passenger vehicles beginning in 2017, aiming to drive down the fuel consumption of new cars by 15% by 2021. In most other major markets, improving efficiency is increasingly recognised as a cost-effective means to reduce oil product demand, greenhouse gas emissions, local air pollutants, import dependence and consumer expenditure, meaning that efficiency standards are likely to strengthen, especially if the cost of energy efficiency measures, such as increased use of electric vehicles, continues to decline.

The impact of lower oil prices on vehicle efficiency

While standards are tightening, the decline in oil prices since late 2014 has moderated efficiency gains in some markets. Since 2014, the average efficiency gain of new passenger vehicle sales in the United States slowed to less than half that of 2005-13 (Figure 1.4). Japan's 2015 fuel economy targets for vehicles were achieved by 2010, which allowed manufacturers some regulatory headroom for the average efficiency of new vehicle sales to fluctuate above the target. Average fuel economy in Japan peaked in 2014, 15% higher than the 2015 target. Higher adoption rates of larger vehicles coupled with a size and weight-based approach (rather than a corporate average approach) to regulating fuel economy saw the average efficiency slide by 4% by 2015 though still 11% than the 2015 target. Japan's 2020 target transitioned to a corporate average approach which should moderate future backsliding in efficiency.

The resurgence of sales for light-duty trucks (sports utility vehicles, pick-up trucks, minivans and crossovers), which typically consume more fuel per kilometre, intensified during the recent fall in fuel prices. This trend was particularly noticeable in the United States, where the relatively large decline in fuel prices, due to lower taxes, led to a seven percentage-point increase in the market share of light-duty trucks and sport utility vehicles (SUV) since 2013 *(EPA, 2016)*. Light truck and SUV sales reached an all-time high in 2015 and now make up over half of all vehicle sales in the United States.

Box 1.1 Efficiency policies curb demand growth (continued)

In other markets, the picture was more mixed with strong growth of light-duty trucks in the share of sales in Turkey, the United Kingdom and Korea, but small declines in France and Germany.

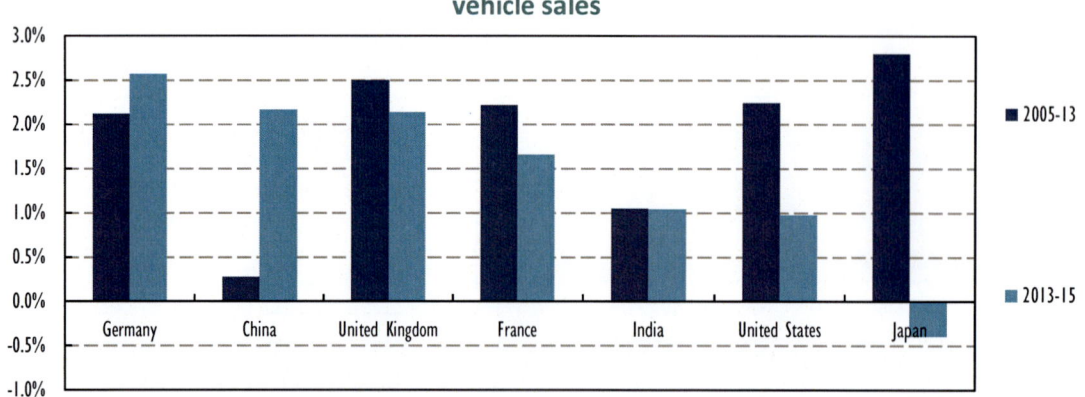

Figure 1.4 Average annual fleet-wide efficiency improvement of new passenger vehicle sales

Source: IHS Polk (2016), *Vehicle Registrations and Other Characteristics at Model Level* (database), IHS, Information Handling Services Markit, London

In China, vehicle sales have been surging and consumers show an increasing preference for light-duty trucks and SUVs. Sales of light-duty trucks grew 66% since 2013, outpacing the 21% growth in all passenger vehicle sales. China's new fuel economy regulations implemented in 2012 (which target corporate average fuel efficiency improvements as opposed to vehicle-specific standards) have sped up the average fuel economy improvement of new vehicles even with increasing truck sales (Figure 1.3). This is expected to continue as the standards for 2016 to 2020 are targeting more ambitious efficiency improvements (ICCT, 2014).

The next phase for efficiency gains in transport: Freight Trucks

There is growing recognition among policy makers of the need to improve the efficiency of medium and heavy-duty trucks. The IEA estimates that only 13% of energy consumption in this vehicle class is subject to efficiency standards (Figure 1.5). Globally, medium and heavy duty trucks make up half of oil consumption in road vehicles and their share is growing. Only four countries (China, US, Japan, and Canada), representing 47% of heavy-duty vehicle sales, have enacted efficiency standards (ICCT, 2016). Further, heavy duty efficiency standards have only recently been implemented, meaning that the measures have not had time to work through the respective national vehicle markets.

The impact of heavy-duty vehicle standards on global oil demand will depend on how widely standards are adopted and the scale of efficiency gains that they will drive. In the United States, Phase 2 will come into effect in 2018 and run until 2027. The Department of Energy estimates that the new standards will save 700 kb/d of demand after being fully phased in. Japan was the first to implement truck standards in 2005 and full enforcement was phased in from 2015. Japanese standards aim to improve truck efficiency by 12% over 2002 levels by 2020. Standards for heavy-duty vehicles are expected to extend to a number of other major vehicle markets. The EU, Korea, and India are in the process of collecting data, and evaluating and developing standards.

DEMAND

Box 1.1 Efficiency policies curb demand growth (continued)

Figure 1.5 Share of global energy consumption in LDVs and medium- and heavy-trucks that is subject to mandatory efficiency standards

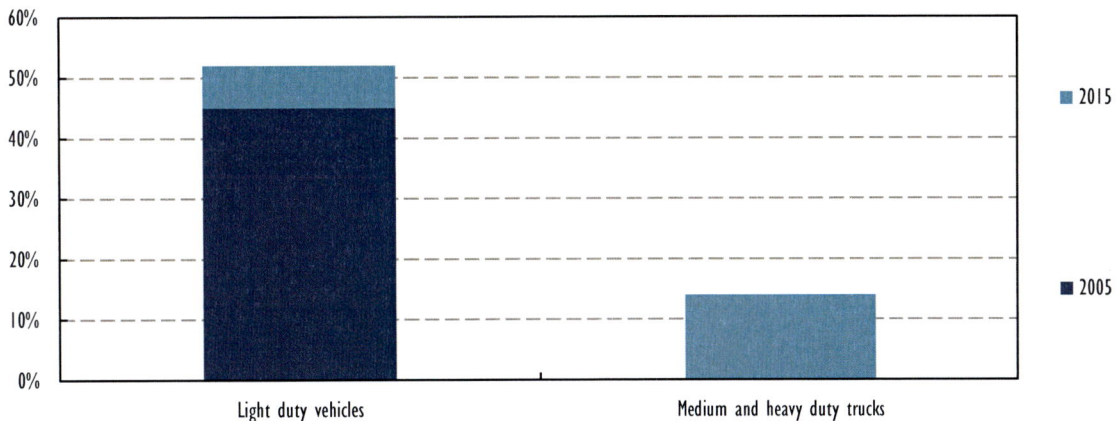

The efficiency improvement that standards will drive is subject to uncertainty. The cost-effective efficiency potential for heavy duty vehicles is presumed to be less than for passenger vehicles. Most trucks already deploy diesel technologies, which are more efficient than gasoline engines.

For more analysis of the impacts of standards on the world's energy system see the Energy Efficiency Market Report 2016 and the forthcoming IEA report on trucking.

Figure 1.6 Product specific breakdown of global oil demand, 2014-22

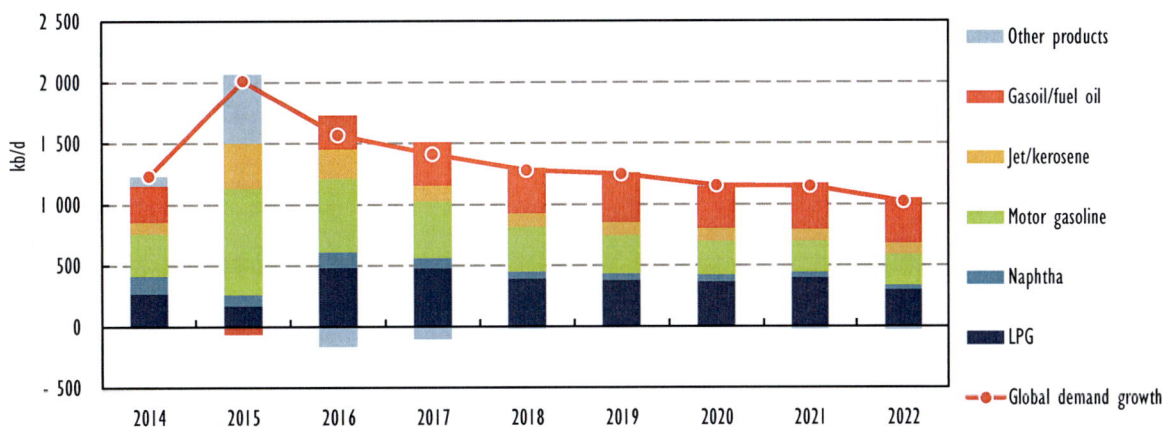

Fuel switching in the power, transport and industrial sectors will act as a drag on growth, although the opposite is true in the residential sector as strong gains in LPG demand, from additional Indian and African residential cooking use, provides a sizeable offset. Potentially lost demand from the road transport sector as a consequence of rapidly expanding electric vehicle sales accounts for a net 0.2 mb/d by 2022 (Box 1.2 Rapid gains in electric vehicle stock forecast but only with muted impact on global demand). A further loss of approximately 0.2 mb/d is foreseen in the shipping industry, as tighter emissions regulations trigger a variety of responses to the IMO's global 0.5% sulphur oxides

DEMAND

limit, including the net loss to oil demand of approximately 0.2 mb/d to ships powered by liquefied natural gas (LNG). Other responses to tighter marine emissions standards include the installation of scrubbers, thus allowing continued use of heavy sulphur fuel oil, switching to marine diesel, LNG-powered ships, refining more low-sulphur fuel oil, non-compliance, and blending other fuels. The net transport fuel demand loss from oil is thus unlikely to exceed 0.4 mb/d through 2022.

Box 1.2 Rapid gains in electric vehicle stock forecast but with only muted impact on global demand

With continuous technological improvements and policy support, the electric vehicle (EV) stock worldwide increased significantly in 2015 to 1.3 million units, 78% higher than 2014. Assuming a continuation of this momentum, the total stock is expected to reach 15 million by 2022.

China, the United States, Japan, Germany, the United Kingdom, France, the Netherlands and Scandinavia are, at present, the main markets for EV development, and will account for over 95% of the global stock during the next five years, resulting from the most conducive policy environment. Incentives include purchase subsidies, tax exemptions, and investments in recharging infrastructure. China also exempts EVs from the strict lotteries for new licence plates in big cities, and it will be the biggest market in 2022, accounting for nearly 50% of the total stock. The implementation of high taxes on oil products in Japan provides a boost for its own EV stock. By 2022 Japan's share of the global fleet will be close to that of the United States, which will see slower growth as a result of lower fuel taxes and a preference for vehicle sizes larger than in other regions.

Figure 1.7 Global electric vehicle fleet

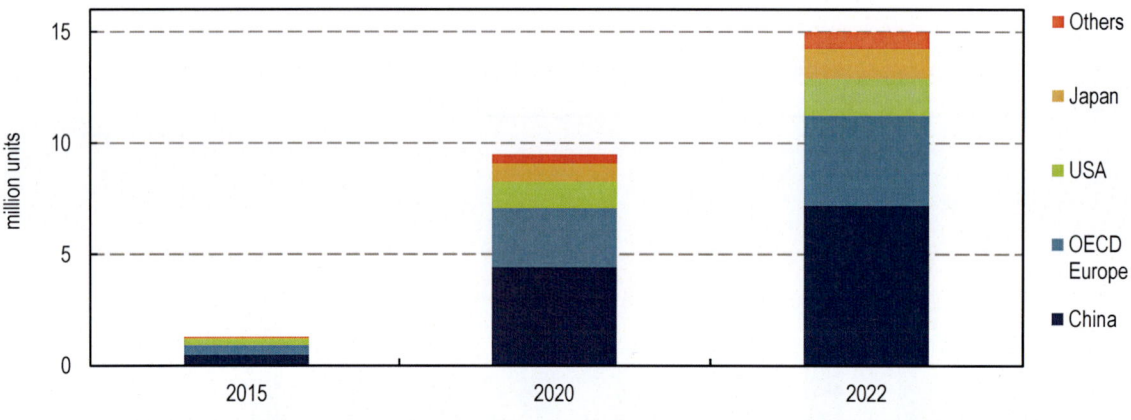

Technology improvements also benefit the development of EVs. Under current assumptions we foresee increasing battery energy densities reducing underlying costs to USD 140/kWh by 2022, from around USD 210/kWh in 2015, offering extended driving ranges at lower costs. Uncertainties around this last assumption will impact the eventual penetration of EVs, with more rapid technological developments likely associated with higher sales figures

Although the forecast growth of EVs is robust, 2016-22, the share in the total fleet remains small. In 2022, EVs will account for only 1.1% of the total fleet, and around half of these are plug-in hybrids, which also consume gasoline. This 1.1% share will replace 0.2mb/d of oil demand by 2022.

Figure 1.8 Relative evolutions of OECD and non-OECD oil demand, 2002-22

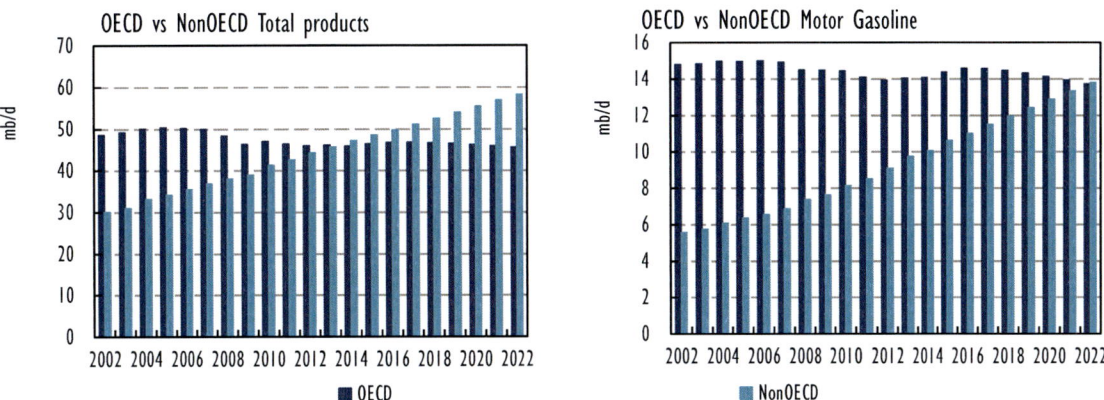

The traditional classification of oil product demand is between OECD and non-OECD countries. The long term trend is for the latter to see demand grow rapidly compared to the relatively sluggish performance in mature OECD markets. Recent years have, however, seen the growth differential narrow. In the five years between 2008 and 2012, non-OECD demand growth outpaced the OECD by an average 5.4%. For example, in 2012 non-OECD oil demand growth came in at 4.0%, whereas OECD oil demand fell by 1.0%. The gap then eased to 3% in 2013-14, before falling below 2% in 2015-16. In our outlook, a non-OECD growth premium is forecast to return, rising to around 3% in 2018-20 and 3.3% by 2021, and then stabilising.

OECD Demand

The sharp oil price decline in 2015 and only partial recovery in 2016 supported that incredibly rare sight of two successive years of rising OECD product demand, a phenomenon last seen in 2005-06. Led initially by the US, with strong year-on-year (y-o-y) gains seen through 1H15, largely driven by gasoline demand, OECD oil demand growth in 2015 came in at its highest level since the post-financial crisis bounce of 2010. Two successive years of European oil demand growth, coupled with persistently strong Korean demand gains post-3Q15, fuelled the OECD's landmark second successive year of growth in 2016.

As efficiency gains bite once more and oil product prices potentially edge higher, 2017-22, OECD oil demand growth will likely vanish, with demand in the region falling by a net 1.2 mb/d over the period. The decline is equivalent to a per annum drop of approximately 0.2 mb/d. OECD Europe and the OECD Americas account for the majority of the decline, falling by 95 kb/d and 60 kb/d respectively.

DEMAND

Americas

Oil demand is forecast to decline modestly in the OECD Americas region, from 24.6 mb/d in 2016 to 24.3 mb/d in 2022, chiefly attributable to falling demand in the United States. Easing gasoline demand leads the way, offsetting predicted gains for LPG (including ethane) and jet/kerosene. The negative impact from potentially higher product prices, 2017-22, coupled with forecast vehicle efficiency gains, offset the predicted benefits from continued economic growth.

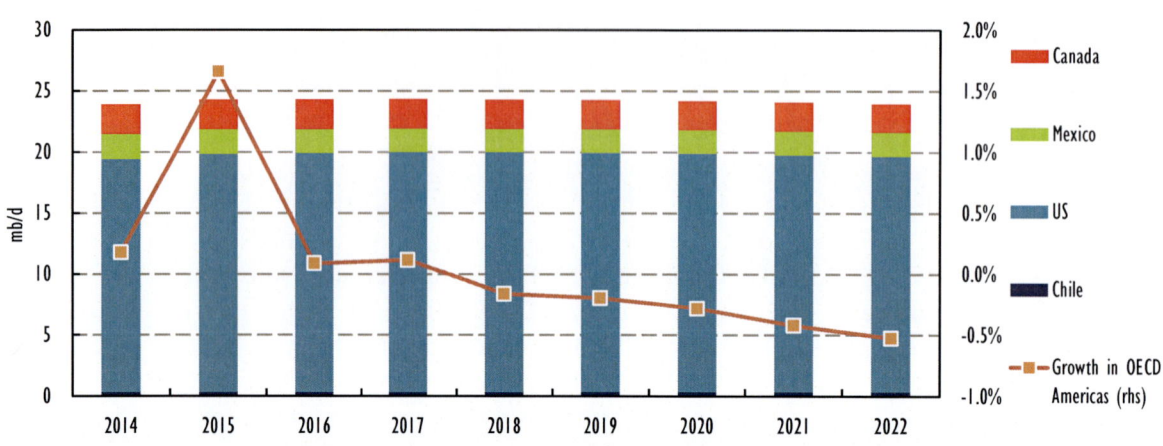

Figure 1.9 OECD Americas: oil demand, 2014-22

The **United States** oil consumer accounts for roughly four out of every five barrels consumed across the OECD Americas. Rising to a peak of 19.7 mb/d in 2018 from 19.6 mb/d in 2016, oil product demand in the United States then edges gently down to 19.3 mb/d in 2022, caused by falls in road transport fuel demand. The net decline of 300 kb/d is at a very gradual rate of 0.3% per annum. On a historical note, it should be remembered that oil demand in the United States peaked in 2005 at 21.2 mb/d. The fact that in 2022, after nearly two decades of economic growth, demand will be 19.3 mb/d is a clear reminder of the major improvements in fuel efficiency in vehicles, as well as the ongoing loss of market share in the power generation and industrial sectors.

Driving the demand picture for the United States, gasoline is forecast to peak in 2017 at 9.3 mb/d, before falling to around 8.8 mb/d in 2022. This decline is chiefly attributable to vehicle efficiency gains outpacing growth in vehicle usage. The net 465 kb/d gasoline demand decline averages out at approximately 1% per annum. This would have been even larger had it not been for the sharp fall in retail gasoline prices from late 2014 onwards which stimulated a dramatic uptick in SUV sales. This boost to the SUV fleet will leave a lasting legacy. Although great strides have been made in increasing the efficiency of all vehicles, SUV engines are less fuel efficient than standard passenger vehicles. With our forecast based on only modestly higher prices through 2022, SUV sales are expected to remain relatively high.

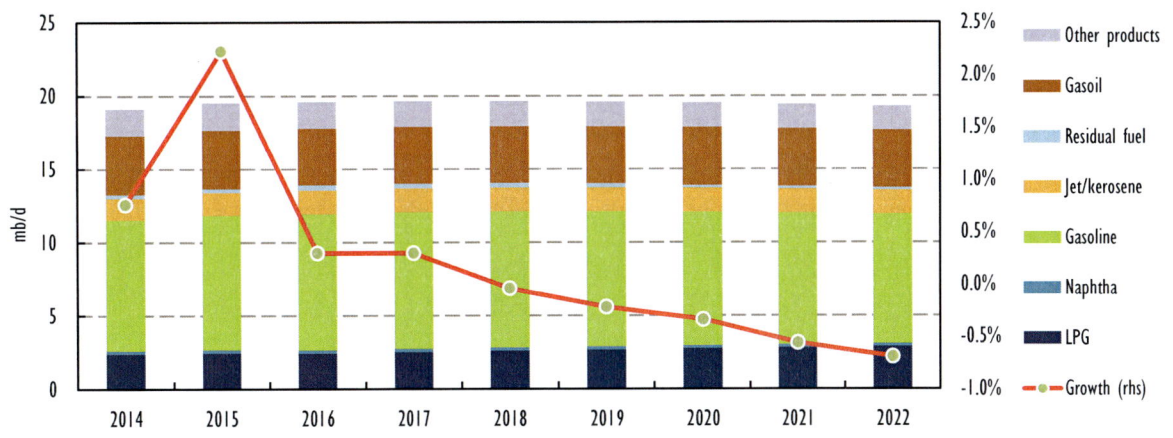

Figure 1.10 United States oil demand, 2014-22

Demand in the industrial and petrochemical sectors will fare better. Gasoil/diesel demand declined heavily in 2015-16 as industrial activity fell sharply in 2H15 through to 3Q16, triggering an estimated net loss of 170 kb/d in demand. This picture changes in our forecast with average gasoil demand in the United States essentially flat to 2022. By way of contrast, there is projected upside for LPG (including ethane) demand, which rises through the forecast to 2.9 mb/d by 2022 (at approximately 3% per annum), supported by continued increases in petrochemical capacity.

Pulled down by sharp contractions in residual fuel oil use and a 1.2% per annum price- and efficiency-driven decline in gasoline, oil product demand in **Canada** shows a net decline of 90 kb/d in the period 2016-22. This is equivalent to an average per annum decline of 0.6%, a significant deterioration from the 0.3% per annum growth seen in 2010-16. Averaging 2.3 mb/d in 2022, total Canadian oil product deliveries are forecast to fall to their lowest level since 2009.

The generally declining **Mexican** demand trend seen in 2013-16 is forecast to reverse post-2017, with a modest net 10 kb/d added in 2017-22. Relatively robust transport fuel demand underpins the forecast, offsetting declines in oil use in the power sector. Transport fuel demand grows from 1.2 mb/d in 2016 to 1.3 mb/d in 2022, while oil used in power generation falls by a similar amount.

Box 1.3 Emissions concerns impact dieselisation

Recent controversies related to diesel particulate emissions will significantly restrain growth through 2022, at least partially offsetting support provided by resurgent industrial oil use and the possibility of additional marine demand from January 2020, as global shipping regulations tighten. With the use of the correct filtration systems cleaner diesel engines will still be developed, but today popular sentiment is very much against choosing diesel vehicles. Furthermore, as crude oil prices fell from late 2014 onwards, and only partially recovered in 2016, the economic argument for buying a diesel vehicle dimmed.

In a sub-USD 60/bbl crude oil price environment, the tide is still somewhat against diesel, versus gasoline, purchases. The UK automotive magazine *What Car?* said that in November 2015, when Brent crude traded at USD 44/bbl, purchasers of the popular Fiat 500 would have to cover 130 000 miles before its more fuel efficient (by nearly 14 mpg) diesel model covered its higher purchase price.

> **Box 1.3 Emissions concerns impact dieselisation (Continued)**
>
> In September 2016, when Brent crude averaged USD 47/bbl, www.carbuer.co.uk concluded that when purchasing a new car, taking into account all differences in purchasing prices/taxes/pump prices/servicing costs, only "if you do over 12 000 miles a year (does) a diesel makes more sense".
>
> Recent efforts to narrow preferential tax treatments for diesel versus gasoline, such as those seen in France, or reducing subsidies on diesel versus gasoline, as occurred in India, provided fundamental support for gasoline, restraining diesel's previously increasing share of the global passenger fleet from 9% in 2000, through to 14% in 2010 and 15% in 2015. A flattening, at around 15% is then forecast through 2022, keeping the road diesel forecast somewhat restrained versus its previous trend.
>
>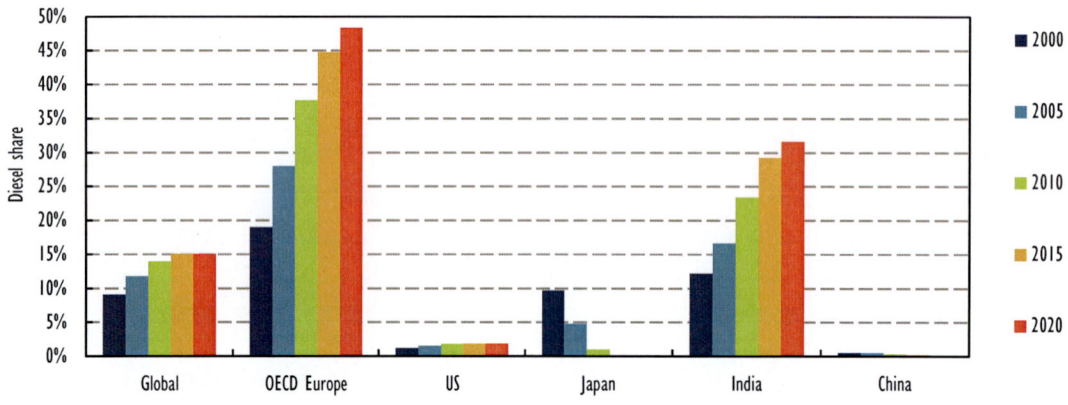
>
> Figure 1.11 Slowing pace of dieselisation

Europe

European oil product demand posted two consecutive years of 0.2 mb/d growth in 2015-16, something last seen in the mid-1990s. This is unlikely to be repeated anytime soon as Europe will continue to see modest economic growth and faces gradually increasing oil prices. Oil product demand is accordingly forecast to decline by approximately 570 kb/d, 2016-22, equivalent to a per annum decline of 0.7%.

The recent resurgence in demand, versus the five-year decline trend seen in 2010-14, was felt across most products and sectors. Increases in gasoil accounted for the largest share of the adjustment (33%), but not all products returned to absolute growth, as residual fuel oil and 'other gasoil' demand continued to fall while gasoline consumption flattened.

Declines across European road transport and industrial oil demand lead the forecast downwards. This includes a deceleration in the pace of dieselisation, reflecting growing concerns about diesel particulate emissions. This change will be particularly apparent in countries like **France**, where there is increasing concern about urban air pollution and thus changes have been made to the taxation treatment of diesel (Box 1.3 Emissions concerns impact dieselisation). Having expanded sharply, 2000-15, the share of diesel vehicles in the European passenger light duty vehicle stock is forecast to slow through 2020; as the share respectively rose from 19% in 2000 to 45% by 2015 but is only forecast to inch up to 48% by 2020 (Figure 1.10).

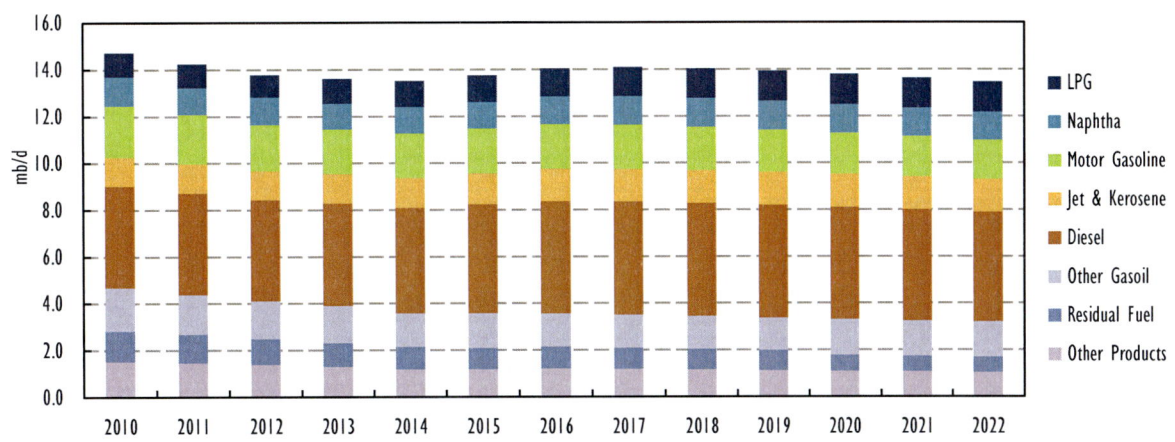

Figure 1.12 OECD Europe oil demand, 2010-22

Exceptions to the overall trend of falling European demand are found in some countries; notably Turkey and a number of Eastern European economies, where lower per-capita oil usage provides support. One of the best examples is Turkey where demand will grow by 175 kb/d between 2016 and 2022, equivalent to an average per annum gain of 2.9%. Over this same time period Turkey's per capita oil consumption rises only very marginally, from 0.012 b/d to 0.013 b/d (Figure 1.12), still less than one half of German per capita oil demand.

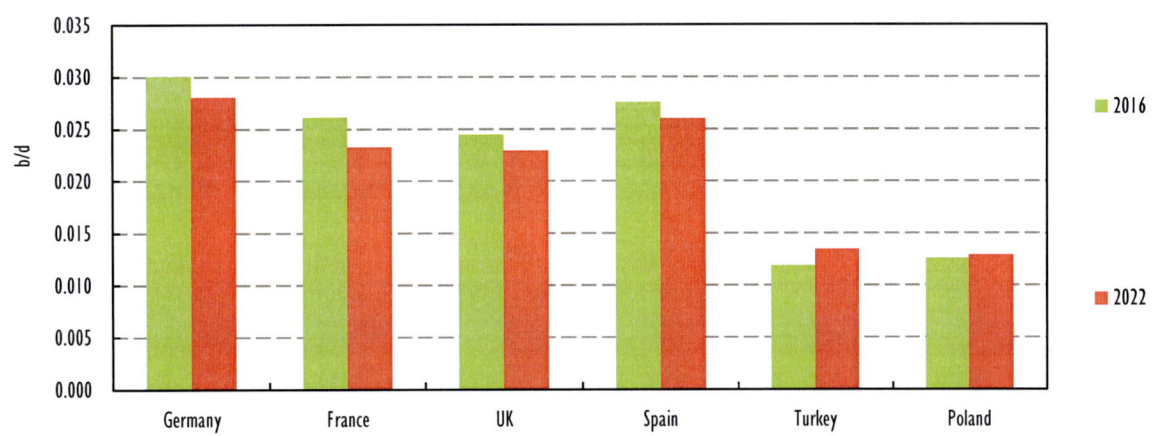

Figure 1.13 Per capita European oil demand, 2016 and 2022

Asia Oceania

Total oil demand in OECD Asia Oceania falls by an average 0.6% per annum or 270 kb/d over 2016-22 in our forecast. The sharpest declines are expected in Japan, followed by Australia, while growth in Korea is forecast to remain positive, supported by its still growing industrial sector.

Losing approximately 375 kb/d through the forecast, **Japanese** demand will be just 3.6 mb/d by 2022, equivalent to an average per annum decline rate of 1.6%, and a level not seen since 1970. Residual fuel oil, 'other products' and gasoline post the largest declines. Demand falls sharply in the power sector, albeit at slower rates than recently seen as the larger scale movements out of oil use have already happened. In 2022 oil's share in power generation will likely fall below 5%, compared to 13% in 2000. Japanese road transport fuel demand falls heavily as vehicle efficiency gains of around 2% per annum, coupled with potential declines in vehicle miles travelled, make a sizeable dent in both gasoline and diesel demand.

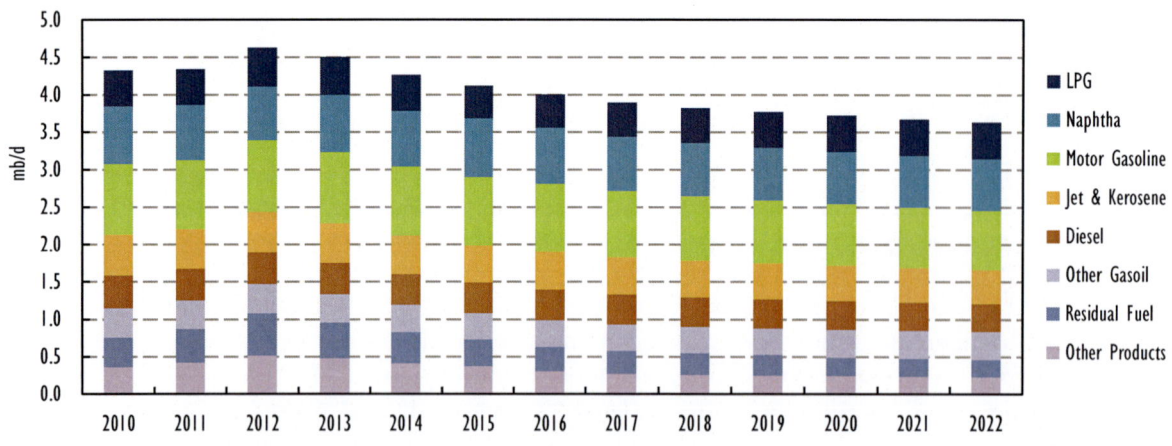

Figure 1.14 Japanese oil demand, 2010-22

Adding approximately 140 kb/d over the six-year period, **Korean** oil demand is estimated to reach 2.7 mb/d in 2022, equivalent to a per annum gain of 0.9%. Growing at just one-third the pace forecast for the Korean economy as a whole, this forecast is based on the assumption that further efficiency gains, deteriorating demographics (as the working age population starts to decrease) and product switching trigger a deceleration in growth. Strong gains in industrial fuels, such as gasoil/diesel and LPG, lead the upside, more than offsetting the weaker performance for gasoline and jet/kerosene demand to 2022.

Non-OECD Demand

For non-OECD economies dependent on commodity exports, demand growth decelerated sharply post-2014 as lower oil prices reduced revenues. Recessions in many countries – notably Brazil and Russia – saw non-OECD demand growth in 2016 fall to a seven-year low of 1.2 mb/d. Supported by stronger economic conditions, growth will recover to 1.5 mb/d by 2021, before plateauing and gently decelerating.

Behind the acceleration in non-OECD oil demand growth is a stronger economic backdrop. In its *World Economic Outlook*, published in January 2017, the IMF noted that growth in its "emerging market and developing economies" classification bottomed out at 4.1% in 2016, and will accelerate to 4.5% in 2017 and then to 4.8% in 2018. Higher oil prices provide an economic support to many large non-OECD exporters, particularly Russia and in the Middle East.

Africa

Although the factors that support strong oil demand growth in Africa remain in place, i.e. relatively strong macroeconomic growth, rapid population gains and exceptionally low per-capita levels of consumption (Figure 1.14), the forecast has been curtailed since last year's *Report*. The main reason is political uncertainty in several countries, e.g. Nigeria, South Africa and Libya.

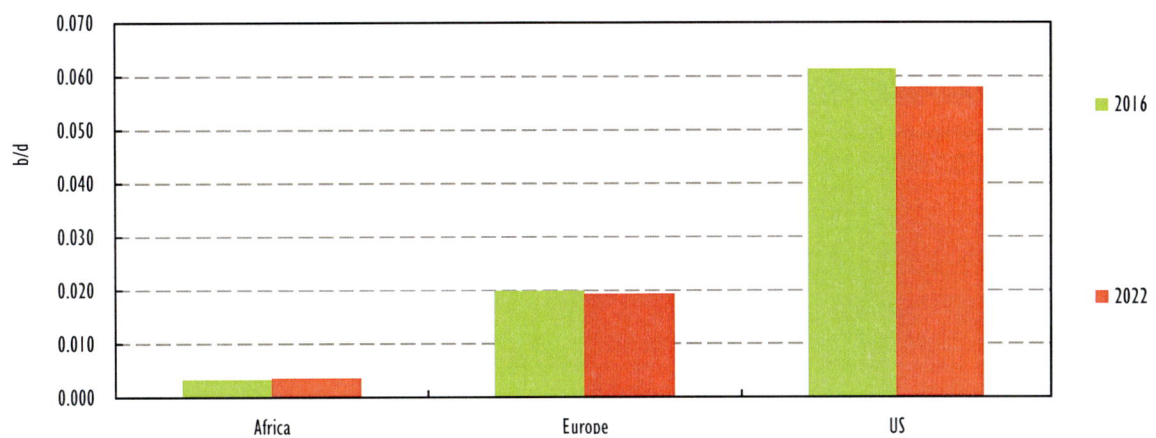

Figure 1.15 Per capita oil demand, Africa, Europe and the US, 2016 and 2022

For **Algeria**, for example, our oil product demand forecast has been curtailed with growth forecast to average 2.8% per annum versus an outlook of 3.5% seen in last year's *Report*. The IMF still forecasts the economy to grow by 3.1% per annum in 2016-21, but the expansion will be shallower than previously assumed. Transport fuels will prove particularly supportive as gasoline demand growth averages 3.2% per annum; jet/kerosene grows by 3.0% and gasoil/diesel by 2.5% per annum. The net Algerian demand addition in 2016-2022 is 85 kb/d.

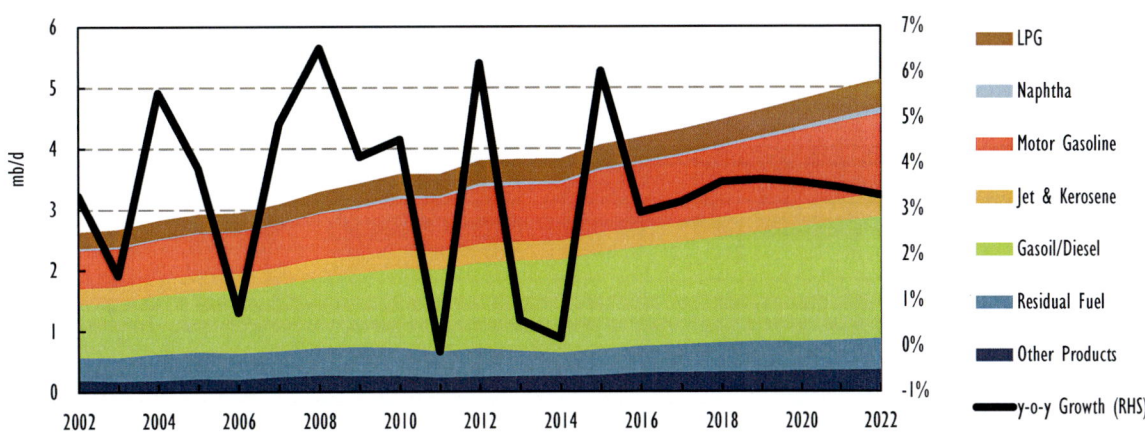

Figure 1.16 African oil demand, 2002-22

Despite our reduced overall demand expectation for Africa, not every country has been downgraded. Notable upgrades since last year's *Report* include Egypt, Libya, Ghana, the Republic of Congo, Cote d'Ivoire and Botswana; countries that are forecast to benefit from higher economic growth according to the IMF. Adding an estimated 250 kb/d between 2016 and 2022, the **Egyptian** demand forecast is particularly strong, with oil demand growth averaging 4.2% per annum supported by gains in the transport and industrial sectors. As with many countries there is some element of political risk, but if Egypt remains stable then the IMF's outlook for economic growth of an average 5% per annum will underpin strong oil demand growth.

Asia (non-OECD)

Non-OECD Asia very much dominates projections of oil demand growth, accounting for roughly seven out of every ten extra barrels consumed globally, 2016-22, or 5.1 mb/d. Averaging just over 3% per annum, or 0.9 mb/d each year, robust Asian gains are based on major expansions in vehicle fleets and further growth in petrochemical capacity, more than offsets savings from fuel switching and efficiency gains. By far the region's most rapid growth is seen in its two largest economies, China, and India.

A net 1.8 mb/d of additional **Chinese** oil demand is forecast to be added in 2016-22, underpinned by supportive economic conditions, big increases in petrochemical activity and a voracious appetite to increase vehicle ownership (20% y-o-y in October 2016, according to the China Passenger Car Association). Equivalent to a per annum gain of approximately 2.4%, the Chinese forecast is notably shallower than previously foreseen as recent vehicle efficiency gains make a major impact on our forecast. Furthermore, the economic growth assumptions that underpin the Chinese oil product demand forecast are reduced; the IMF cites economic growth of around 6.0% per annum, 2017-21, roughly two-tenths of a percentage point below their forecast of a year ago, while vehicle ownership levels have risen to above 200 per thousand people.

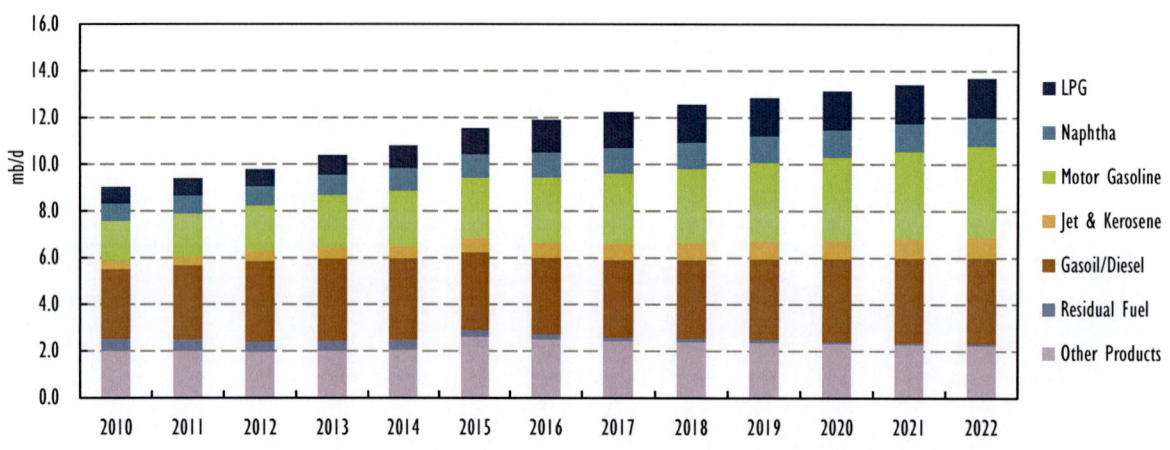

Figure 1.17 Chinese oil demand, 2010-22

Underpinned by rapid growth in the transport and residential sectors, **India** will see demand grow by 1.6 mb/d in the period 2016-2022, equivalent to an average per annum gain of 5.4%. Growth will be led by gasoline, gasoil/diesel and LPG, with the latter benefitting from the government's drive to increase its use as a cleaner cooking fuel. The plan is to convert 1.5 million low income households to LPG in the financial year 2016-17 and to convert 5 million in total by 2019. As of December 2016, Indian LPG coverage had reportedly reached 70% of households, up from 61% at the start of the year. Also, rapid vehicle sales growth support strong transport fuels gains. With a very modest, sub-20 vehicles per thousand people, the potential growth in the Indian transport fleet is vast.

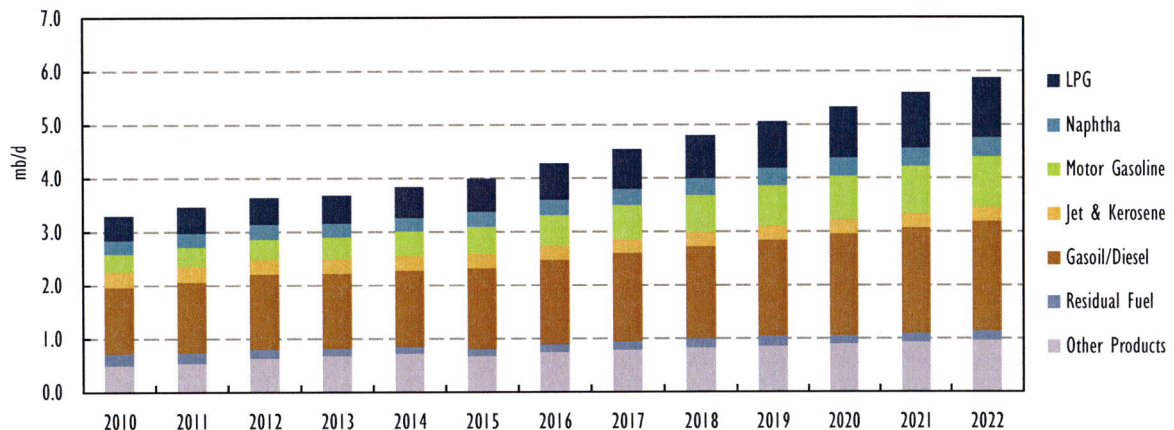

Figure 1.18 Indian oil demand, 2010-22

One major uncertainty exists at the start of our forecast for India arising from the government's withdrawal of two of the most common denomination bank notes. The resultant shortage of cash has hampered daily life for millions of people. The extent and duration of the cash shortage is not known as we write this *Report*, but it is clearly a risk to the early part of our forecast.

Exceptions to the rule that oil demand will grow strongly in Asia are found in Hong Kong and Chinese Taipei, both are economies that have embarked upon more fuel efficient road transportation. In **Hong Kong**, for example, only 30 kb/d of additional oil product demand is forecast to be added, with the total rising from 375 kb/d in 2016 to 405 kb/d in 2022. The growth is dominated by gasoil, as the already highly efficient vehicle fleet remains not only size-constrained but also sees continued average per annum efficiency gains close to 2%. A similarly small net 50 kb/d gain is forecast in **Chinese Taipei** where demand grows from 1.0 mb/d in 2016 to 1.1 mb/d in 2022.

Table 1.3 Asian oil demand; total (kb/d), per capita (b/d)

	2015	2016	2017	2018	2019	2020	2021	2022
China	11,545	11,905	12,235	12,555	12,850	13,135	13,415	13,685
Per capita	0.008	0.009	0.009	0.009	0.009	0.009	0.010	0.010
India	3,990	4,275	4,540	4,800	5,060	5,330	5,600	5,880
Per capita	0.003	0.003	0.003	0.004	0.004	0.004	0.004	0.004
Indonesia	1,740	1,805	1,885	1,962	2,040	2,115	2,190	2,265
Per capita	0.007	0.007	0.007	0.007	0.008	0.008	0.008	0.008
Malaysia	770	805	835	865	920	945	965	990
Per capita	0.028	0.029	0.029	0.030	0.032	0.032	0.032	0.033
Singapore	1,255	1,325	1,365	1,405	1,440	1,465	1,485	1,510
Per capita	0.224	0.233	0.237	0.241	0.243	0.244	0.246	0.248
Thailand	1,335	1,390	1,435	1,470	1,505	1,530	1,555	1,580
Per capita	0.020	0.020	0.021	0.022	0.022	0.022	0.023	0.023

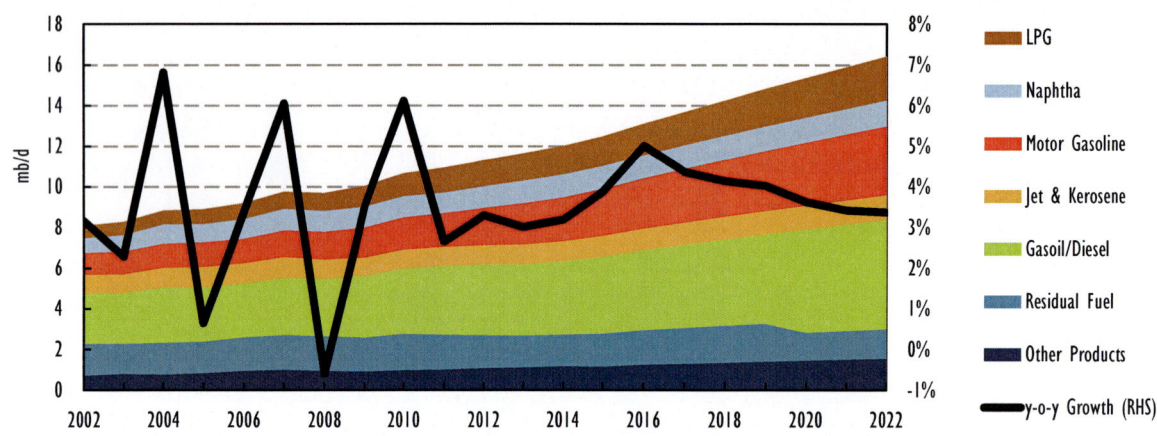

Figure 1.19 Non-OECD Asia (excluding China) oil demand, 2002-22

Rapid demand gains will still consistently be seen in many non-OECD Asian economies, although they largely remain the preserve of the relatively poorer economies such as Bangladesh, Myanmar, Cambodia, Indonesia, the Philippines, Sri Lanka and Pakistan. These countries will expand sharply from a low base in terms of overall per capita consumption and vehicle ownership levels. **Malaysia**, for example, is forecast to see average per annum demand growth of approximately 3.5% in the period 2016-22, or a net gain of 185 kb/d. Gasoline provides the majority of the upside to the forecast, adding approximately 95 kb/d as rapid vehicle sales growth far exceeds any modest efficiency savings. Strong gains are also anticipated for LPG and gasoil/diesel, the latter largely due to additional industrial usage.

Analysis of the world's eighth most populous country, **Bangladesh**, puts in context the massive growth potential that non-OECD Asia still possesses. Consuming an average of 135 kb/d of oil products in 2016, total Bangladeshi oil demand, from a population of 170 million, is equivalent to just one-tenth that of Spain, with a population of 48 million. By 2022, Bangladesh's oil demand will reach 185 kb/d, an average growth rate of 5.6% per annum. Bangladesh's population density is very high and this will partially restrain the pace of growth.

Europe (non-OECD)

Non-OECD Europe, the smallest of our non-OECD regions, is forecast to add approximately 95 kb/d of additional oil product demand to 2022, equivalent to roughly 2% per annum. The sharpest growth is seen in Malta, Albania, Gibraltar, Bosnia and Herzegovina, Kosovo and Serbia. In contrast there will be only modest or no growth in Croatia and Bulgaria.

Table 1.4 Non-OECD European oil demand, kb/d

	2016	2017	2018	2019	2020	2021	2022	2016-22
Non-OECD Europe	**700**	**715**	**730**	**750**	**765**	**780**	**795**	**95**
Bulgaria	95	95	95	100	100	100	105	10
Gibraltar	70	70	75	80	85	90	95	25
Romania	200	205	210	210	215	215	215	15

Box 1.4 Jet fuel demand continues to fly

Rising by approximately 1.4% per annum to 2022, global jet/kerosene demand will increase by 640 kb/d, making it the fourth fastest growing petroleum product after LPG (including ethane), gasoil and gasoline. Unlike LPG, where ample supplies contribute to the growth, or the vast gasoline market, which is underpinned by rapid gains in emerging market vehicle fleets, or gasoil, which is forecast to benefit from resurgent industrial demand and some product switching from high-sulphur fuel oil in the shipping industry, projected jet/kerosene growth derives mainly from stronger economic growth.

Pure jet fuel demand accounted for roughly seven out of every eight barrels of jet/kerosene consumed in 2016, with kerosene still used for residential heating and/or cooking in a few countries, chiefly Japan and India. Heating kerosene demand has been steadily declining since 2000; and to 2022 the aviation sector will account for all future growth. Rising air transport demand in developing countries drives this trend, with the only restraint coming from any deceleration in economic growth and efficiency gains.

Whereas emerging economies overtook the OECD in total oil use terms in 2014, this is not so for jet fuel demand, which remains heavily dominated by richer OECD economies. Non-OECD demand is, however, catching up fast and will continue to do so, with growth of 3% per annum forecast for 2016-22, versus flat OECD demand. Faster non-OECD demand growth reflects rapidly rising incomes and the emergence of a non-OECD middle class, plus the establishment of many non-OECD countries, such as Dubai, as international airline hubs. As recently as 2005, the only non-OECD location among the world's 15 busiest airports was Beijing. By 2015, Beijing was joined by Dubai, Shanghai, and Hong Kong. This trend is forecast to continue through 2022, with other Chinese, Asian, African and Middle Eastern airports expected to expand rapidly, pulling up non-OECD jet fuel demand.

A combination of technological advancements and better fleet management techniques restrain growth. The International Air Transport Association (IATA) estimates the fleet replacement's contribution to rising fuel efficiencies at 1.5% per annum. Improved airline management systems raised passenger load factors from 73% in 2004 to 80% in 2016. IATA's 'Technology Roadmap' highlights further ways to improve airline efficiencies, including better aerodynamics, retrofitting old planes, and developing new windowless and hybrid-wing-body planes.

Non-OECD Asia dominates jet/kerosene demand growth in 2016-22, with the region forecast to account for roughly three-quarters of global demand. China alone accounts for nearly half of this. Relatively strong gains are also forecast in Africa and the Middle East, respectively accounting for 9% and 21% of global growth. Absolute declines are forecast in the OECD, however, as the market has been saturated to a point that efficiency gains and the evolution of airline transport hubs, out of the OECD increasingly towards non-OECD countries, offsets otherwise supportive jet fuel demand growth.

Former Soviet Union (FSU)

Having suffered from lower oil prices since late 2014, and to some extent from economic sanctions after the Crimea episode, **Russian** oil product demand growth returned with vigour in 2016, as the economy appeared to bottom out. Although many forecasters, including the IMF, still foresee an absolute GDP contraction in 2016, the scale is clearly easing as can be seen from the recent uptick in industrial activity, and the 3.3% gain in oil product demand that has ensued. Oil demand growth is forecast to ease back to a more reasonable 2.6% in 2017, as the economy is bolstered by industrial demand.

DEMAND

Table 1.5 Oil demand growth (kb/d) in the major economies of the former Soviet Union

	2016	2017	2018	2019	2020	2021	2022	2016-22
Former Soviet Union	**170**	**115**	**110**	**85**	**80**	**80**	**75**	**545**
Russia	150	95	80	50	45	40	35	340
Turkmenistan	10	10	10	10	10	10	10	55
Ukraine	5	5	5	5	5	5	5	40
Kazakhstan	0	0	5	5	5	10	10	30
Uzbekistan	5	5	0	0	5	5	5	15

Average annual demand growth then eases to around 1.3% over the period 2018-22, as projections of absolute declines in road transport demand trim the otherwise persistent gains from the petrochemical and jet fuel markets. Entrenched vehicle efficiency gains, coupled with relatively small expansions in the Russian vehicle fleet (less than 2% per annum), will curb road transport fuel demand through the forecast.

Figure 1.20 Russian oil demand, 2010-22

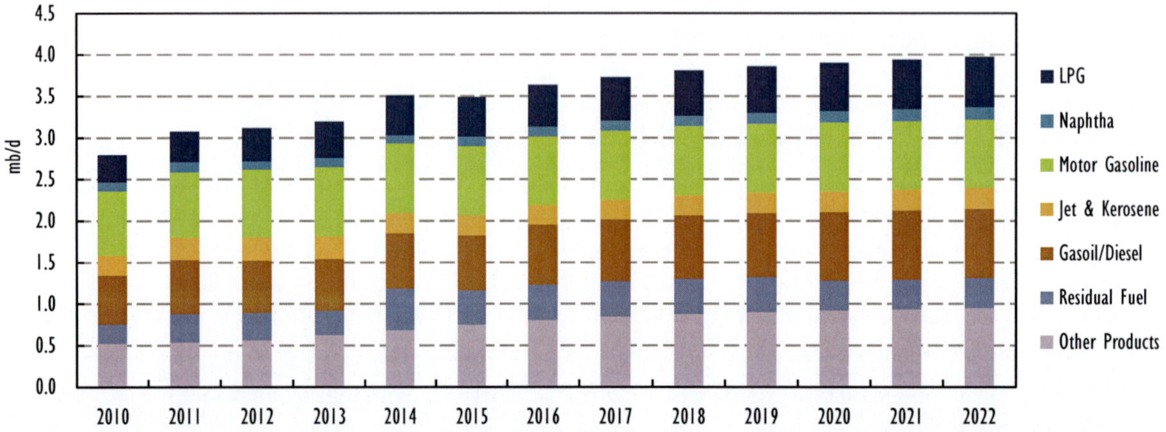

Strong gains for oil demand are also forecast in Armenia, Georgia, Latvia, Lithuania, Moldova, Tajikistan, Turkmenistan, Uzbekistan and the Kyrgyz Republic. In contrast, Belarus is forecast to show little-to-no growth in 2016-22, as prospects likely remain restrained by the beleaguered state of the economy.

Latin America

Having seen an exceptionally tough couple of years, non-OECD Latin America is forecast to return to relatively strong growth conditions post-2017. Over the forecast period, 2016-22, a net gain for oil product demand of approximately 0.6 mb/d is expected, equating to a modest per annum gain of 1.3%. Although this assumes slower growth momentum than in last year's *Report*, non-OECD Latin America remains an important region post-2017.

Falling sharply in both 2015 and 2016, with a net loss in demand of 170 kb/d, **Brazilian** oil product demand looks set to return to growth once more. Initially, it will be modest in 2017, then accelerating through 2020 as underlying economic growth picks up.

Table 1.6 Latin American oil demand (kb/d)

	2016	2017	2018	2019	2020	2021	2022	2016-22
Latin America, non-OECD	**6,645**	**6,670**	**6,755**	**6,860**	**6,965**	**7,080**	**7,195**	**550**
Argentina	770	775	785	795	805	815	820	50
Brazil	3,075	3,080	3,110	3,150	3,195	3,240	3,280	205
Colombia	350	360	365	380	390	400	410	60
Ecuador	285	280	280	280	280	285	290	5
Panama	150	155	160	170	180	185	195	45
Peru	255	265	270	280	280	285	290	35
Venezuela	630	610	600	595	595	600	610	-20
Annual Change	-120	25	85	100	105	115	120	

As was the case during the slowdown, Brazilian gasoline and gasoil/diesel will be the key drivers of change, contributing 80% of the total growth seen in 2017-22. To 2022, a net gain of approximately 205 kb/d is foreseen, 100 kb/d of which will be gasoline and 70 kb/d gasoil/diesel. The legacy of the recent downturn will be long-lasting, however; total Brazilian demand is not forecast to return to 2014 levels until 2021-22 at the earliest.

Figure 1.21 Brazilian oil demand, 2010-22

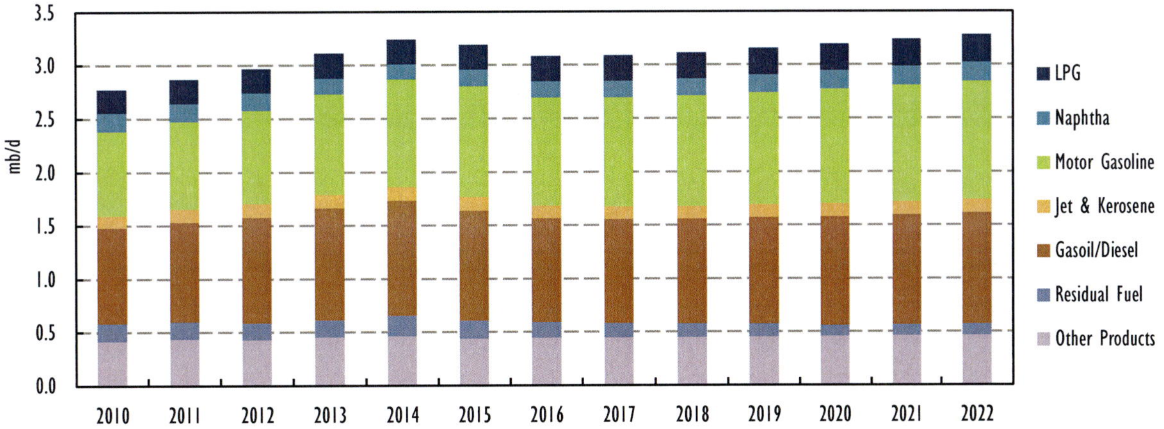

Other Latin American countries that see notable oil demand growth include Colombia, Argentina, Costa Rica, the Dominican Republic, Guatemala, Haiti, Honduras, Nicaragua, Panama, Peru and Uruguay. As with Brazil, albeit to a lesser degree, oil demand in **Argentina** has suffered in recent years at the hands of its hamstrung domestic economy. Post-2016, a recovery is foreseen supporting a re-acceleration in oil demand growth, particularly in transport fuels and the agriculture sector, largely towards gasoil. The ailing economy saw oil demand ease back by around 20 kb/d in 2015, before flattening in 2016. With economic growth, according to the IMF, likely to escalate to around 3% by 2020, after a contraction of 2% in 2016, a net gain of approximately 60 kb/d for oil demand is foreseen in 2016-22. For **Colombia**, even more rapid economic growth is projected, reaching 4% per annum by 2020.This supports oil demand growing by an average 2.7% to 2022, equivalent to a net gain of 60 kb/d over the period. Additional gasoil/diesel, gasoline and jet/kerosene demand accounts for almost all of the forecast Colombian demand gain, as the vehicle fleet continues to expand rapidly and industrial activity accelerates.

Middle East

Oil demand in the major net oil exporting countries in the Middle East has suffered from lower oil prices since 2014 but it seems likely to stage a recovery from 2017 onwards. This is based partly on the expectation of higher international prices for crude oil and products supporting stronger economic growth, and also on a strong expansion of the petrochemical sector with a number of major projects set to start up. Particularly strong demand gains are foreseen in Qatar and Kuwait.

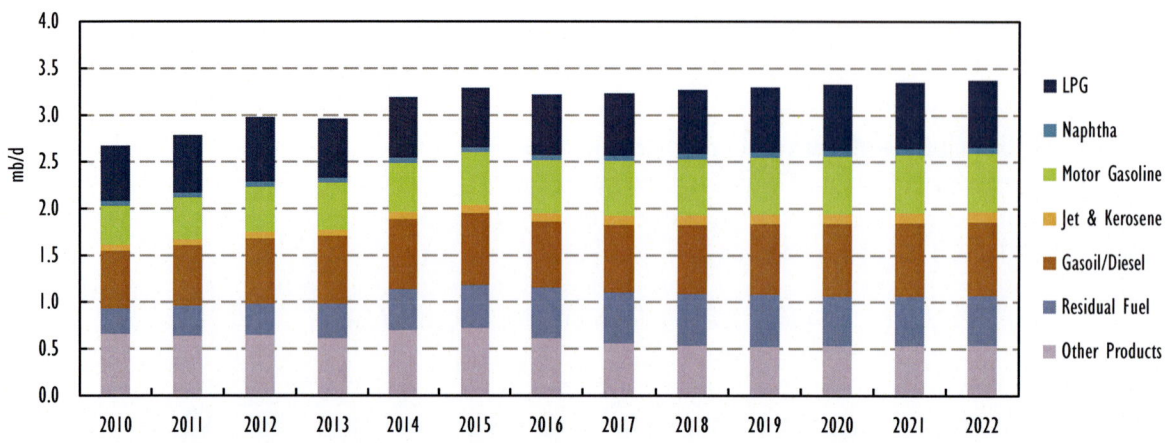

Figure 1.22 Saudi Arabian oil demand, 2010-22

Saudi Arabia is set to recover from the economic uncertainty seen in 2016 with oil export revenues likely to stabilise and probably increase after four years of contraction from the most recent peak in 2012. The ramp up of the huge 2.5 billion cubic feet per day Wasit gas facility will reduce the enormous use of crude oil in the power sector, particularly in the summer when it can reach as much as 0.9 mb/d. The government is determined to introduce more stringent efficiency measures and this partly explains why growth in the once rapidly expanding oil demand base dips below a 1% per annum average through the forecast to 2022. This is sharply below the prior six-year average of close to 3%. Most significantly, recent efforts to reduce subsidies on transport fuels have sharply trimmed the growth forecast for gasoline to a relatively muted 1.7% per annum 2016-22, dramatically below the near 5% per annum growth rate seen in the previous six-year period, 2011-16.

Table 1.7 Middle Eastern oil demand (kb/d)

	2016	2017	2018	2019	2020	2021	2022	2016-22
Middle East	8,460	8,615	8,800	9,015	9,230	9,500	9,690	1,230
Iran	1,960	2,030	2,100	2,160	2,215	2,275	2,330	370
Iraq	850	865	890	915	935	945	960	110
Saudi Arabia	3,220	3,235	3,270	3,300	3,325	3,350	3,375	155
UAE	845	865	885	905	925	940	965	120

Changing IMO bunker fuel specifications from 2020 have a particularly pronounced impact on the **UAE** forecast, with a near 120 kb/d swing projected in 2020 from higher sulphur fuel oil to marine diesel, although uncertainties could impact this forecast either way. Overall, the UAE demand forecast is for an average per annum gain of 2.2% to 2022, just under half the average gain seen in the previously comparable six-year period, as transport fuel demand growth, in particular decelerates.

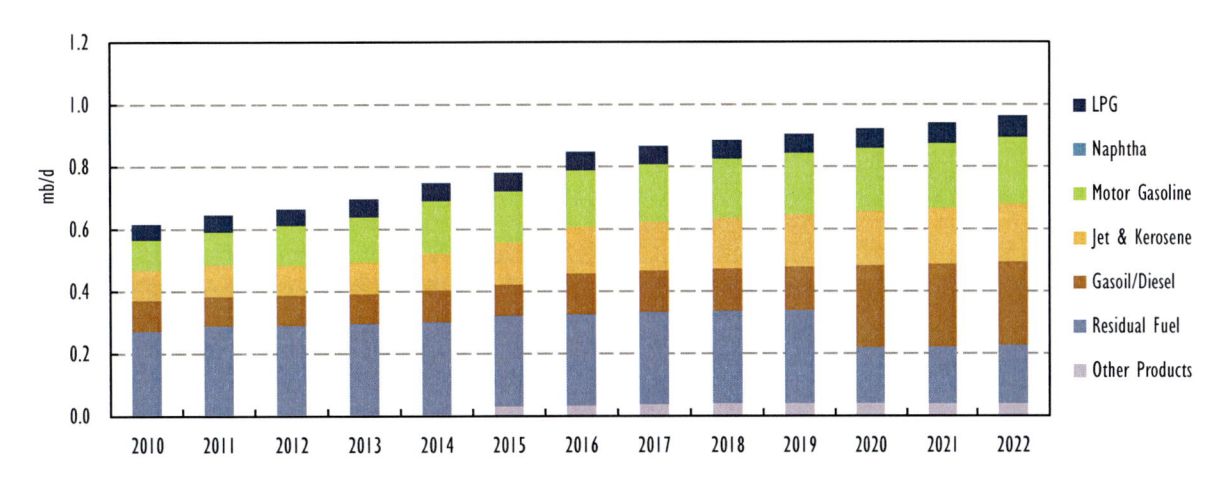

Figure 1.23 UAE oil demand, 2010-22

The **Iranian** demand picture is likely to reverse sharply from its beleaguered recent history, as three consecutive years of falling net oil demand in 2014 to 2016 are replaced by gains averaging 3.0% per annum in the period 2016-22. Led by transport and industrial fuels, the total forecast Iranian oil demand gain is equivalent to 380 kb/d through the forecast, nearly triple the gain of the previous six years as the macroeconomic dynamics for Iran significantly improve. The caveat that must be entered here is uncertainty around the policy of the new US Administration towards sanctions. Clearly, if nuclear-related sanctions were re-imposed, this would have a detrimental impact on growth.

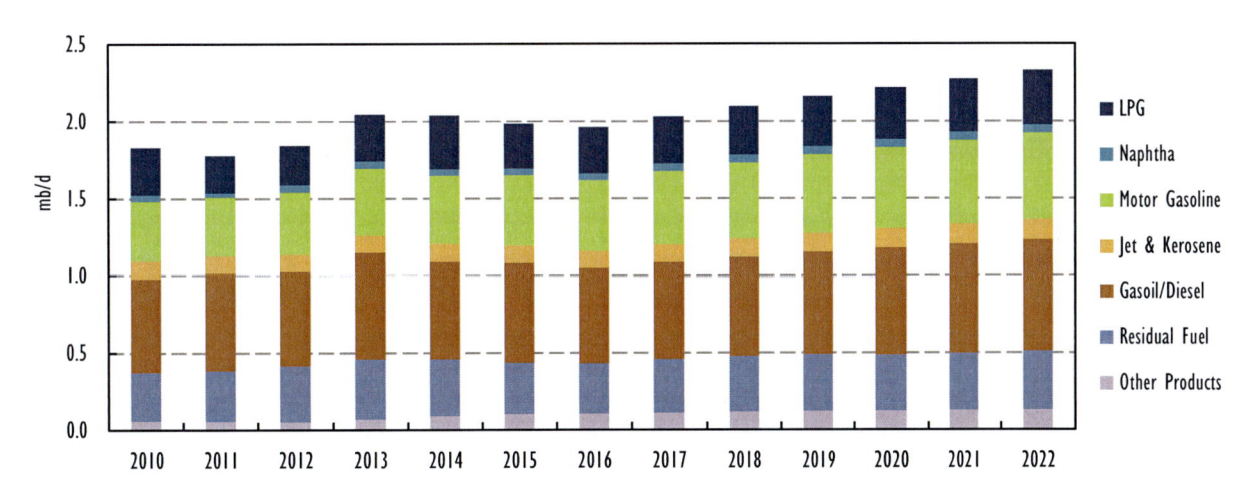

Figure 1.24 Iran oil demand, 2010-22

Petrochemical sector expansions in the region raise the LPG and naphtha demand forecasts by a combined 570 kb/d to 2022, with particularly strong gains forecast in Kuwait, Saudi Arabia, Oman, Qatar and Iran. Middle Eastern petrochemical demand growth ranks second only to the OECD

Americas, supported by the availability of cheap feedstock and relative proximity to the world's major demand centres in Asia. Growing natural gas production, and with it natural gas liquids, provides a ready source of cost competitive ethane that makes the Middle East the world's cheapest ethylene producing region worldwide. However, as Middle Eastern petrochemical production increases faster than ethane supply, a gradual shift towards heavier feedstocks is projected.

References:

US EPA (United States Environmental Protection Agency) (2016), Light-Duty Automotive Technology, Carbon Dioxide Emissions, and Fuel Economy Trends: 1975 through 2016, https://www.epa.gov/sites/production/files/2016-11/documents/420r16010.pdf.

IEA (2016), Energy Efficiency Market Report, OECD/IEA, Paris.
ICCT (International Council on Clean Transportation) (2014), Policy Update: China Phase 4 Passenger Car Fuel Consumption Standard Proposal:
http://www.theicct.org/sites/default/files/publications/ICCTupdate_ChinaPhase4_mar2014.pdf.
ICCT (2015), Factsheet: Japan, Light Duty Vehicle Efficiency Standards. International Council on Clean Transportation.
http://www.theicct.org/sites/default/files/info-tools/pvstds/Japan_PVstds-facts_jan2015.pdf.

ICCT (2016), International policy developments for heavy-duty efficiency 2014-2015 (blog post) [accessed 25 January 2017], http://www.theicct.org/sctp-hdv-e.

2. SUPPLY

Highlights

- **Global oil production capacity is forecast to expand by 5.6 mb/d to 2022 as a potential price recovery tempts producers to invest after two lean years.** Growth is heavily front-loaded and supply looks ample through the early part of the forecast. Unless further projects are sanctioned quickly, growth all but stalls from 2020.

- **After a 25% decline in 2015, global upstream spending was slashed by an additional 26% in 2016, to USD 433 billion.** Following the consolidation of oil prices above USD 50/bbl, there are tentative signs of producers rethinking their capital expenditure (capex) plans. Global upstream investment is expected to marginally increase in 2017, led by robust growth in North America.

- **Non-OPEC supply growth is poised to recover in 2017, following a 0.8 mb/d decline last year.** Total liquid supplies are expected to expand by 0.4 mb/d, fuelled by renewed expansion in the US, along with longer term growth projects in Brazil, Canada, and Kazakhstan.

- **Non-OPEC supply growth is set to accelerate over 2018-19 before slowing markedly towards the end of the forecast period.** By 2022, non-OPEC oil production will reach 60.9 mb/d, 3.3 mb/d higher than in 2016.

- **The Americas continue to dominate growth over the forecast period.** The United States remains the number one source of supply growth, adding 1.6 mb/d, followed by Brazil (1.1 mb/d) and Canada (0.8 mb/d).

- **The outlook for Russia has materially improved following a significant increase in development drilling over the past year.** Total liquids output is expected to hold steady through 2022, at around 11.3 mb/d.

- **Lower prices led producers in China and Colombia to scale back activity last year, resulting in sharper-than-expected output declines.** Production will continue to fall over the forecast period, albeit at a shallower rate than seen in 2016.

- **OPEC crude production capacity rises by 1.95 mb/d by 2022 to 37.85 mb/d in anticipation of higher demand.** Indeed, the call on OPEC crude rises to 35.8 mb/d in 2022 from 32.2 mb/d in 2016. Capacity growth is concentrated in the low-cost Middle East, with Iraq leading the gains. Iran, the UAE and Libya, assuming political stability in the latter, also post solid growth.

- **Some OPEC members outside the Middle East fare less well, with declines in capacity of 20 kb/d to 110 kb/d.** Venezuela posts the biggest loss due to chronic under-investment as well as economic and civil strife. Capacity also shrinks in Algeria, Nigeria and Angola.

Trends in global oil supply

Global oil supply grew last year despite a weak oil price environment as low-cost producers from the Middle East to Russia pumped at record rates. In North America and other higher-cost regions, however, supply shrank as investment fell sharply. OPEC hiked total output by more than 1.1 mb/d and Russia lifted production by 0.25 mb/d, more than offsetting declines elsewhere. As a result, world supply rose by 0.4 mb/d in 2016 to 97 mb/d.

After a 25% decline in 2015, global upstream spending was slashed by an additional 26% in 2016 to USD 433 billion. This year, the recovery in oil prices in the wake of a coordinated OPEC/non-OPEC output cut may tempt some oil companies to open their wallets and raise investment in oil fields around the world. Tentative signs are emerging that producers are rethinking capital expenditure (*capex*) plans, with global upstream investment expected to see a marginal increase this year.

Global oil production capacity expands by 5.6 mb/d by 2022, of which non-OPEC contributes 60%. Growth is heavily front-loaded. Indeed, the supply situation looks comfortable throughout the early part of our forecast. By 2020 however, global oil capacity growth slows considerably as a two-year spending drought of 2015-16 has left few projects in the pipeline. It is not too late to avert a supply crunch, provided companies start to sanction development work without delay.

Figure 2.1 Global liquids capacity growth

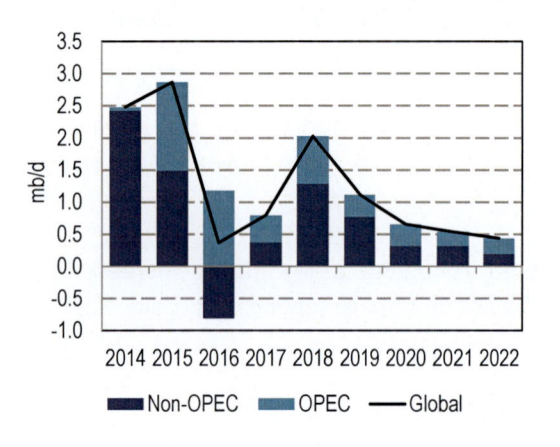

Figure 2.2 Global capacity growth 2016-22

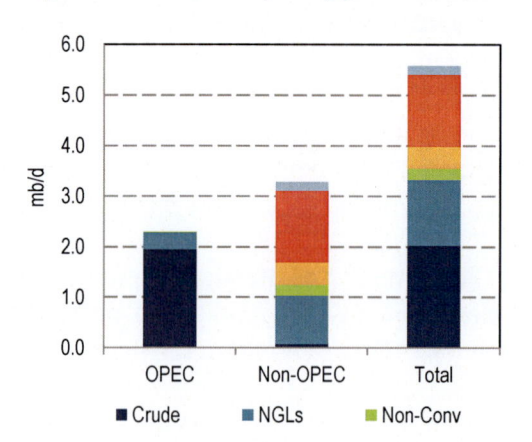

After falling by 0.8 mb/d in 2016, non-OPEC supply growth is poised to recover in 2017. Growth accelerates over 2018-19 but then slows markedly. By 2022, non-OPEC oil production will reach 60.9 mb/d, 3.3 mb/d higher than in 2016. The Americas continue to dominate non-OPEC growth and producers there are expected to lead any increase in spending. The US remains the single largest source of output growth even before any potentially favourable policy changes by the new US administration are factored in.

As for OPEC, the group is building capacity – even as it reduces production in 2017 – in anticipation of higher demand. Indeed, the call on OPEC crude and stock change rises to 35.8 mb/d in 2022 from 32.2 mb/d in 2016. At the same time, crude capacity expands to 37.85 mb/d in 2022 from 35.9 mb/d in 2016, implying a reduction in spare capacity. Growth is concentrated in the Middle East, while some OPEC producers outside the region struggle. Other OPEC supplies, including condensate, natural gas liquids and non-conventional production grow by roughly 0.35 mb/d over the period.

Box 2.1 Upstream investment sees modest increase in 2017, but costs rise too

Following an unprecedented collapse in upstream oil and gas investment over the past two years, there are now tentative signs of a modest recovery. As oil prices plunged from more than USD 100/barrel in 2014 to a low of USD 30/bbl in early 2016, global upstream capital expenditures (capex) were cut by 25% in 2015, and by an additional 26% in 2016 to USD 433 billion. Some companies are signalling increased capital expenditure plans for this year, but for the industry as a whole, the recovery is expected to be modest and partly offset by rising costs.

Amongst international oil companies, only ConocoPhillips, ExxonMobil and Statoil have announced higher spending. The remainder plan to cut investment from 2016 levels. Shell intends to spend 17% less this year, while Chevron plans to curb capex by a further 14%. All the companies that have provided production guidance for the year are suggesting higher output as they do more with less and as longer term projects with sunk costs come on line. We are also seeing major oil firms, such as Exxon and Chevron, increasingly shifting their attention towards shorter cycle investments, most notably in US LTO.

Table 2.1 Selected company spending and production plans

Company	2016 Capex actual	2017 Capex guidance	Change% 2016-17	Prod 2015 kboe/d	Prod 2016 kboe/d	Prod guidance 2017
BP	16.0	14.3	-11%	3 279	3 263	↑
Chevron	20.2	17.3	-14%	2 622	2 594	+4-9%
ConocoPhillips	4.9	5.0	2%	1 589	1 567	+up to 2%
Eni	9.1	8.1	-11%	1 598		
ExxonMobil	14.5	16.6	14%	4 098	4 053	↑
Royal Dutch Shell	21.6	18.0	-17%	3 080	3 668	↑
Total	14.3	12.9	-10%	2 347	2 452	+over 4 %
OMV	1.5	1.7	13%	309	311	+3%
Repsol	3.1	3.0	-3%	559	690	-1.4%
Statoil	10.1	11.0	9%	1 812	1 825	+4-5%
Galp	1.0	0.9	-10%	46	68	+33-40%

Source: Company financial reports.

As was the case during the downturn, the biggest investment change is expected to come from US independents who are already responding to higher prices. Several companies revised up their 2016 spending plans towards the end of last year as they increased activity, especially in the Permian basin. Activity is expected to accelerate further over 2017, and firms such as Chesapeake, Devon and Noble Energy have all announced higher capex plans. While capex trends and objectives vary across LTO operators, improving financial conditions seem to be a priority many, including Devon and Apache as well as traditionally heavily leveraged players such as Continental Resources and Noble Energy. A shift in company focus towards repairing balance sheets and generating positive cash flow might dampen growth in the near term.

As spending levels slowly pick up, costs are also expected to increase. According to the IEA's upstream Investment Cost Index (UICI), over the past two years upstream costs fell by roughly 30% to levels last seen more than a decade ago[*]. IEA's *World Energy Investment 2016* found that as capex

[*] The projects included within the UICI are fixed, i.e. the UICI does not account for changes in the complexity or geography of upstream projects that have been executed. A combination of these changes with changes in the UICI would be reflected in the global average cost of producing a barrel of oil.

Box 2.1 Upstream investment sees modest increase in 2017, but costs rise too (continued)

fell, cost deflation underpinned around two-thirds of the reduction in while lower activity made up for the remainder. Globally, upstream costs dropped by 15% in 2015 and 17% in 2016. Cost deflation seen in the US shale industry was even higher - at 30% in 2015 and 22% in 2016.

In order to reduce costs, operators have renegotiated or terminated contracts, deferred or cancelled projects and retendered new projects. In an attempt to capture long-term efficiencies, companies have made efforts to consolidate their pool of suppliers, and standardized equipment and processes. While variations exist across regions and industry sectors, there is a growing perception that around 50-60% of cost reductions achieved will not be sustainable in the near future. As such, the reinforcement of cost-efficiency strategies has been emphasized in companies' financial filings.

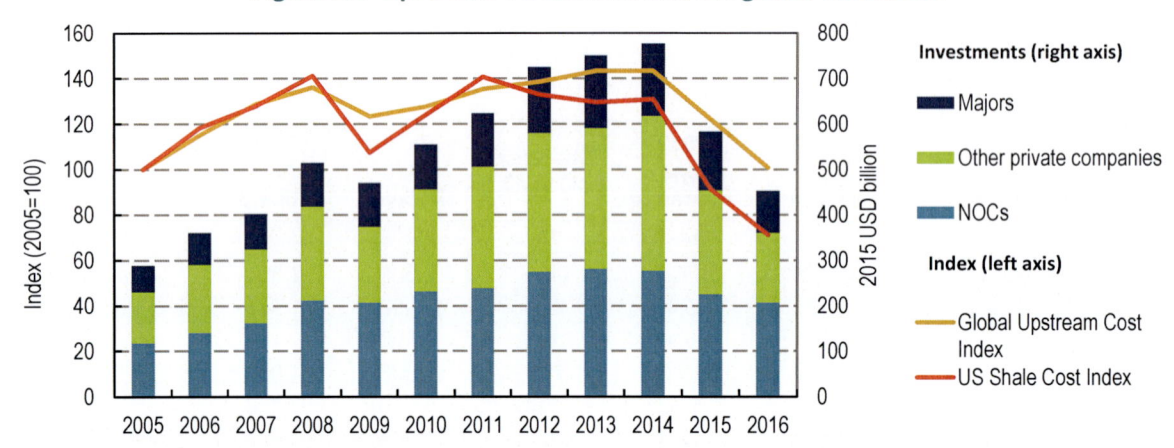

Figure 2.3 Upstream investment and IEA global cost index

Source: IEA (2016) *World Energy Investment*

Signs of cost inflation are already emerging, with pressure pumping and land drilling costs seen rising the most. Logistic services costs are also expected to increase, and for activities such as drilling and completions, most of the cost reductions have likely already been achieved. Companies do, however, expect data acquisition, subsea and engineering services to see further decreases in the coming 12 months. Additional declines could also come from the offshore sector, as investment (with the exception of Brazil) remains muted and could even contract further. Reductions could also come as some high-cost contracts (especially for drilling ships) are ending and new ones will likely better reflect the current market situation and show significant savings. As such, while overall upstream costs might increase modestly in the US this year, elsewhere they could remain under pressure for a while longer.

The industry has also shown its ability to adapt to a lower-for-longer price environment by cutting operational costs by an average 26% since the 2013 peak. Over the period of rising oil prices, companies shifted their strategies to increase and diversify the portfolio of upstream assets with less concern over operational expenditures. As a result, lifting costs[*] increased by 50% in the sector between 2010 and 2013, and by as much as 68% in the case of majors, suggesting not only the development of more expensive resources but also growing inefficiencies in the companies' operational procedures. Judging by the latest earnings reports, however, companies remain focused on continuing to capture efficiencies to drive costs even lower.

* Lifting cost is the total production cost of operating a well divided by the total production. This typically refers to the cost of producing oil and gas after drilling is complete, including transportation costs, labor costs, supplies, costs of operating the pumps and electricity used.

Non-OPEC supply overview

Non-OPEC oil production is expected to return to growth this year after a difficult 2016. Higher prices are encouraging increased investment in the US, while a number of long lead-time projects will be completed and brought on stream elsewhere. Growth should accelerate in 2018 and remain relatively robust in 2019, though the hiatus in new investment decisions since 2014 will significantly slow growth thereafter. For the 2016-22 period, non-OPEC supplies are forecast to grow by 3.3 mb/d, to reach 60.9 mb/d in 2022.

The twin force of lower oil prices and unprecedented spending cuts slashed roughly 0.8 mb/d of non-OPEC liquids output in 2016. The steepest drop came, as expected, from light tight oil (LTO) regions in the US. More surprising was the extent of the declines seen in China and Colombia. As prices plunged below USD 40/bbl, producers in both countries reduced spending and shut in uneconomic wells.

Equally surprising was the resilience of Russian production. Although dollar earnings from exports fell dramatically, the drop in the value of the rouble was a major offsetting factor which allowed companies to maintain or increase spending on domestic operations. Rosneft, for example, increased development drilling by more than 50% year-on-year to manage field decline. Operators in the North Sea also defied expectations by posting a third consecutive year of growth, after most observers had written off the region as being in terminal decline.

In our forecast period, the Americas will continue to dominate growth. The United States is the number one source of extra supply, adding 1.6 mb/d by 2022. LTO output is forecast to expand by 1.4 mb/d over the period, with growth strongest in the early years before stabilising in the absence of higher prices or further technological breakthroughs. A higher price than shown in the futures strip used to model these projections would be required to see more substantial growth (Box 2.2). The output of natural gas liquids (NGLs) will grow by 0.9 mb/d, while conventional crude production (excluding LTO) declines.

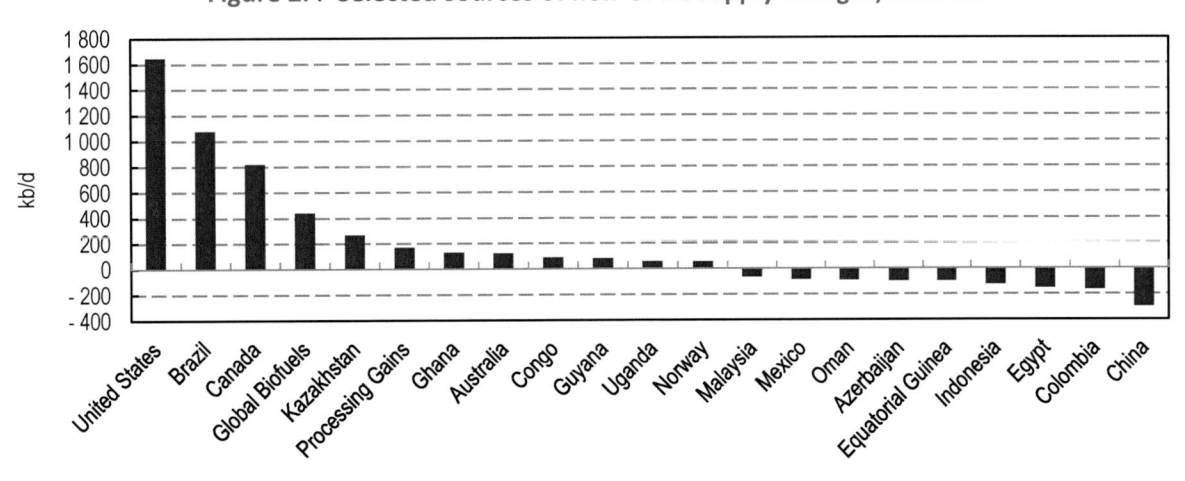

Figure 2.4 Selected sources of non-OPEC supply changes, 2016-22

Other gains will come from Brazil (1.1 mb/d) and Canada (0.8 mb/d) where long lead-time projects in the pre-salt polygon and in oil sands, respectively, come on stream. Smaller increases come from Kazakhstan and global biofuels output. Output from non-OPEC's top five sources of growth over the next six years - the US, Canada, Brazil, Kazakhstan and global biofuels -will increase by a combined 4.3 mb/d by 2022, while the rest of non-OPEC declines by nearly 1 mb/d in total.

Figure 2.5 Supply from non-OPEC top five sources of growth vs others

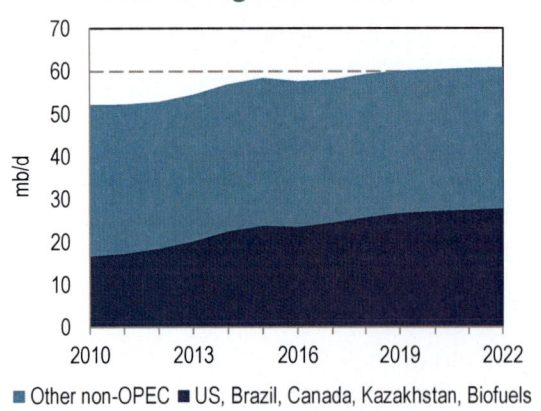

Figure 2.6 Annual increase from non-OPEC top five sources of growth vs others

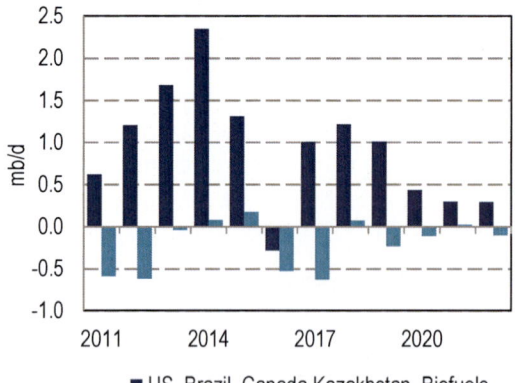

Following a significant increase in development drilling over the past two years, the outlook for Russian oil output has materially improved. A weak rouble and a progressive tax system have allowed oil companies to maintain spending through the downturn, with the government budget taking the biggest hit from the drop in oil prices. Boasting lower production costs than anywhere but the Middle East, Russia is expected to hold total liquids output more or less steady at around 11.3 mb/d over the forecast period.

Table 2.2 Non-OPEC supply (mb/d)

	2016	2017	2018	2019	2020	2021	2022	2016-22
OECD	23.4	23.6	24.4	24.9	25.3	25.7	25.8	2.4
Americas	19.5	19.8	20.5	21.1	21.4	21.7	21.8	2.4
Europe	3.5	3.4	3.4	3.3	3.4	3.5	3.4	-0.1
Asia Oceania	0.4	0.4	0.4	0.5	0.6	0.6	0.5	0.1
Non-OECD	29.6	29.6	30.0	30.1	30.0	29.9	29.9	0.2
FSU	14.2	14.3	14.6	14.6	14.5	14.4	14.3	0.1
Europe	0.1	0.1	0.1	0.1	0.1	0.1	0.1	-0.0
China	4.0	3.8	3.8	3.8	3.7	3.7	3.7	-0.3
Other Asia	3.6	3.5	3.4	3.3	3.3	3.2	3.2	-0.4
Americas	4.5	4.7	4.8	5.1	5.2	5.3	5.4	0.9
Middle East	1.3	1.2	1.2	1.2	1.2	1.2	1.2	-0.0
Africa	1.9	2.0	2.0	2.0	2.0	1.9	1.9	-0.1
Non-OPEC Oil Production	53.0	53.3	54.4	55.1	55.3	55.6	55.7	2.7
Processing Gains	2.3	2.3	2.3	2.3	2.4	2.4	2.4	0.2
Global Biofuels	2.3	2.5	2.6	2.7	2.8	2.8	2.8	0.4
Total-Non-OPEC Supply	57.6	58.0	59.3	60.1	60.4	60.7	60.9	3.3
Annual Change	-0.8	0.4	1.3	0.8	0.3	0.3	0.2	0.5
Changes from last *MTOMR**	-0.1	0.3	0.9	1.1	0.8	0.3		

* Including Indonesia, excluding Gabon throughout

In contrast, 2016 provided a valuable reminder of how fast output can fall if spending levels and drilling rates are not maintained. China and Colombia, both characterised by mature and naturally declining output, saw output plunge by 7% and 12% year-on-year, respectively, in 2016 as producers cut back drilling and shut marginal fields. While higher spending and the application of advanced technology will help mitigate the decline rate going forward, it will likely not be enough to reverse the structural trend. China, along with Colombia and Egypt sees the largest production declines in the medium term.

United States

The United States is expected to be the largest contributor to non-OPEC supply growth in the medium term. Increased drilling, helped by cost deflation and efficiency improvements, sees US output expanding by nearly 1.6 mb/d through 2022, even assuming stable crude oil prices of around USD 60/bbl over the period. Roughly half the gains are expected to come from natural gas liquids as infrastructure developments, both in terms of expanded export capacity and new US petrochemical plants, support growth in coming years. Crude and condensate production grows by 0.8 mb/d, as declines in conventional production partly offset output gains from LTO formations.

Figure 2.7 US total oil production

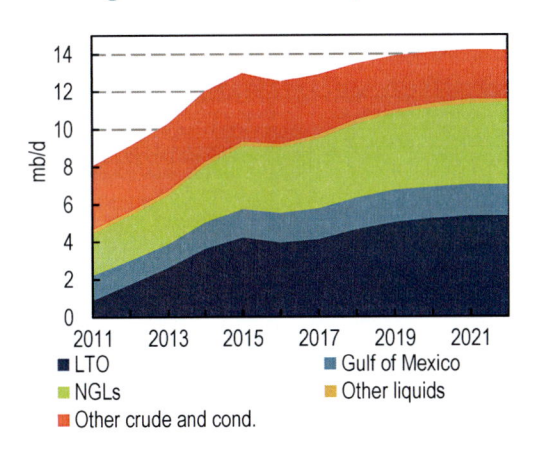

Figure 2.8 US oil output growth by type

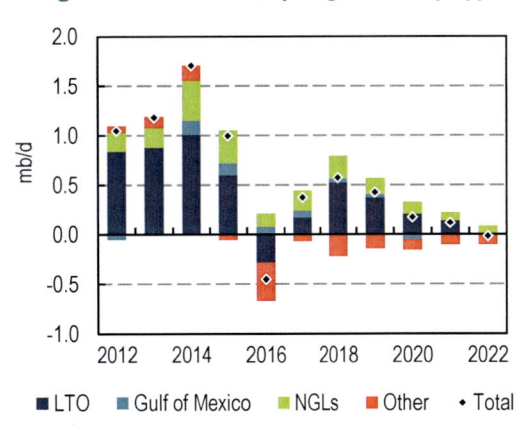

With US WTI crude oil prices recovering from below USD 30/bbl at the start of 2016 to around USD 55/bbl a year later, LTO production is set to return to growth during 2017. After hitting a low of 316 last May, the number of active oil rigs in the US has risen steadily, reaching a total of 525 at the end of 2016 and 602 by the end of February. The pace of the increase picked up markedly towards the end of 2016 and at the start of 2017, as the OPEC/non-OPEC agreement to restrict output appeared to set a floor under prices, providing operators with enough certainty to increase activity. In December, 48 new rigs were brought into operation, the highest increase since early 2014. While up 66% since the May 2016 low, the number of rigs still fell short of the year-ago level. Only in early 2017, with operators adding another 77 rigs over January and February, did we see year-on-year (y-o-y) increases in the number of operational oil rigs in the US.

As only the best acreage was tapped, US operators continued to show impressive productivity gains in 2016. According to data from Rystad Energy, average well performance, as measured by cumulative production by well, increased by 25% in 2016. The Energy Information Administration's (EIA) *Drilling Productivity Report* shows similarly improvements in production per rig.

Supply

Figure 2.9 Average oil well performance by US Shale play

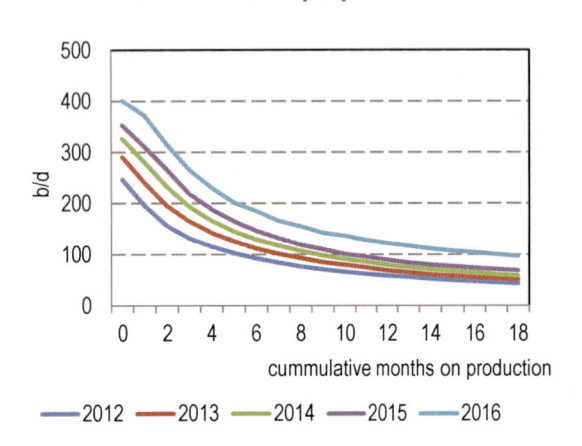

Figure 2.10 Oil production per rig

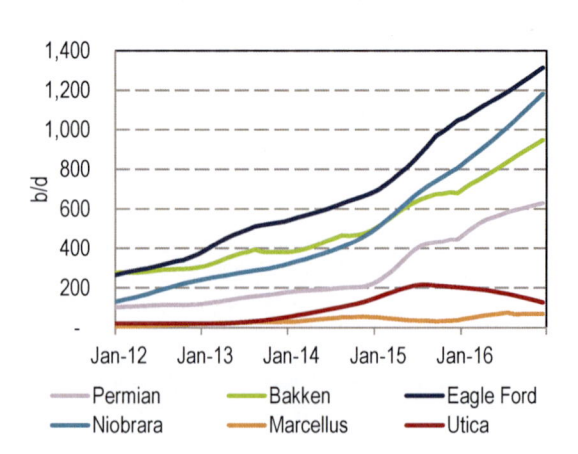

Sources: Rystad Energy; EIA Drilling Productivity Report.

LTO production is forecast to expand by 1.4 mb/d through 2022, with the strongest growth seen in 2018. Due to the time lag between spudded and completed wells, which generally averages between four to six months, growth in 2017 will be restricted to around 180 kb/d. Output picks up rapidly, however, rising by more than 500 kb/d during the course of the year to a new all-time high by end-2017. More substantial growth will come in 2018, when annual average output is expected to be 530 kb/d higher. From there, growth tapers off as producers are unlikely to support further increases in activity in the absence of incremental price increases and/or additional cost/technology improvements. As production rises, more wells will have to be drilled just to maintain output levels. Furthermore, as the best resources are developed and less productive areas are next to be tapped, and as input costs (such as steel, sand, labour, etc.) are likely to increase, the economics of new wells will again deteriorate.

Figure 2.11 US rig count vs oil price

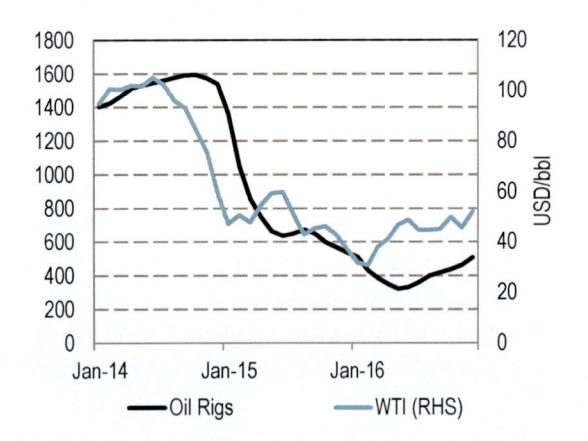

Figure 2.12 US light tight oil production

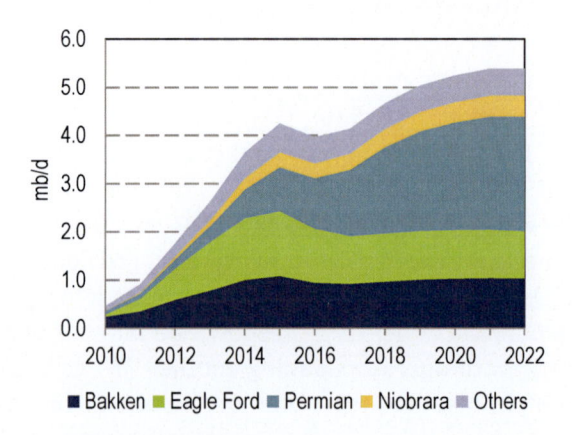

The estimate for LTO production is nevertheless higher than last year's *Report*. Not only have cost reductions and efficiency improvements over the past two years lowered the financial break-even price for most plays, but crucially, the total resource estimate for recoverable reserves has been lifted. In its 2016 Annual Energy Outlook (AEO), the EIA increased its estimate for technically recoverable LTO resources from 88 billion barrels to more than 100 billion barrels, which suggests that a higher number of wells will be economical at a given set of prices.

Box 2.2 If the price is right

This *Report* derives its price assumptions for modelling purposes from the futures curve. At the time of writing, prompt month Brent futures were trading at USD 58/bbl and staying at roughly this level through 2022. The futures curve is not a price forecast and is an imperfect modelling tool. It nevertheless represents the level at which market participants can hedge today and, as such, still influences investment and business decisions – at least in the near term.

The steady price trajectory through 2022 suggests that market participants expect plentiful US LTO supplies coupled with continued OPEC market management to keep oil trading in a narrow range. In reality, oil prices are likely to be volatile and deviate from those indicated by the current futures strip. Factors on both the demand and supply side of the oil market balance, downstream bottlenecks and geopolitical events at some point or another may see oil prices take a different course.

The production response of shale at different price levels is therefore critical, as it will play a key role in balancing the market over the medium term. As witnessed over the past two years, US LTO responds more rapidly to price signals than other sources of supply. Still, output did not fall as quickly and as deeply as many had anticipated due to the time-lag between drilling and oil flowing. Moreover, operators had hedged parts of their production and launched cost-cutting and efficiency measures. Our base case sees US LTO expand by 1.4 mb/d over the forecast period, if prices remain in the USD 55-60/bbl range suggested by the futures curve.

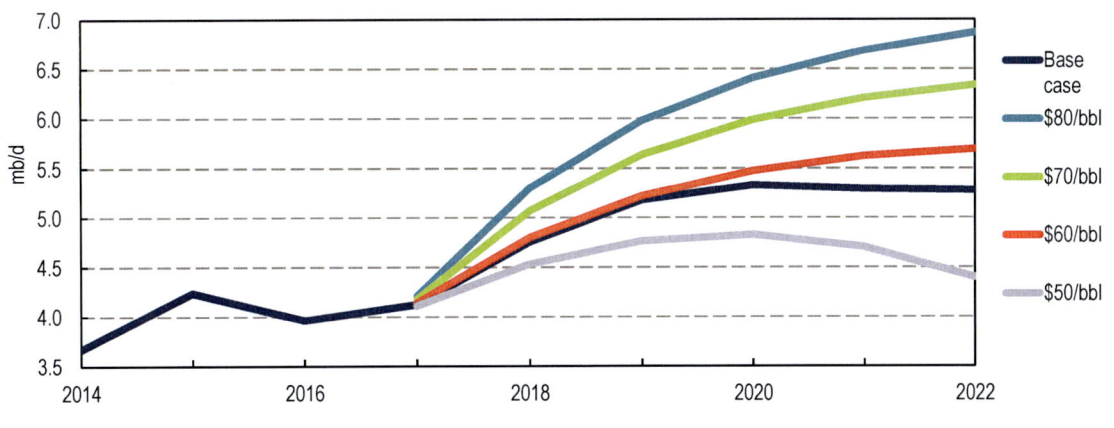

Figure 2.13 US light tight oil production sensitivities

Should prices for any extended period of time veer outside this band, however, LTO production is expected to respond accordingly. If prices climbed to USD 80/bbl – which is the reference price assumed in the World Energy Outlook's New Policies Scenario - production could be 1.6 mb/d higher than our base case by 2022. Alternatively, a price of USD 50/bbl would cause LTO output to decline from the early 2020s.

Of course, the price of oil is not the only variable that will affect LTO production. The size of remaining technically recoverable resources, for which estimates were raised by the EIA from 88 to 103 billion barrels in the 2016 AEO, is important as the implied intensity of sweet spots rises proportionally.

Future technological improvements and productivity gains as well as cost inflation will be equally important. Growth will likely be tempered by inflation in service costs, after idle capacity during the

SUPPLY

> **Box 2.2 If the price is right (continued)**
>
> downturn led the industry to cut margins to the bone. Signs of cost inflation are already emerging, with pressure pumping and land drilling costs seen rising the most.
>
> While the industry does not cease to impress with improvement in productivity rates, gains are unlikely to continue at the same rates. Operators have optimized drilling and completion techniques, and are operating more efficiently. Many of the recent gains, however, stem from the fact that only the most prolific acreage made economic sense during the downturn. But even when capital was allocated to only the very best wells it was not enough for the industry to generate positive cash flow. Going forward, further improvements in well productivity will be constrained as drillers move away from the sweet spots and start developing second and third-tier wells.

Crude and condensate production in the **Gulf of Mexico**, meanwhile, is expected to average just under 1.7 mb/d by 2022, 80 kb/d more than in 2016. Growth slowed last year, to around 85 kb/d, compared with 120 kb/d in 2015 and 140 kb/d in 2014. Spending cuts have resulted in lower activity in the Gulf, and relatively few new projects are due to come online in the coming years. Growth will taper off entirely by 2020 unless further projects are brought forward.

In the near term, capacity increases will come from Shell's 50 kb/d Stones project which was commissioned in September 2016, and from Noble's 20 kb/d Gunflint project, Exxon's 34 kb/d Julia project and Anadarko's 80 kb/d Heidelberg spar, which also started up last year. In 2017, Freeport McMoRan plans to bring online its 30 kb/d Horn Mountain Deep development. BP will increase the capacity at its Thunder Horse field, first by 25 kb/d through a water injection programme, and by a further 50 kb/d from its South Expansion Project brought on-stream at the end of 2016.

In 2018, first oil is expected from Chevron's 75 kb/d Big Foot platform and Hess's 80 kb/d Stampede project. Towards the end of the decade, Shell is planning to start production from its 175 kb/d Appomattox project, while BP recently sanctioned its Mad Dog Phase 2 project at less than half the original cost estimate. Mad Dog 2, which will include a new FPSO with the capacity to produce 140 kb/d of oil, is targeting production start-up in late 2021.

> **Box 2.3 New outlets spur US NGL supply boom**
>
> US natural gas liquids (NGLs) will be a leading source of non-OPEC production growth in the medium term as new export terminals and domestic petrochemical plants offer outlets for products. Production of NGLs – including ethane, propane, normal butane, isobutane and natural gasoline – is forecast to increase by 0.9 mb/d by 2022 to 4.5 mb/d.
>
> The supply of NGL has expanded by an impressive 1.4 mb/d, or nearly 70%, to 3.5 mb/d over the past six years. Crude oil output grew at nearly the same rate, adding 3.36 mb/d. During our forecast period, however, the share of NGLs in total US oil supplies, already at 28% (when excluding biofuels) in 2016, will increase as more liquids are stripped out of the gas stream.
>
> Ethane is set to drive NGL growth over the coming years. New deep-water export facilities in Pennsylvania (Marcus Hook) and Texas (Morgan's Point) will fuel the growth. Product is now being shipped to Europe and India on specially designed carriers. Until recently, ethane was consumed only by North American ethylene plants. With no available export outlets, the economics did not favour full ethane recovery. As a result, increasing volumes were reinjected in the gas stream and in 2015 we

Box 2.3 New outlets spur US NGL supply boom (continued)

estimate that the volume was nearly 500 kb/d. Volumes declined to 360 kb/d over 2016 and will continue to fall as new offtake capacity comes online.

Domestic demand for ethane is expected to increase as new ethylene production facilities are completed. During 2017, feedstock capacity at ethylene cracking plants is set to rise by 6 700 thousand metric tons/year, or the equivalent of an additional 400 kb/d of ethane feedstock. In addition to expansions and feedstock conversion projects, five new ethylene plants are to start up in Texas this year. These are Dow Chemical Co.'s Freeport, OxyChem/MexiChem JV's Ingleside, Chevron Phillips Chemical's Baytown, ExxonMobil Chemical's Baytown and Formosa Plastics Corp's plant at Point Comfort.

Figure 2.14 Estimated US ethane rejection

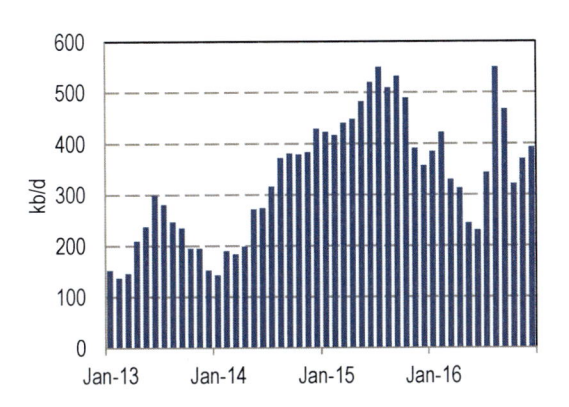

Figure 2.15 US LPG exports

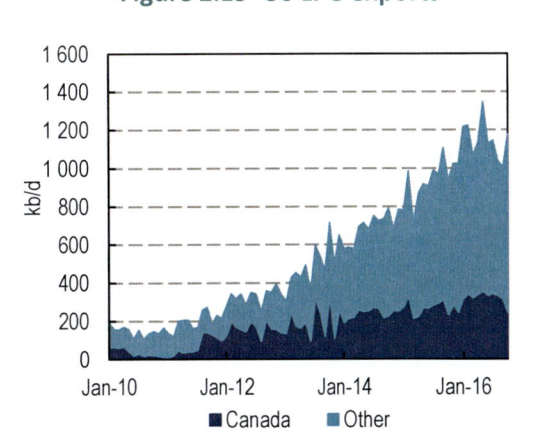

The US has also seen a remarkable expansion of its propane/butane export capacity. Capacity has increased from only 200 kb/d at the start of 2013 to 1.3 mb/d in early 2017. The latest addition was Phillips66' Freeport, TX 150 kb/d propane/butane export facility, which started up in 3Q16. As such, NGL and LPG exports have increased five-fold in only four years to more than 1 mb/d.

Canada

Despite the prolonged slump in oil prices and the deferral of a number of projects, Canada will remain a key contributor to non-OPEC supply growth in the medium term. In 2016, growth was derailed by devastating wildfires across Alberta, but, as infrastructure was largely left intact, production is set to rebound sharply in 2017, and indeed this was already seen towards the end of 2016. Recently completed oil sands projects, and sites already under construction, will drive growth to 2022. Oil sands production, including upgraded synthetic crude, is forecast to expand by 900 kb/d over the outlook period to reach 3.3 mb/d in 2022. Total Canadian oil supplies are forecast to grow by 820 kb/d, to 5.3 mb/d in 2022, from 4.5 mb/d in 2016.

Growth will be heavily front-loaded, with production rising 150 kb/d in 2017 and around 170 kb/d in both 2018 and 2019. In addition to the rebound from last year's shut-ins, gains will come from the ramping up of ConocoPhillips' Surmont project, Cenovus's Foster Creek expansion and Canadian Natural Resource Ltd.'s (CNRL) Horizon mining and upgrading expansion. During 2018, Suncor is planning to commission its Fort Hills site, which will add an extra 160 kb/d once fully operational. From 2020, growth slows to around 100 kb/d per year, as a number of projects were put on hold for financial reasons or still awaiting regulatory approval from the Albertan provincial government.

SUPPLY

Figure 2.16 Canada total oil production

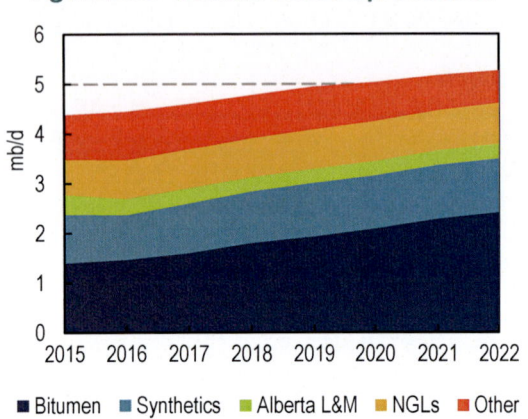

Figure 2.17 Canada annual supply growth

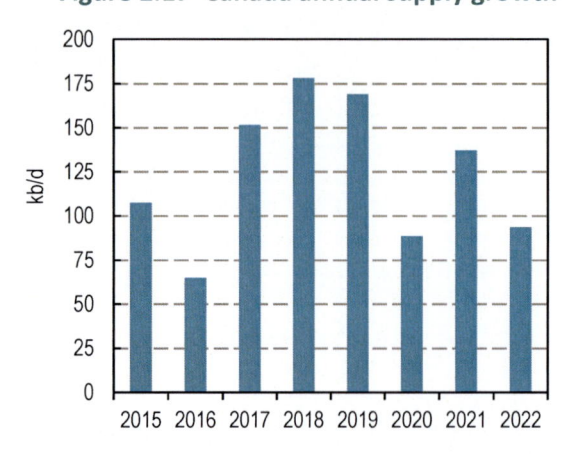

Following the long awaited approval of two new pipeline projects at the end of 2016 (Box 2.4), and significant cost reductions, Canadian producers are considering increased investments. Cenovus Energy, for example, announced in December 2016 that it plans to invest USD 1.2-1.4 billion in 2017, an increase of 24% from last year and proceed with the expansion of its Christina Lake project, after having put it on hold when prices plunged. The expansion will raise capacity by 50 kb/d when completed during 2H19. CNRL also said lower costs were among the factors allowing it to move forward with its 40 kb/d Kirby North oil sands project.

Conventional crude oil output is set to decline over the forecast period, despite new offshore supplies. Offshore Newfoundland and Labrador, the Exxon-led 150 kb/d Hebron project is scheduled to come online in late 2017, while new production from satellite fields supports output at Hibernia, where output already ramped up to four year highs at end-2016. Natural gas liquids (NGLs), including pentanes plus, is projected to increase steadily, from 775 kb/d in 2016 to 825 kb/d in 2022.

Box 2.4 Canadian producers eye export expansion, rail use to rise

As Canadian oil output continues to grow, producers are looking ahead to an urgently needed expansion of the export network. Two pipeline projects set to boost export capacity by a combined 960 kb/d were approved at the end of last year, but they will only alleviate bottlenecks from 2019-20. Until then, rail shipments will increase to around 250 kb/d and producers will have to discount heavy Canadian benchmarks such as Western Canada Select (WCS) in order to stay competitive.

Currently, roughly 75% of Canada's crude oil production is exported, mainly by pipeline. The remainder is shipped by rail and barge. Four major pipelines (Kinder Morgan Trans Mountain, Enbridge Mainline, Spectra Express and TransCanada Keystone) move around 3 mb/d of crude from Western Canada to domestic refining centres in the east or to consumers in the US.

The biggest new stretch of proposed pipeline will be Kinder Morgan's Trans Mountain Expansion, which will increase capacity of the existing system that moves crude from Edmonton, Alberta, to Burnaby, British Columbia by 590 kb/d to 890 kb/d. Enbridge's Line 3 Replacement Project, that extends from Edmonton, Alberta to Superior, Wisconsin, will restore the line to its original 760 kb/d nameplate capacity, an increase of 370 kb/d from current maximum throughput rates regulated to about 390 kb/d.

Box 2.4 Canadian producers eye export expansion, rail use to rise (continued)

The proposed in-service date of both projects is 2019. The Canadian government rejected Enbridge's Northern Gateway Pipeline project, designed to ship 525 kb/d of crude from Bruderheim, Alberta to Kitimat, British Columbia, on environmental grounds.

Other pipeline proposals are being considered. TransCanada's Energy East project, if approved, will transport 1.1 mb/d of crude oil from Hardisty, Alberta to the three largest refineries in eastern Canada (Suncor, Valero, and Irving) and to international markets via the port of St John, New Brunswick, by the end of 2021. The new US administration has also revived TransCanada's Keystone XL project: the 1 179-mile project would deliver 830 kb/d of crude oil from Hardisty to Steele City, Nebraska, where it will link up with the existing US network.

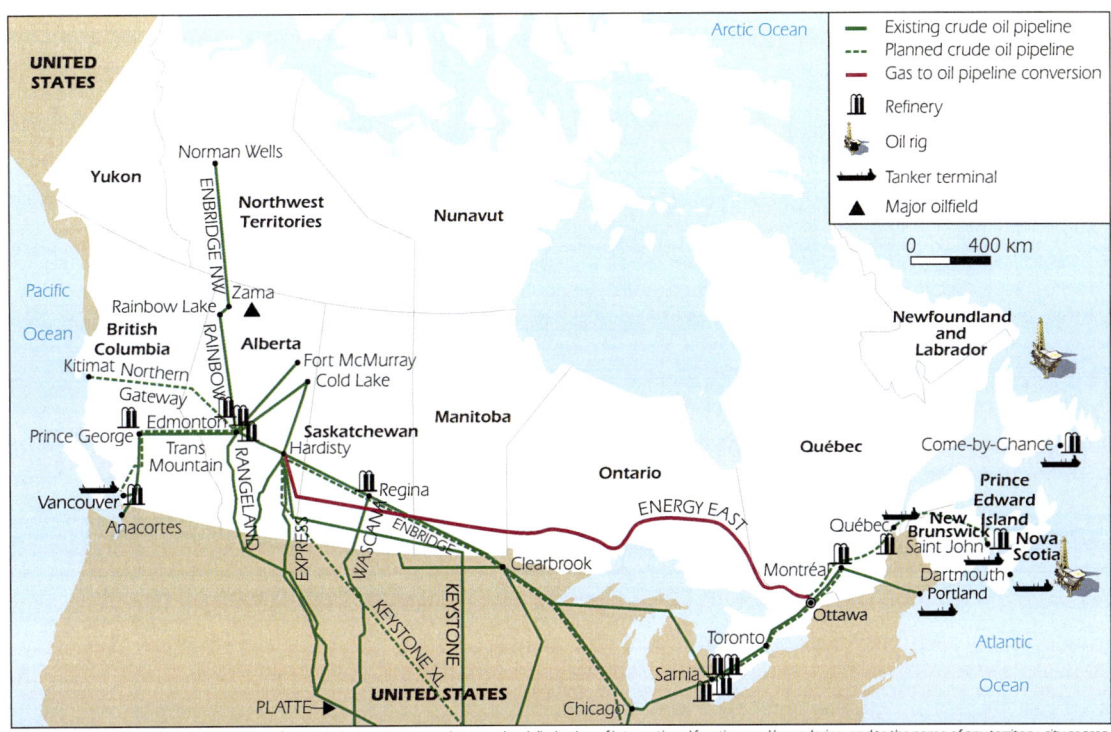

Map 2.1 Canada oil infrastructure

Despite being a significant net oil exporter, Canada relied heavily on imports for more than a third, or roughly 0.5 mb/d, of its refinery feedstock in 2015. With restricted pipeline capacity to move crude from Alberta to the East Coast, and little upgrading capacity to convert heavy and high-sulphur feedstocks into transportation fuels, eight refineries located in Eastern Canada, with a total crude throughput capacity of 1.2 mb/d, imported three quarters of their feedstock, mostly light crude oil, during 2015.

Over the medium term, there are a number of projects designed to increase the share of Canadian crude oil refined at home. In addition to the proposed East Canada pipeline project, the three-phase North West Redwater Sturgeon bitumen refinery project in Alberta will enable the conversion of an additional 240 kb/d of bitumen blend into fuels, but only the first 80 kb/d phase is scheduled to come online within the timeframe of this Report in late 2017. A number of other projects to increase domestic crude conversion capacity are being proposed in British Columbia, though given the recent rejection of the proposed Northern Gateway Pipeline, these are less likely to move ahead.

Box 2.4 Canadian producers eye export expansion, rail use to rise (continued)

When pipeline capacity has not been available or domestic needs have fallen, rail shipments offer a vital relief valve. That is sure to be the case again. As no new pipeline capacity will be added before 2019, crude exports by rail could jump from 80 kb/d in 2016 to 520 kb/d in 2017 before falling back to 430 kb/d in 2018. Implied rail export requirements will, however, decline to an average 105 kb/d over 2019-22 as supply growth eases and as additional pipeline capacity comes online. According to the National Energy Board, total crude oil rail loading capacity in Western Canada is 1 mb/d, well above crude-by-rail needs in 2017 and 2018.

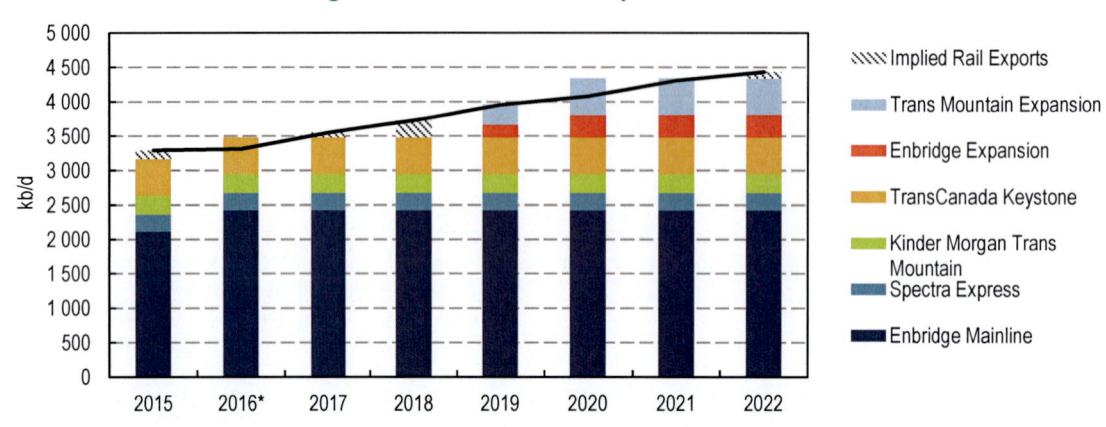

Figure 2.18 US crude receipts from Canada

* 2016 supply affected by wildfires.

The export bottleneck is also expected to have a significant impact on prices. The differential between WCS and West Texas Intermediate (WTI), the US light oil benchmark, typically reflects the difference in quality and the cost to move crude from origin to destination. The cost to transport heavy crude from Western Canada to the Gulf Coast by rail is now around USD 15-20/bbl compared to USD 7-10/bbl for pipeline exports. As infrastructure constraints led to an increased need for rail shipments, the price differential between WTI/WCS widened to around USD 20/bbl on average over 2011 to 2014 and reached as much as USD 39/bbl in December 2013. As oil prices fell, however, the discount narrowed to USD 13-14/bbl over 2015 and 2016, barely enough to cover rail costs.

Figure 2.19 Crude oil prices

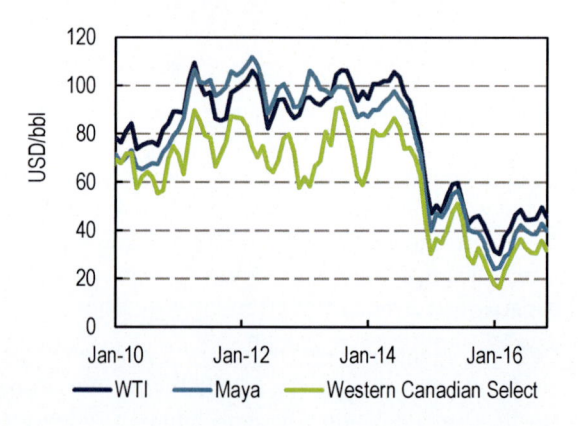

With rail shipments set to rise, producers in Alberta will have to offer a discount to WTI and other crudes such as Mexican Maya, which can be shipped to the US Gulf Coast for a few dollars a barrel. From 2020 onwards, the WCS-WTI spread is likely to narrow provided that new infrastructure is built. The reliance on US markets and associated transport costs may maintain the pressure on Canadian crude prices. As such, a diversification of export outlets and spare transport capacity is desirable. Otherwise, Canada might face restricted access to markets where the highest growth in crude oil demand is concentrated – namely Asia.

Mexico

While making good progress towards opening up of its upstream sector to foreign and domestic competition, it will take time for new projects to reverse the declining trend in oil output. Mexican oil production is set to decline to a low of just 2.2 mb/d in 2019. From 2020 onwards, however, increased investment is set to reverse the trend. Total oil production, including NGLs, is forecast to average 2.4 mb/d in 2022, only slightly lower than the 2016 average. Of this, crude oil and condensates account for roughly 2.1 mb/d.

Since embarking on its historic oil sector liberalisation in late 2013, the Mexican government has completed the first round of the Upstream Reform. Last December, it concluded the fourth, and last, bid opening of Round 1, by awarding eight out of 10 deep water blocks on offer to companies including China Offshore Oil Corp., Total, ExxonMobil, Chevron, Inpex, Statoil, BP and a handful of smaller independents. The success of the latest bid opening, known as 1.4, is seen as pivotal to the outlook and to the overall success of the reform because the deep water leases on offer are the most likely to reverse a decline in supply over the longer term. Previously, the government had awarded 30 contracts in the shallow water and onshore to 33 private companies.

Figure 2.20 Mexico total oil production

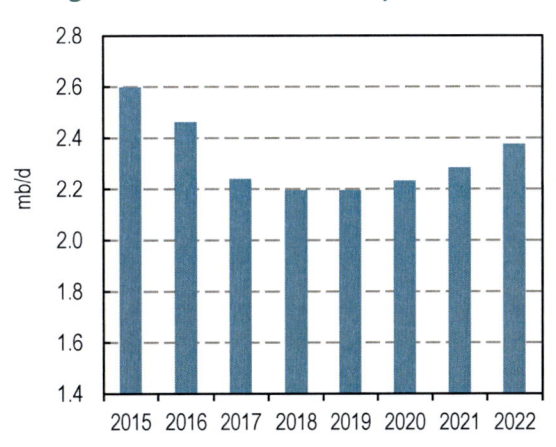

As part of its upstream opening, Mexico's state oil company, Pemex, laid out a new strategy last November that highlights a dramatic shift to the use of partnerships in the exploration and production sector. The plans open up more than 160 new opportunities for private companies. As part of the last bid opening of Round 1 Pemex has already signed its first joint venture deal under the new sector framework with BHP Billiton to develop the Trion deep-water development near the maritime border with the US, and the company expects that 2017 will also bring other farm-outs in the shallow-water area of Ayin-Batsil and the onshore areas of Ogarrio and Cardenas-Mora. In 2017, upstream regulator Comision Nacional de Hidrocarburos (CNH) plans to auction 15 shallow-water blocks, which could hold reserves of almost 1.6 billion barrels of oil equivalent. The CNH also plans to auction off this year 26 onshore blocks, including 12 seen as highly prospective for gas. Also, three more auctions might be added to the 2017 schedule or 2018.

Pemex's latest 2016-21 business plan lists 2017 as its target date for partnerships in the extra-heavy oil field of Ayatsil-Tekel-Utsil and in the Chicontepec region, as well as seven more unspecified onshore areas in the northern and southern parts of the country. The strategy sets out ambitious plans for 2018, with six deals proposed for shallow northern waters, 64 onshore agreements in the north and south and 86 natural gas contracts in the Burgos and Veracruz areas.

Brazil

Despite numerous challenges, the outlook for **Brazilian** oil production remains promising, with another 1.1 mb/d to be added to supply by 2022. State-owned Petrobras and its partners have lifted output by 0.8 mb/d over the past decade, and growth is set to accelerate with a number of new production systems being commissioned over the coming years. The removal of Petrobras's mandatory minimum 30% operating stake in unlicensed acreage in the pre-salt polygon and a lowering of local content requirements will likely spur more foreign investment.

While Petrobras again has taken the axe to investments, it still plans to raise its domestic oil production by 700 kb/d over 2017-21, from an expected 2.07 mb/d targeted for this year. In a revised business plan released last September, Petrobras said it expects to spend USD 74.1 billion over the coming five years, a 25% decrease from the USD 98.4 billion outlined in the previous plan. Petrobras, which will continue to focus its investments in the upstream, said that improved operating performance and the application of new technologies will underpin growth despite lower spending. The company has already reduced the average time needed to build an offshore well in the Santos Basin from 152 days in 2010 to only 54 days in 2016. Furthermore, it said that average lifting costs had declined to less than USD 8/bbl compared to an industry average of around USD 15/bbl, while pre-salt wells productivity – at around 25 kb/d per well – is much higher than originally expected.

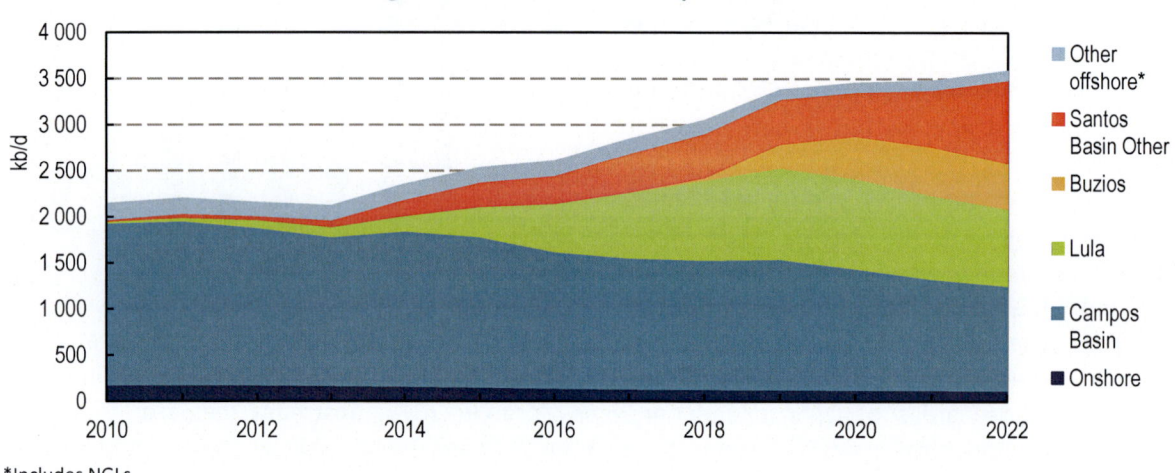

Figure 2.21 Brazil total oil production

*Includes NGLs.

Petrobras' business plan foresees 19 new production systems being brought online over the coming five years. In 2017, the Tartaruga and Mestiça projects, in the post-salt Campos Basin, will be brought online followed by new units at the Lula Norte and Lula Sul fields in the Santos Basin pre-salt as well as the Libra Extended Well Test (EWT). In 2018, Petrobras plans to start operations at Berbigão, Lula Extremo Sul, and Búzios 1, 2 and 3, all in the pre-salt cluster. The target date for first commercial oil from Libra has been kept at 2020. Petrobras is currently tendering for a floating production, storage and offloading vessel (FPSO) with capacity to produce 180 kb/d and 12 million cubic metres per day of natural gas in the area. Also in 2020, Petrobras plans to start production from Sepia, Buzios 5 and the first floater to revitalise output in the Marlim field in the Campos basin. Petrobras unveiled plans to contract new units to enter operations in 2021, including Libra 2, Itapu, the integrated development at the Parque das Baleias complex and a second FPSO to be installed at Marlim.

Meanwhile, the giant Lula pre-salt field in the Santos Basin continues to expand and is expected to reach production of 1 mboe/d next year, seven years after commercial production started via a pilot FPSO. Petrobras and partners Shell (through its takeover of BG Group) and Portugal's Galp Energia are currently producing about 700 kb/d from Lula from six FPSOs, of which four — Cidade de Angra dos Reis, Cidade de Paraty, Cidade de Mangaratiba and Cidade de Itaguai — have already reached their plateau rates. A further two floaters — Cidade de Marica and Cidade de Saquarema —were deployed in 2016. The Cidade de Itaguai FPSO is set to reach peak production in just 13 months while the Cidade de Marica and Cidade de Saquarema are expected to top their respective production capacity of 150 kb/d in less than 12 months. The Lula full field development calls for the installation of 10 FPSOs in all. Petrobras has postponed production from Lula West until after 2021, however, following disappointing reservoir data.

Brazil is also making important progress in opening up its upstream sector to international oil companies. Late last year, the government approved guidelines for upcoming bid rounds, including the second offering of production-sharing contracts in pre-salt acreage. On 29 November, Brazilian president Michel Temer sanctioned a law removing Petrobras's mandatory minimum 30% operating stake in unlicensed pre-salt acreage. Under the new law, Petrobras will retain preferential rights to new pre-salt areas awarded under the PSA contract regime and may participate in licensing rounds if it wants to bid for more than a 30% stake. Furthermore, the government has approved regulatory changes that lower the local content percentages for areas to be offered under the PSA regime. Brazil, which only held three bid rounds using the concession contract regime and tendered only one new pre-salt block over the past seven years, plans to hold three auctions in 2017. More frequent licensing rounds, with reduced NOC participation, as well as expanded partnerships and divestments by Petrobras, will open up increased opportunities for IOC investment.

IOCs are already scaling up their investments in Brazil. Shell recently allocated USD 10 billion to its projects over the next five years, in addition to any potential acquisitions of new upstream assets. The capital is set to go mainly towards increasing sub-salt output and most notably towards the development of the 8 - 12 billion barrel Libra field, in which it holds a 20% stake alongside Petrobras (40%), Total (20%), CNOOC (10%) and CNPC (10%). Shell forecasts its Brazilian production to reach more than 800 kboe/d by 2020, from around 300 kboe/d currently. Total and Petrobras signed a strategic partnership in October 2016, and in December Total acquired a 35% operating stake in the Lapa field - which started production in December - and a 22.5% stake in the Berbigão and Sururu fields for USD 2.2 billion. Statoil, meanwhile, paid USD 2.5 billion for a 66% stake in the BM-S-8 block containing the Carcara discovery in July, in what was Petrobras's first major subsalt sale.

Petrobras reported total debts of USD 122.7 billion in 2016, and it has taken steps to reduce this burden by increasing the sale of non-core assets. The company has said it plans to expedite the ongoing divestment process, setting a new target to sell USD 19.5 billion-worth of assets in the next two years starting in 2017 – following a USD 15 billion divestment program for 2015-2016. While making some important sales in 2016, a court ruling in early December forced the company to put on hold the sale of a number of assets, including 100 onshore upstream assets as well as its BR Distribuidora subsidiary, which operates the company's largest fuel distribution network. Petrobras secured a 10-year loan deal with China Development Bank for USD 5 billion in December, following a USD 10 billion lending agreement signed in February 2016. In the February deal, Petrobras committed to supply a total of 100 kb/d of crude oil to Chinese refiners for 10 years.

Other Latin America

After posting one of non-OPEC's largest output reductions in 2016, **Colombia's** decline is expected to ease in 2017, as higher prices and government incentives spur renewed investment. Colombian crude oil supplies fell by as much as 120 kb/d last year, or 12%, to an average of 890 kb/d, after producers cut spending to the lowest level since 2004. The fall in production is expected to slow to around 40 kb/d in 2017. According to the Colombian Petroleum Association, oil firms plan to invest more than USD 3 billion in exploration and development projects in 2017, a 30% increase from the USD 2.3 billion spent last year.

As a result of the spending declines, the number of exploration and production wells drilled in 2016 totalled only 25 and 150 compared with 25 and 710, respectively, in 2015 and more than 130 and 1000 in 2013 when Colombia was seeing strong growth in crude output. Drilling activity is already trending higher, however, as the rig count hit 19 in December, after bottoming out at two in April, according to the latest Baker Hughes International Rig Count data.

Figure 2.22 Colombia total oil production

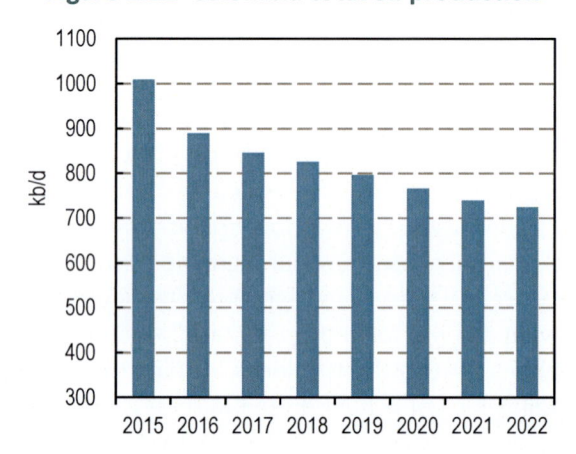

The Colombian government is also planning to provide incentives to spur new investments. Congress is expected to pass a bill that includes tax credits, new investment rules to boost oil field cash flow and the refund of value-added taxes to companies that explore offshore plays. The government has also promised to take action to cut the number of community blockades, which forced oil companies to suspend drilling. Colombian oil production is nevertheless expected to decline to an average 725 kb/d in 2022.

Oil production in **Argentina** is also expected to fall over the medium term. Developments in the tight oil formations in Vaca Muerta slowed as oil prices dropped. The government decided to lift a 15-year-old export duty on oil and oil products, effectively slashing its domestic crude prices to bring them into line with international benchmarks, scrapping a longstanding upstream subsidy that was aimed at stimulating domestic production. The government led by President Mauricio Macri, who took office at the end of 2015, has been trying to spur energy investments to boost lagging production. Argentina's many independent oil producers and provincial officials have warned that cutting the price subsidy would reduce industry employment and even bankrupt some smaller upstream companies.

Developments in **Guyana,** meanwhile, are moving ahead at full speed. ExxonMobil, through its Esso Exploration and Production Guyana Limited subsidiary, submitted an application for a production license and an initial development plan to the Ministry of Natural Resources for the Liza field in December, only 17 months after announcing its discovery. The company, which also awarded contracts for a FPSO vessel to be deployed at the field, hopes to take a final investment decision on the project in 2017. The field has potential recoverable resources in excess of 1 billion oil-equivalent barrels and is located in the Stabroek block approximately 120 miles (193 kilometres) offshore

Guyana. Esso Exploration and Production Guyana Limited is the operator and holds a 45% interest in the Stabroek block. Hess Guyana Exploration Ltd. holds a 30% interest, and CNOOC Nexen Petroleum Guyana Limited holds a 25% interest. If all goes to plan, Guyana could become an oil producer by 2021 and quickly ramp up output to 80 kb/d in 2022.

North Sea

North Sea oil production once again surprised with its resilience in 2016. After posting growth of nearly 160 kb/d in 2015, total North Sea supplies increased by a further 85 kb/d, to 3.1 mb/d, in 2016, significantly overshooting official government projections for both Norway and the UK. While a number of new projects are still to come online, declines at mature fields are expected to keep overall output in check through 2020, before the launch of the Johan Sverdrup field returns output to growth. After dipping to a low of 3 mb/d in 2019, North Sea production recovers to 3.2 mb/d by the end of the decade.

Norway

After posting three years of growth, **Norwegian** oil production is forecast to decline in 2017 and through 2019, before the start-up of the giant Johan Sverdrup field again boosts output. Following slightly higher than expected production in 2016, the outlook for the early part of the forecast period has been marginally lifted since last year's *Report*. Sharp investment cutbacks have yet to show a material change to decline rates at existing fields. Observed declines at mature fields are nevertheless expected to keep output on a downward trend until 2020, despite the start-up of a number of new fields.

Last year, growth was largely fuelled by the ramp-up of the Knarr and Edvard Grieg fields which were commissioned in 2015, and from Eni's Goliat project that finally saw first oil last March. The three fields produced a combined 210 kb/d in October 2016. In 2017 fresh supplies will be seen from Aker BP's 60 kb/d Ivar Aasen project - which started up last December - and from the Statoil-led Gina Krog field which is set to be commissioned later in the year. Also, new production will come from Total's Martin Linge oil and gas field in 2Q18. Total recently raised the resource estimate of the field to 255 mb, 37% higher than its initial estimate, and plans to produce 80 kboe/d at peak, of which roughly half is expected to be oil.

Finally, the giant Johan Sverdrup field is scheduled to start production in 2020. The consortium developing the field, led by Statoil, raised their first phase production target to 440 kb/d, from 315-380 kb/d envisaged earlier, while at the same time cutting planned capital expenditures by 20%. The first phase is projected to break even at oil prices below USD 25/bbl, according to the consortium. Full field development is expected to yield 550-650 kb/d and is still targeted for 2022. It is not only projects currently sanctioned that are benefitting from cost reductions. According to the Norwegian Petroleum Directorate, offshore operators have pushed down development costs for eight planned field developments by more than 40% over the past two years due to the selection of simpler concepts, cheaper equipment and more efficient drilling.

Plans for development and operation of five of the projects were filed with the ministry last year: Statoil's Utgard, Byrding and Trestakk, Dea's Dvalin, and Centrica's Oda field. The other projects are Snilehorn, Johan Castberg, Snorre Expansion, and the second phase of Johan Sverdrup as well as the

Dea-operated Zidane. While not included in these projections, both the Johan Castberg and Snorre expansions, as well as the second phase of Johan Sverdrup, could start production within the timeframe of this report. The Johan Castberg project in the Barents Sea, which is estimated to hold 400-650 million barrels of reserves, could start production by 2022 if a final investment decision is made shortly. Statoil and its partners have cut the planned investment cost for the project by around 50% compared with initial estimates, in part due to a simpler project design selection. All in all, Norwegian total oil supplies are forecast to decline from around 2 mb/d in 2016 to 1.8 mb/d in 2019 before rebounding to just shy of 2.1 mb/d by the end of the forecast period.

Figure 2.23 Norway oil production

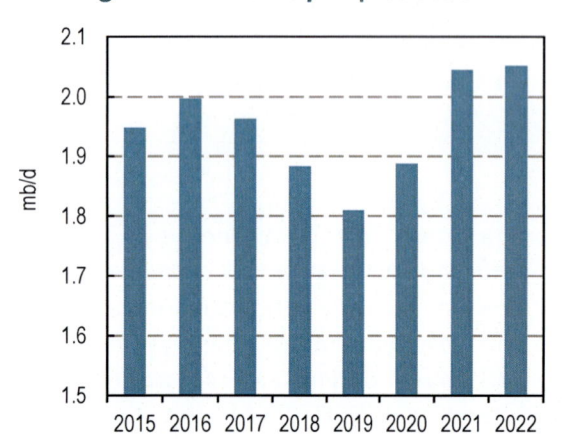

Figure 2.24 UK oil production

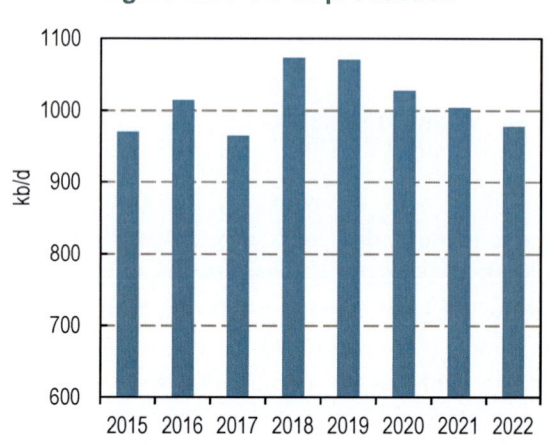

United Kingdom

After posting growth in both 2015 and 2016, oil production in the **UK** is projected to decline by 50 kb/d in 2017 year to 965 kb/d. Output is then expected to recover in 2018 as a number of large new projects ramp up output. Notably, BP is on track to start its Quad 204 (Schiehallion) and its Clair Ridge redevelopment projects later in 2017. The two projects will add roughly 120 kb/d of new production each once fully operational. Kraken and Great Catcher will also produce first oil in 2017, adding roughly 45 kb/d each. In 2018, Statoil plans to commission its Mariner field, one year behind schedule, anticipating a fast ramp up towards its 55 kb/d capacity. UK oil production is expected to return to decline from 2019 and through the forecast period. By 2022, output is expected to average 980 kb/d, slightly lower than in 2016. If we see further cutbacks in investments at already producing fields and an increase in decline rates, there is a risk that output towards the end of the forecast period could be significantly lower.

Australia

Australian oil production is set to grow by 120 kb/d over the forecast period, to reach 475 kb/d in 2022. Faced by high decline rates across its conventional resource base, growth is entirely driven by condensate and natural gas liquids output from new LNG projects. Notably, after more than six years in construction, Chevron's USD 54 billion offshore Gorgon gas project finally started production in 2016 and it is expected to yield around 20 kb/d of condensates. Gorgon is part of a wave of new gas projects that will lift Australian LNG capacity to 118 bcm by 2018 and make it the world's largest LNG exporter. Additional condensate and NGL volumes will come from Wheatstone LNG, Prelude and, most importantly Ichthys, which will add an estimated 130 kb/d once fully operational.

People's Republic of China

The outlook for **Chinese** oil production has been severely curtailed since the 2016 *Report*, after spending cuts saw output last year plunge by 300 kb/d, or 7%, accelerating over the course of the year to nearly 400 kb/d in 4Q16. to its lowest level in nearly a decade. There is little evidence of the decline being arrested and China's total oil production is forecast to drop to 3.7 mb/d in 2022, compared with the 4 mb/d produced in 2016.

As crude oil prices started to fall in mid-2014, PetroChina, Sinopec and CNOOC reduced its total upstream spending by 40% in 2015 to USD 44.7 billion. The Chinese companies cut upstream investments by a further 19% in 2016. While upstream players are looking to raise spending levels in 2017, they warn that output is likely to continue to fall. CNOOC is planning to increase spending by 26%, but has said that it expects its oil and gas output to fall by up to 5.5%, to 1.23-1.26 mboe/d this year. Both CNPC and Sinopec have warned of further spending and output cuts at the country's two largest, but ageing fields, Daqing and Shengli.

Figure 2.25 China oil production

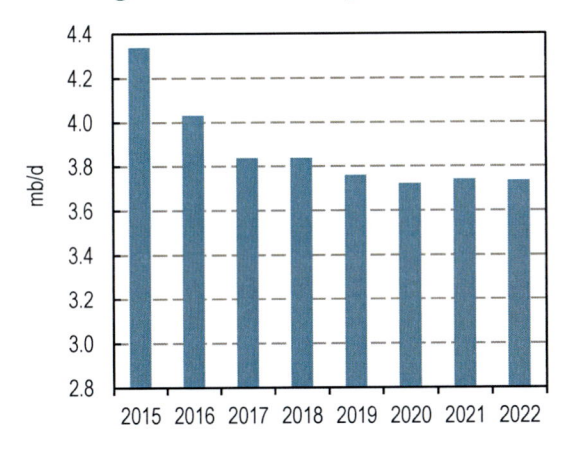

Figure 2.26 China 2016 annual output change

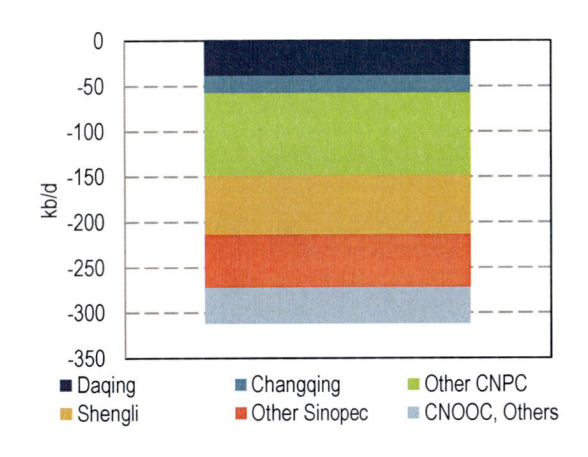

While Chinese field level data is only sporadically made available, annual data show that it was Daqing and Shengli, which in 2015 accounted for 18% and 13% respectively of China's total crude supply, that saw the sharpest output drops in 2016.

Supply from Daqing fell by 5% to 730 kb/d due to reserves depletion and the costs and technical challenges of having to deal with a water cut as high as 90%. According to Chinese industry officials, more than one third of drilling facilities at Daqing are being mothballed due to its high production cost. CNPC plans to cut spending on exploration and engineering by 20% this year, and is looking to restructure the Daqing Oilfield Company (DOC) into a service-focused international player. As CNPC looks for overseas opportunities, and its remaining domestic resources are mostly high-cost, Daqing's production is forecast to decline over the medium term. According to company officials, the current lifting cost at Daqing is about USD 45/bbl.

In response to lower prices, Sinopec cut its costs and reduced high-cost oil production. It shut four Shengli oil blocks: Xiaoping, Yihezhuang, Taoerhe and Qiaozhuang. Output at Shengli, which accounted for 65% of Sinopec's domestic crude output last year, declined by 12% last year and a further 2% decline is planned for 2017.

SUPPLY

> **Box 2.5 China slows pace on overseas oil investment**
>
> Energy-hungry China has for decades invested in overseas oil and gas production in a bid to secure supplies and develop technical expertise. From 1992 to 2015, cumulative investment reached USD 270 billion, including USD 90 billion of loans. But lower oil prices have seen spending slow down.
>
> Initial investments were made by national oil companies (NOCs) in overseas oil and gas fields. By 2015 more than 20 Chinese oil companies had invested in nearly 200 oil and gas projects in 54 countries. In 2009 Beijing started to offer loans to producer countries which were repaid with oil. Venezuela, Russia, Angola, Brazil, Ecuador, Bolivia, Turkmenistan and Kazakhstan have all signed "loans for oil" contracts with China. As oil prices fell, volumes due under these deals have increased to roughly 1.5 mb/d.
>
> As a result, China's total overseas equity oil amounted to 3.1 mb/d in 2016, nearly five times the 2009 level of 0.7 mb/d. That is over 25% of total domestic demand and is equivalent to 40% of crude imports. The top three NOCs - CNPC, Sinopec and CNOOC - accounted for over 90% of total overseas equity oil production.
>
> **Figure 2.27 Chinese overseas investment M&A and equity oil output**
>
> However, the rapid expansion of the NOCs' investment portfolios increased their management risks. Some high-cost acquisitions experienced heavy losses after the oil price slumped in 2014. The price drop also hurt their domestic output and earnings, piling more pressure on overseas investment budgets.
>
> Additionally, more than half of China's international investments are in Africa, the Middle East and Latin America – regions that experienced political instability that has hit their production and thus Chinese companies' ability to lift oil output.
>
> Chinese NOCs thus reconsidered their strategy and became more conservative. In 2014, overseas oil investment dropped sharply by 80% year-on-year to less than USD 5 billion. More than 70% of the investment came from private Chinese companies and the NOC share continued to decline in 2015 and 2016. The next five years will see them optimizing their investment profile and focusing on countries – such as Russia, Iran and Iraq - that form part of the government's Belt and Road Initiative, which links China to key economic partners in Eurasia, Africa and the Middle East.
>
> Meanwhile, overseas investment by private enterprises grew rapidly to reach USD 4 billion in 2016. The government is tightening its monitoring of NOCs' overseas spending, while encouraging private companies to do more. In the near future, private companies' strategy will likely focus on two directions: following the government's call to develop the Belt and Road Initiative as well as taking advantage of lower oil prices to gain foothold in developed countries by mergers and acquisitions. But without strong participation of the NOCs, China's overseas investment and equity oil output will see only modest growth in the next five years.

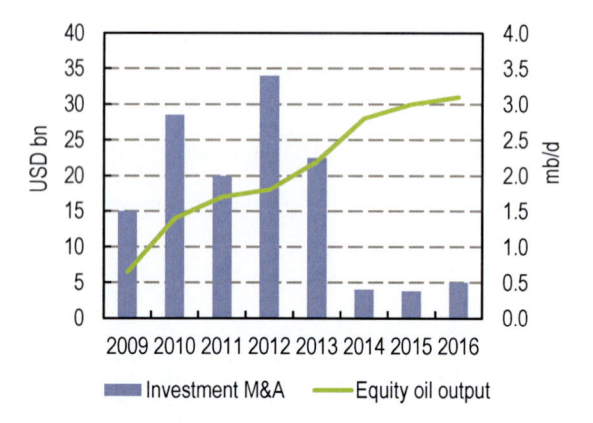

Other Asia

Oil production in other Asian countries is forecast to drop by 410 kb/d by 2022 to 3.2 mb/d. The biggest decline will come from **Indonesia** (-125 kb/d). Output is expected to fall also in **India** (-65 kb/d), **Malaysia** (-65 kb/d), **Thailand** (-40 kb/d) and **Viet Nam** (-30 kb/d) as natural declines will more than offset growth from the few new upstream projects currently planned for the period.

Russia

Following a significant increase in development drilling over the past year, the outlook for Russian oil output has materially improved. A weak rouble and lower taxes has allowed oil companies to maintain spending through the downturn, with the government budget taking the biggest hit from the drop in crude oil prices. Lower production costs than all but the lowest cost Middle East countries support growth through the forecast period when a number of new projects are set to come online. Total liquids output is expected to hold flat, at around 11.3 mb/d.

Figure 2.28 Russia total oil production

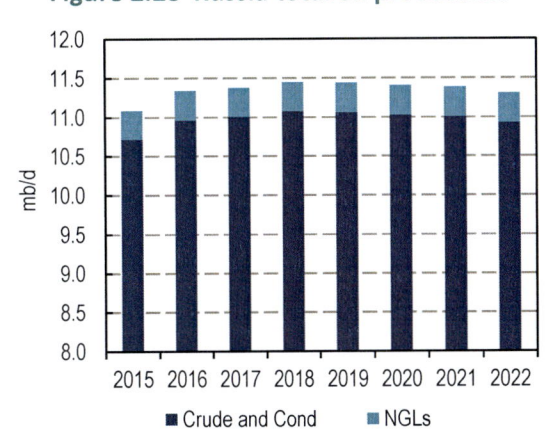

Figure 2.29 Russia y-o-y supply growth 2015-22

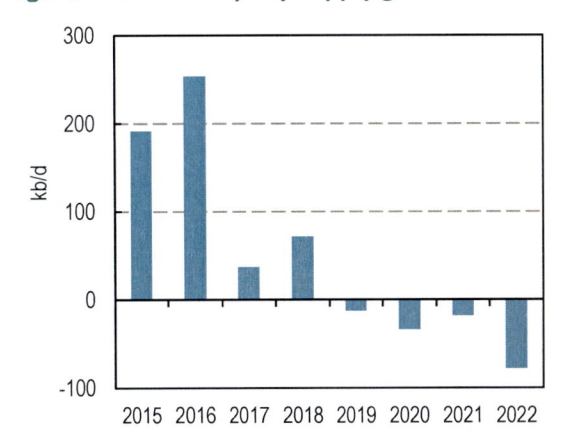

Contrary to expectations, Russian oil production surged ahead in 2015 and 2016, by 190 kb/d and 250 kb/d respectively. Output hit a record 11.34 mb/d on average last year, with small and medium-sized producers Gazpromneft, Novatek, Tatneft, Russneft and Bashneft posting higher production. Novatek alone accounted for 30% of the net production increase. Growth has not only been driven by greenfield developments but was also helped by a marked deceleration in decline rates across mature fields. Investment in upstream activity continued apace despite lower prices, thanks to the devaluation of the rouble and Russia's progressive tax system – which means that companies pay a much smaller tax rate at lower prices. The rouble oil price in 4Q16 was only 20% lower than in 1Q14 compared with a 53% drop in the USD price. At the same time, net of export tax and mineral extraction tax, Urals priced in roubles is actually higher than at the start of 2014.

Rouble devaluation, as well as increased use of in-house drilling and lower service company margins, has also led to favourable economics for infill drilling and other intensification measures at mature fields. Over 2015 and 2016, Russian producers increased drilling rates at mature fields, by around 15% per annum. The most significant increase came from Rosneft, which doubled the metres drilled from 2014 to 2016. The share of horizontal drilling metres rose to more than 30% last year, from only 10% in 2010.

Pressured by a fragile economic situation, Russia agreed with OPEC and other non-OPEC producers to cut its oil production by up to 300 kb/d from early 2017. If not extended beyond the current six-month term, output will still be higher this year than the 2016 average. Production will grow more substantially in 2018, as new projects offset brownfield declines. Notable new projects include Lukoil's Filanovskoe, Gazpromneft/Rosneft's Messoyakha, Gazpromneft's Novoport and Rosneft's Suzunskoe. Thereafter production growth stalls unless further projects are sanctioned, and on the assumption that brownfield decline rates return to more normal levels of around 3%, from less than 2% currently. The pace at which decline rates accelerate, as well as companies' ability to maintain spending levels, will be key to determining future production levels.

Figure 2.30 Average production costs (incl. taxes) of key producers in 2015

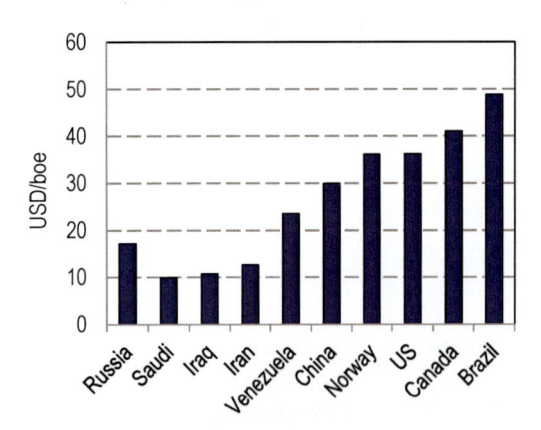

Figure 2.31 Evolution of production drilling rates in Russia, 2013-2016E

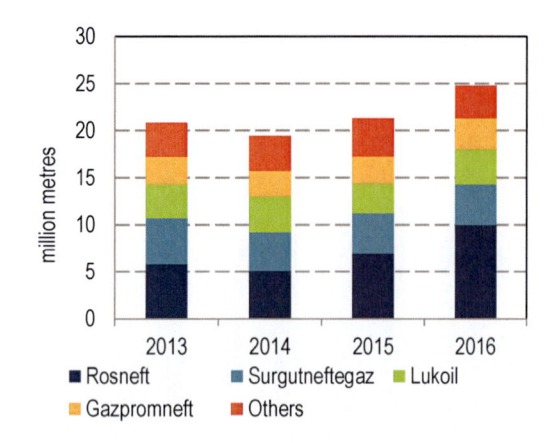

Sources: Rystad Energy; CDUTEK, Deloitte.

Kazakhstan

After years of delays, Kazakhstan's giant Kashagan field finally restarted last September, with oil flowing at a rate of around 100 kb/d by year-end. The 13 billion barrel field, which was originally planned to commence production in 2005, was briefly brought on line in 2013 but had to be shut down almost immediately after serious pipeline corrosion was discovered. The restart of production from Kashagan is expected to lift Kazakh output to 1.8 mb/d in 2017, an increase of 145 kb/d compared with the 2016 level, even as the Kazak government agreed to curb output from 1 January along with other non-OPEC and OPEC countries.

As the field continues to ramp up towards its 370 kb/d nameplate capacity, output should continue to rise through 2018. Originally, the consortium developing the field envisaged raising output to as much as 1 mb/d, but the second phase of the project seems to have been put on hold. Towards the end of the forecast period, additional growth is set to come from the Tengiz field. The Chevron-led Tengizchevroil consortium plans to increase output to 860 kb/d by 2022, from around 600 kb/d currently. In all, Kazakh oil production is expected to increase by 270 kb/d to reach 1.9 mb/d in 2022.

Azerbaijan

In Azerbaijan, BP will double the capacity at its Shah Deniz gas field by 2018. Phase 1, which started operations in 2006, produced around 10.8 bn m^3 of gas and 55 kb/d of condensate in 2016. Crude production from the BP-led Azeri-Chirag-Guneshli (ACG) project produced 645 kb/d of oil over the first three quarters of 2016, unchanged from a year earlier. Azerbaijan and the BP-led consortium recently reached agreement to extend the life of the field to 2050, beyond the previous agreement terminating in 2024. BP and state SOCAR are setting up a new production sharing agreement for the 25-year extension, and hope to squeeze out an extra 2.5 billion barrels of oil using enhanced oil recovery technology, for a total investment of USD 20 billion.

Africa

Oil production in non-OPEC Africa - not taking into account Gabon which re-joined OPEC last August - is forecast to decline by around 75 kb/d over the 2016-22 period, to 1.9 mb/d. Production will fall in all countries with the exception of Congo, Ghana and, later on, Uganda.

The largest increment to supplies will come from **Ghana**, which is set to double its oil output from less than 100 kb/d currently to around 220 kb/d in 2022. Increased supplies will come from the Tullow-operated Tweneboa, Enyenra and Ntomme fields that started producing in August 2016. The project is expected to ramp up to just shy of 80 kb/d at its peak. Further gains will come from Eni's Offshore Cape Three Points project, which is expected to yield around 45 kb/d of oil output at its peak. The project is expected to launch by August 2017.

Substantial growth will also come from **Congo**, with the start-up of a number of fields early in the forecast period. Moho Marine Nord, which was commissioned in 2016, will add around 100 kb/d of new supplies while Nene Marine, which started up in 2016, will ramp up to around 90 kb/d at the end of the forecast period. Congo's production is expected to decline later, however, limiting the net gain over the forecast period. Output rises by 90 kb/d from 240 kb/d in 2016 to just over 350 kb/d in 2018, but then declines to 330 kb/d by 2022.

Towards the end of the forecast period, oil production should also start in **Uganda**. Last September, Tullow Oil and Total were finally granted production licences after years of delays. This paves the way for Tullow, Total and China's CNOOC, which has already secured a licence for its Kingfisher field, to push ahead with the development of multiple oil discoveries in the environmentally sensitive Lake Albert area.

Total, which in early 2017 agreed to increase its stake in the Lake Albert Basin project to 54.9%, by acquiring an additional 21.57% interest from Tullow, says the project can now effectively move ahead. Construction of a 1 443 km crude export pipeline through Tanzania is set to start in June 2017, for a targeted completion in 2020. Tullow says that the agreement will allow the Lake Albert Development to move ahead swiftly, increasing the likelihood of a final investment decision in 2017 and first oil by the end of 2020. The project is expected to achieve peak production of around 230 kb/d. In our projections we assume that output will commence in mid-2021, averaging 60 kb/d, with more substantial growth to come beyond the horizon of this *Report*.

A Tullow Oil-led partnership with Africa Oil and Maersk Oil is also stepping up its exploration efforts in **Kenya**'s prospective South Lokichar basin in order to finance an export pipeline to the port of Lamu. The partners hope to take a final investment decision for the project by late 2018, but production is most likely to start beyond the timeframe of this *Report*. An early production scheme has already been approved by the partners, however, that would see output of around 2 kb/d by mid-2017, with crude to be transported by road from Lokichar to the port of Mombasa.

OPEC

OPEC is building up production capacity, despite the group's deal to cut supplies at the start of 2017, in anticipation of higher demand for its crude. Indeed, the call on OPEC rises to 35.8 mb/d in 2022 from 32.2 mb/d in 2016. A dramatic drop in revenue from oil sales has forced OPEC to do more with less. This is particularly the case in the Middle East, which has capitalised on the fall in oil development and service costs to boost output from its vast, relatively low-cost reserves. The region's producers raised supply by 2.8 mb/d from 2014 to 2016, while African and Latin American members saw output fall by 650 kb/d.

The expansion effort extends throughout our forecast period as crude production capacity rises by 1.95 mb/d, driven largely by Iraq. Iran, the UAE and Libya, assuming political stability in the latter, are also projected to post notable growth. The heftiest gains are expected in the first half of the period, as Libya is showing early promise and assuming a restart in 2018 of the Neutral Zone oil fields shared between Saudi Arabia and Kuwait. After 2020, capacity rises only modestly as, so far, few major upstream projects have got off the drawing board.

Figure 2.32 Low-cost Middle East drives growth

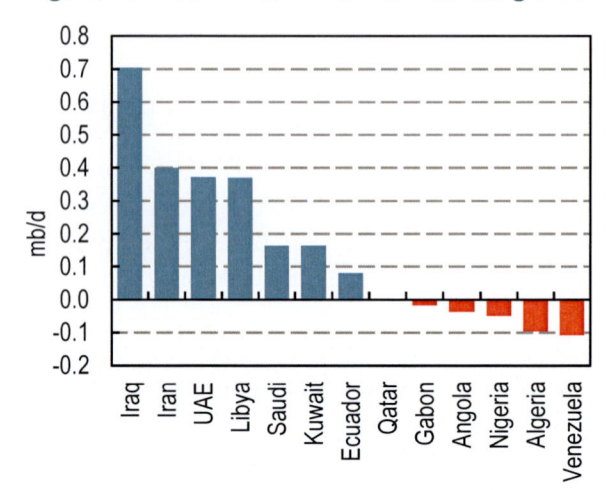

The exception could prove to be Iran, which is working to attract the foreign capital necessary to push production beyond the 4 mb/d mark. Following the lifting of nuclear-related sanctions in 2016, crude flows were boosted swiftly to a pre-sanctions level of 3.75 mb/d. Assuming relatively limited outside investment during the next six years, our forecast shows Iran's sustainable crude oil capacity rising to 4.15 mb/d by 2022. Whether or not the P5+1 nuclear agreement remains in force during the medium term will be a crucial factor in how much spending takes place. If capacity does increase by 400 kb/d over the six-year period, that would represent solid growth, but not enough to allow Iran to regain its former position as OPEC's second biggest producer after Saudi Arabia.

Iraq will easily retain OPEC's number two spot at least through 2022. Since its oil development effort got under way in earnest in 2010, crude output has doubled to reach nearly 4.7 mb/d. A costly battle against the Islamic State of Iraq and the Levant (ISIL) and a dramatic fall in oil revenues has slowed the pace of production growth from nearly 700 kb/d in 2015 to 400 kb/d last year. Capacity-building eases to an annual average of 120 kb/d over the forecast, but that is enough to push Iraq to 5.4 mb/d. The UAE is expected to show robust growth of 370 kb/d from 2016-2022.

Some countries outside of the Middle East fare less well, with declines in capacity of between 20 kb/d to 110 kb/d. Venezuela posts the biggest loss due to chronic under-investment and its wider economic crisis. Algerian capacity slides, but an efficiency drive within the oil and gas sector has helped to stem the decline. Capacity also shrinks in Nigeria and Angola, where a number of capital-intensive deep water projects are unlikely to start up before the early 2020s.

Table 2.3 Estimated sustainable OPEC crude production capacity (mb/d)

Country	2016	2017	2018	2019	2020	2021	2022	2016-22
Algeria	1.14	1.13	1.10	1.08	1.07	1.06	1.05	-0.09
Angola	1.81	1.81	1.91	1.88	1.84	1.81	1.77	-0.04
Ecuador	0.57	0.59	0.60	0.61	0.62	0.63	0.65	0.08
Gabon	0.23	0.22	0.22	0.21	0.21	0.21	0.21	-0.02
Iran	3.75	3.80	3.85	3.90	4.05	4.10	4.15	0.40
Iraq	4.70	4.82	4.92	5.03	5.14	5.27	5.40	0.70
Kuwait	2.94	2.94	3.05	3.08	3.09	3.09	3.10	0.16
Libya	0.65	0.81	0.90	0.96	0.98	1.00	1.02	0.37
Nigeria	1.83	1.81	1.82	1.82	1.83	1.80	1.78	-0.05
Qatar	0.67	0.66	0.66	0.66	0.67	0.67	0.67	0.00
Saudi Arabia	12.23	12.23	12.34	12.38	12.39	12.40	12.40	0.16
UAE	3.15	3.20	3.32	3.40	3.45	3.49	3.52	0.37
Venezuela	2.22	2.15	2.12	2.10	2.10	2.10	2.12	-0.11
OPEC	35.90	36.18	36.82	37.13	37.43	37.61	37.85	1.95

Box 2.6 OPEC takes charge

OPEC's deal to cut supply by 1.2 mb/d from January 2017 heralded a return to market management for the first time since 2008 following two years of a market share policy with no limits on production. The explicit aim of the six-month pact is to work off a massive inventory excess that built up – on average 900 kb/d from 2014 to 2016 inclusive - in large part because of record Middle East OPEC output. An implicit goal is to steady the price of oil between USD 50-60/bbl. Oil below USD 50/bbl was a cause of concern for all - even those with substantial foreign reserves, such as Saudi Arabia. OPEC revenues sank to an estimated USD 440 billion in 2016, down from a recent peak of USD 1.19 trillion in 2012 when the average price of Brent crude was close to USD 100/bbl.

The point of OPEC's pump-at-will strategy was to defend market share by driving out high-cost output. It worked up to a point. Non-OPEC supply fell by 800 kb/d in 2016, with the US accounting for more than half of this.

But towards the end of the year, even with oil prices languishing around the mid-USD 40s/bbl level, it became evident that non-OPEC supply would return to growth in 2017 as companies worked more efficiently in a lower oil price environment. As OPEC ministers gathered in November there was a real possibility that - unless something changed - oil prices could fall again as they did at the start of the year.

Figure 2.33 OPEC's cash crunch

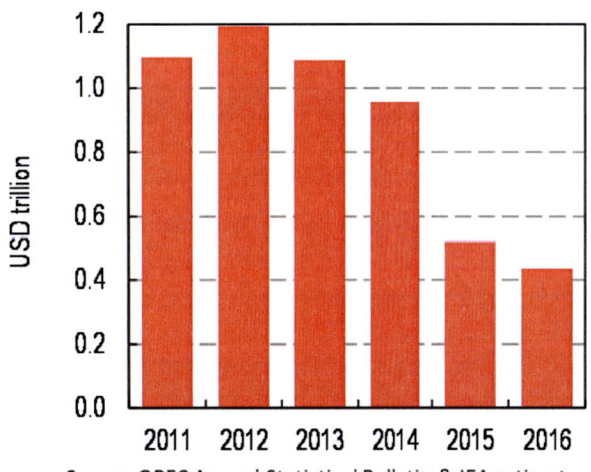

Source: OPEC Annual Statistical Bulletin & IEA estimate

> **Box 2.6 OPEC takes charge (continued)**
>
> Although it has not been explicitly stated as an official target for OPEC, a sustained oil price above USD 50/bbl became the top priority and a coordinated round of supply cuts from OPEC and non-OPEC countries was seen as a necessity.
>
> So, will OPEC market management last through the course of our medium term forecast? Of course, it is impossible to know. But we can be sure that in the next few years there will be solid increases in demand. Supply growth from non-OPEC countries will not completely satisfy this higher requirement. More OPEC oil will be necessary, but the need is less urgent in the early years of our forecast period. Whether OPEC members maintain output restraint for a prolonged period is unclear. However, it is difficult to imagine a return to the unbridled production that sent prices crashing to their lowest level in more than a decade.

Within OPEC, **Iraq** will post the biggest gains (over a third of overall capacity growth) although its expansion effort is likely to slow until a vital water injection scheme to boost reservoir pressure is up and running. Crude oil output capacity is projected to rise to 5.4 mb/d by 2022, for annual average growth of 120 kb/d over the forecast period. As always, there are risks to this projection: to the upside given Iraq's vast, low-cost reserve base and budgetary pressure to raise production and to the downside given security, financial and institutional obstacles.

For two years running, Iraq has managed to shatter production records, raising flows by more than 1 mb/d, even as it wages a costly battle against ISIL and struggles under severe budgetary strain. At the start of 2016, expectations were that output would remain stable due to budget cuts on mega-projects run by international oil companies (IOCs) in the south. But Iraq defied the odds and emerged as the world's second biggest source of crude oil supply growth, second only to Iran. The lower oil price environment encouraged flat out production in 2016 to achieve year-on-year growth of 410 kb/d. The southern oil fields - such as Zubair, West Qurna-1 and Missan - helped to fuel the gains.

Iraq's oil heartland around Basra will provide the bulk of the growth over the forecast period. In the north, complicated geology, security risks and lower oil prices have frustrated the development drive. The Kurdistan Regional Government (KRG) is producing around 700 kb/d from fields under its control, but is struggling to meet export payments to foreign contractors. Additionally, the performance of the core Taq Taq field is expected to deteriorate further with production having already fallen from 120 kb/d in 2014 to around 45 kb/d at the time of writing. ExxonMobil's withdrawal from half of its six explorations blocks has also dented confidence in the region.

In contrast, flows of Basra crude from the southern fields have risen steadily following the commissioning in mid-2015 of a new system to separate heavy and light oil and the construction of more storage tanks at the Fao terminal. It will be essential for southern export capacity, now just over 3.5 mb/d, to expand in line with rising output. New storage tanks, pumps and pipelines are expected to be sufficient to handle the anticipated rise in supply. An expansion that doubles capacity at the Khor al-Amaya terminal to 1.2 mb/d and the installation of a fourth single point mooring system are expected to be finished by mid-2017.

Iraq's prized southern oil fields will not come close to achieving their full potential - and an official target of 6 mb/d by 2020 looks unattainable - unless a long-delayed project to supply water gets off the ground. Baghdad has scaled down the planned mega-project, reducing its scope from 7.5 mb/d to 5 mb/d to be brought on in two stages. Until then, alternative sources will have to suffice at mature fields such as Rumaila, Zubair and West Qurna-1.

In the early part of the forecast, work at Zubair, Rumaila, Halfaya, Missan and so-called national effort fields such as Nassiriya and Luhais will help boost production. In setting 2017 budgets the ministry has urged companies to make further cuts in operating costs but has still managed to raise the expected level of expenditure from USD 10.7 billion in 2016 to USD 11.6 billion in 2017. Much of the increased spending is intended to raise output at state-run oil fields, which account for roughly 10% of Iraqi output.

A substantial chunk of additional capacity could also be provided by the Royal Dutch Shell-operated Majnoon field, near the border with Iran. At the start of 2017, Shell signed a USD 210 million contract with Halliburton to drill 30 wells which could lift production from the field to about 400 kb/d in three years from current levels of 220 kb/d. Other recently tapped fields such as West-Qurna-2, Halfaya and Gharraf – which do not require near-term water injection to boost reservoir pressure – are also expected to ramp up.

Baghdad is also planning to bolster its production capacity by offering a dozen small and mid-sized oil fields in its first upstream opening since 2012. The oil ministry pre-qualified 19 companies including Rosneft, Inpex, Glencore, Mubadala and Crescent Petroleum. It will, however, take several years for most of the 12 fields, located in southern and central Iraq, to start pumping. The projects are being offered on terms more akin to a production-sharing contract. Under service contracts awarded to IOCs since 2009, the ministry repays contractors a fixed fee for every barrel of oil produced. When oil prices were high, the contract worked well, but now Baghdad is paying out the fee from dramatically lower revenues. Foreign firms typically receive payment in crude that equates to the value of cash owed.

Figure 2.34 Iraq leads growth

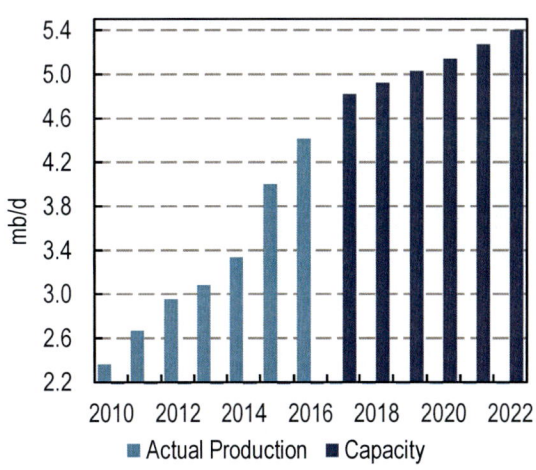

For their part, the IOCs appear to be re-thinking their exposure in both the north and south of the country. Shell, seeking to shed USD 30 billion in global assets, reportedly is evaluating its position in technical service agreements at the southern West Qurna-1 oil field project, where it has a stake of just under 20%, and the Majnoon oil field, where it is the operator. West Qurna-1, run by ExxonMobil, is pumping roughly 470 kb/d, and Majnoon about 220 kb/d. Shell also has two other core projects on its books: it leads the Basra Gas Co joint venture, which processes and markets associated gas and natural gas liquids from the oil fields of Rumaila, West Qurna-1 and Zubair. It is also planning the USD 11 billion Nibraas petrochemical project.

SUPPLY

In the north, the military campaign against ISIL has put the KRG budget under enormous strain. The government is struggling to pay foreign investors and investment has slowed considerably, even at the biggest foreign-operated oil fields of Tawke and Taq Taq, where reserves estimates have been downgraded.

> **Box 2.7 Iran bounces back**
>
> Production surged back above 3.7 mb/d within months of sanctions being eased in 2016, and Iran is set for further crude oil capacity growth of 400 kb/d over the forecast period. Modest annual gains are expected to push output above the 4 mb/d mark by the end of 2020. Growth beyond that level is likely to require foreign technology and finance, which could prove tougher to attract given uncertainty over the new US administration's position on the P5+1 nuclear agreement with Iran. The government set a production target of around 5 mb/d for the end of the decade, although this appears to be ambitious.
>
> In hindsight it seems clear that, under the leadership of oil minister Bijan Zanganeh, engineers had properly prepared the country's oil network before sanctions were eased. Core fields such as Ahwaz, Marun and Gachsaran, were revived and provided a swift boost which saw Iran emerge as the world's largest source of supply growth. Sustainable capacity of 3.8 mb/d, the level assigned Iran under OPEC's end-2016 supply pact, appears to be achievable for 2017. The West of Karun oil fields on the border with Iraq are expected to ramp up and provide the additional 50 kb/d of capacity.
>
> **Figure 2.35 Iran rebuilds**
>
> On the marketing front, the National Iranian Oil Co (NIOC) was quick to launch a post-sanctions sales drive to recapture its European customer base, even in an oversupplied and highly competitive market. Shipments rose steadily and by the end of 2016 had returned to pre-sanctions levels of roughly 900 kb/d or nearly 40% of overall sales of around 2.4 mb/d.
>
> Over the medium term, Iran's investment and political climate will be crucial factors when it comes to determining supply growth. NIOC is confident that it will finalise upstream deals with IOCs in 2017 under its new Iran Petroleum Contract (IPC). Some foreign investors are wary: they are awaiting the development of the US administration's policies towards and the outcome of the Iranian presidential election in May. The threat of snap-back sanctions under the terms of the P5+1 nuclear agreement may also give potential investors pause. In any event, US companies remain out of the picture while Washington's non-nuclear-related sanctions remain in place.
>
> Some international firms are willing to strike initial deals with Iran whatever their concerns over a shift in US policy. Total was the first IOC to seal a preliminary development deal – Phase 11 of the South Pars gas field - under the new IPC. It plans to take a final investment decision on the USD 2 billion project by mid-2017 if nothing changes with regard to sanctions. NIOC has also signed a number of memoranda of understanding, including with Shell, which will study the offshore Kish gas field, Yadavaran and South Azadegan, which borders the Shell-operated Majnoon field in Iraq.
>
> Much will depend on contract terms the oil ministry is still refining. To lure the IOCs, Tehran hammered out the IPC that it believes is better than what is on offer in Iraq.

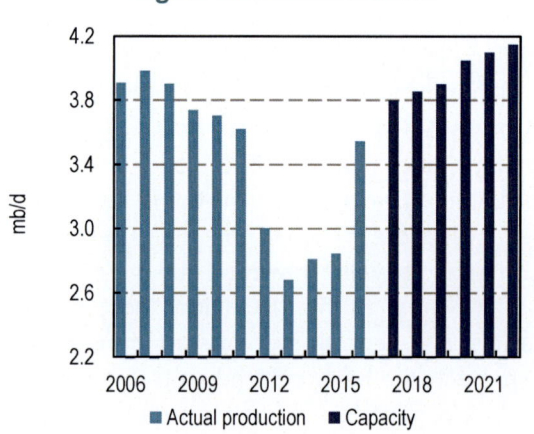

Box 2.7 Iran bounces back (continued)

Iran's low-cost reserves, offered in a stable environment, are hugely attractive but corporate cost cutting means IOCs will drive a hard bargain. While the 20-year IPC is an improvement on the unpopular buy-back model, which compensated foreign firms with production, potential investors are still waiting to see the fine print.

The South Azadegan project is tipped to become the first oil development scheme offered to the IOCs. NIOC has selected 29 firms - including Total, Shell, Eni, China National Petroleum Corp (CNPC) and Lukoil - to qualify for bidding on 50 oil and gas projects. The list did not include BP, which has substantial assets in the US.

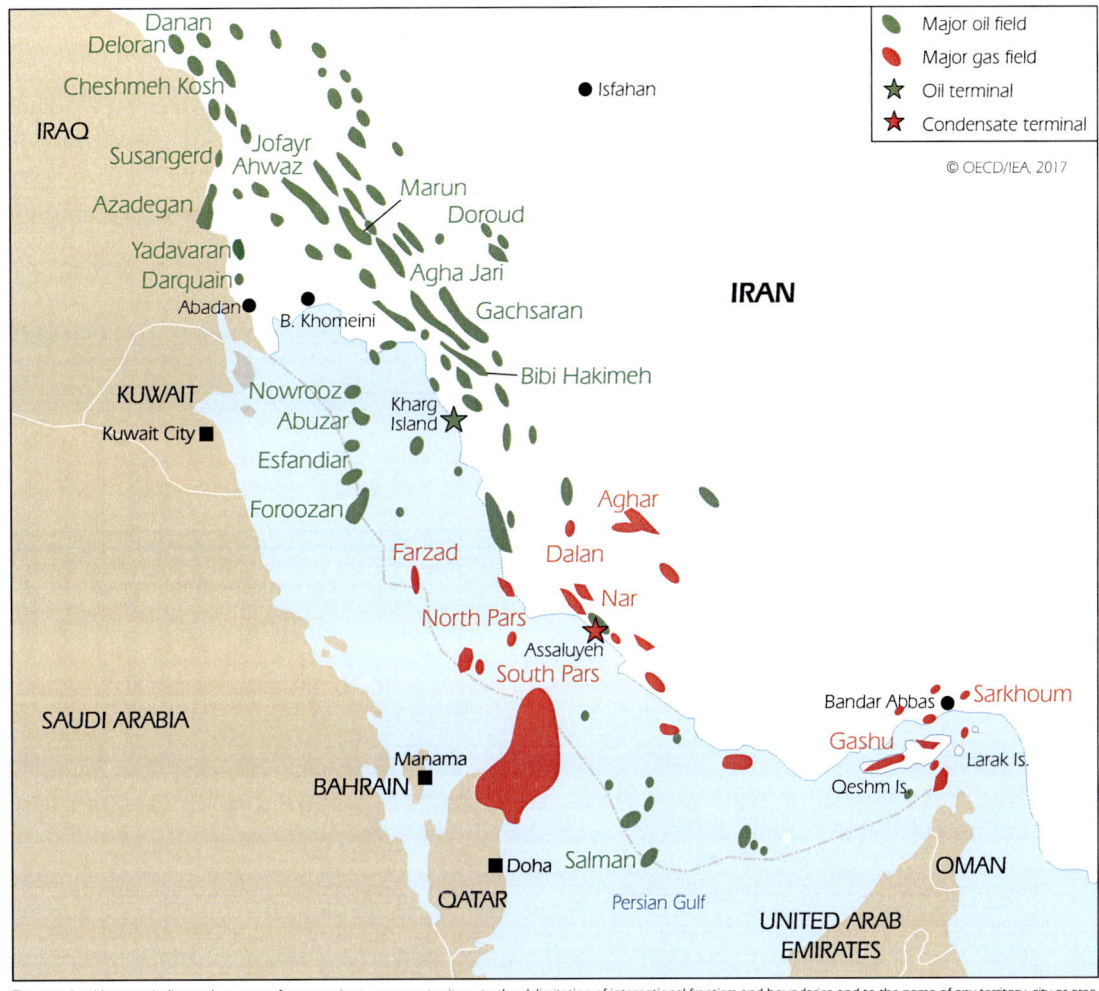

Map 2.2 Iran's oil and gas fields

This map is without prejudice to the status of or sovereignty over any territory, to the delimitation of international frontiers and boundaries and to the name of any territory, city or area.

Following years of chronic under-investment, Iran hopes to attract the foreign cash and technology that is vital to raise output. Development of the vast reservoirs of South Azadegan, North Azadegan and Yadavaran, which straddle the border with Iraq, is a top priority. Their development, along with the rehabilitation of older fields, is vital to maintaining output at the 4 mb/d level.

SUPPLY

> **Box 2.7 Iran bounces back (continued)**
>
> Target production from Azadegan and Yadavaran is 1 mb/d versus current flows of about 240 kb/d but achieving that goal will require the help of Western oil companies. Oil Minister Zanganeh says some USD 20 billion in investment will be needed to increase the fields' recovery rates and boost output.
>
> CNPC developed the first phase of the onshore North Azadegan oil field, which is now producing around 75 kb/d. South Azadegan is churning out around 50 kb/d. China's Sinopec is at work on the first phase of development at Yadavaran, which is pumping roughly 115 kb/d.

Despite continued belt-tightening, the **UAE** is building up capacity, which is expected to rise by 370 kb/d to 3.52 mb/d by 2022. The Abu Dhabi National Oil Co (Adnoc), started to reduce spending in 2015 when oil prices tumbled and was striving for budget cuts of up to 25% last year.

The lower oil price environment has, however, made the UAE's relatively low-cost reserves look even more alluring. After lengthy negotiations, Adnoc has lined up foreign partners for a 40% holding in the Abu Dhabi Co for Onshore Petroleum Operations (Adco), which accounts for half the UAE's crude output. CNPC and a private Chinese firm paid a combined USD 2.67 billion for a 12% stake. CNPC secured 8% and CEFC China Energy got a 4% share.

BP, a partner in the original 75-year Abu Dhabi onshore concession that expired in January 2014, agreed to take a 10% stake. In 2015, Total won a 10% share in the onshore fields (including Bab, Bu Hasa, Shah and Asab) after paying a reported USD 2.2 billion signature bonus. Abu Dhabi asked BP in 2015 to match the bonus to stay for a further forty years in a new production-sharing pact for the fields that pump Abu Dhabi's flagship Murban crude. BP finally agreed to meet the asking price and Abu Dhabi will accept the payment in BP shares.

Figure 2.36 UAE posts solid growth

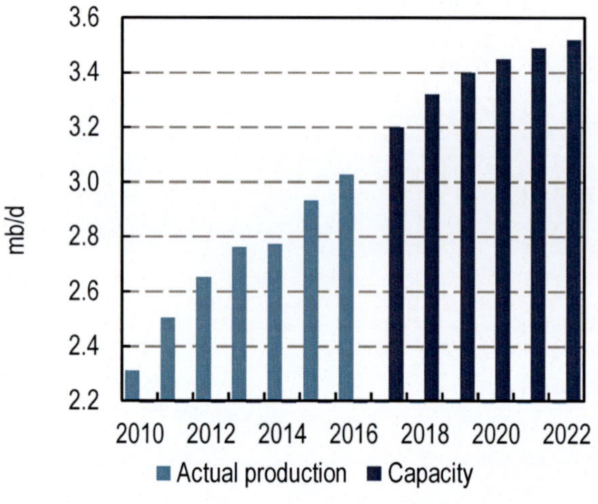

As part of the BP deal, the company becomes the Bab field asset leader. Total was awarded Bu Hasa and Southeast in 2015. Total is also due to take on Northeast Bab. Inpex of Japan and GS Energy of South Korea won smaller stakes of 5% and 3%, respectively. Adco now pumps around 1.6 mb/d and the official target is 1.8 mb/d by 2018.

In the medium term, the offshore Upper Zakum field, one of the world's largest, will provide the most significant expansion to UAE capacity. Output from the technically challenging field reached 670 kb/d last summer and is on track to hit 750 kb/d by 2018 after the completion of a USD 10 billion project. The next target capacity for the field is 1 mb/d. Zakum Development Co (Zadco), the joint venture that operates the field, is held 28% by Exxon, 12% by Jodco and 60% by Adnoc.

Adnoc is also planning to merge its two offshore operating companies into a single unit. The so-called NewCo would produce 1.3 mb/d to 1.4 mb/d by combining the operations of Abu Dhabi Marine Operating Co (Adma-Opco) with Zadco. The Adma-Opco contract expires in 2018, while the Zadco concession extends to 2041. Adnoc reportedly may still re-tender Adma-Opco along the same lines as Adco. Adnoc holds 60% in the joint-venture, with international partners - BP (14.67%), Total (13.33%) and Japan's Jodco (12%) – holding the remainder. It operates a group of offshore oil fields including the core Lower Zakum and Umm Shaif. The Sarb, Umm Lulu and Nasr fields, which are expected to produce 270 kb/d between them, are due to start pumping in 2018.

Box 2.8 Libya's fragile recovery

Following more than two years of oil sector attacks and civil unrest, a tentative recovery in Libya lifted production above 700 kb/d in early 2017 for the first time in two years. It will be a challenge to boost production further, but there is potential for capacity to rise gradually from 650 kb/d kb/d in 2016 to just over 1 mb/d by the end of 2022.

Sustainable capacity in the medium term is unlikely to come close to the 1.6 mb/d that was achieved prior to the 2011 overthrow of Muammar Gaddafi. It may even be a struggle to reach the 1 mb/d mark that was touched briefly in October 2014. Libya's resilience has been proven in the past, however, and the National Oil Corp (NOC) says it aims to reach a production level of 1.25 mb/d by the end of 2017. This ambitious target depends upon a steady flow of cash from the central bank to cover the cost of infrastructure repairs, as well as political stability. For 2022, a more aspirational output goal of 2.1 mb/d has been set.

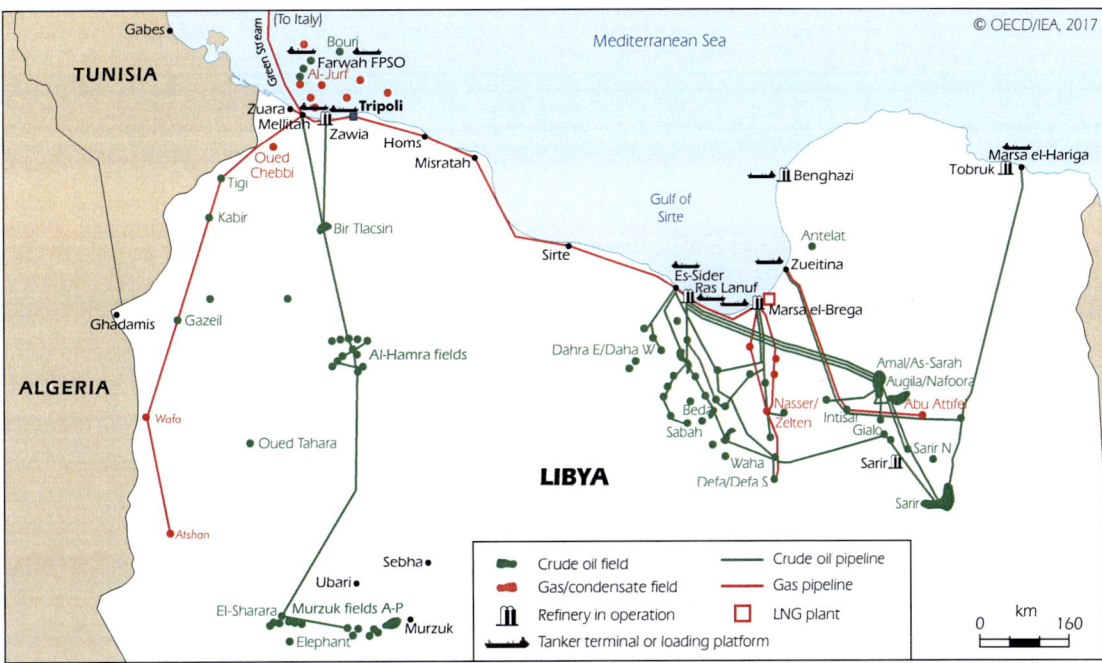

Map 2.3 Libya's oil infrastructure

2.8 Libya's fragile recovery (continued)

In the short term, Libyan officials say production of 775 kb/d could be reached with relative ease after the reopening of a pipeline that links the Repsol-operated El Sharara field, which can ramp up to 330 kb/d, with the Eni-managed El Feel, which can pump roughly 90 kb/d. All of the country's main export terminals have reopened and shipments from El-Sharara loaded at the port of Zawiya in January.

Libya's comeback may prove fleeting, however, given the challenges of maintaining security and the need for cash to fund critical infrastructure repairs. Demonstrating the fragility of Libya's recovery, NOC temporarily lost 60 kb/d of production in mid-January after a fire at a substation at the Sarir oilfield in the Sirte Basin oil heartland in the east. And some 70 kb/d of output from Mesla, another eastern field, was halted briefly due to a pipeline leak.

The wider threat to the oil sector comes from a simmering feud between the UN-backed Government of National Accord (GNA) in Tripoli and the Tobruk-based eastern government supported by the Libyan National Army (LNA). Libya's production comeback began last September following the LNA's removal of the Petroleum Facilities Guards (PFG) from export outlets in the east.

NOC is now keeping close watch over those eastern oil ports - Es Sider, Ras Lanuf and Zueitina. Only a quarter of the 19 storage tanks are reported to be operational at Es Sider, but sufficient repairs have been made at the 320 kb/d terminal, damaged by sabotage at the start of 2016, to allow for shipments of up to two cargoes per month. Nearby Ras Lanuf, with capacity of just over 200 kb/d, is shipping roughly the same amount. The two eastern export outlets were shut from December 2014 until July 2016 by the PFG due to a dispute over payments.

In early 2016, militants set fire to oil storage tanks at Es Sider and Ras Lanuf, which forced the closure of the Waha oil fields, the main contributors to Libya's benchmark Es Sider crude. Waha restarted in October and production was restored to around 80 kb/d at the time of writing. NOC has also been relying heavily on oil that is pumped out of the Sirte Basin by the state Arabian Gulf Oil Co (Agoco), operator of the Sarir and Mesla fields that have cranked out around 250 kb/d between them.

Libyan officials say that significant investment is not needed to return El Sharara and the nearby El Feel oil field to capacity, but a swift injection of cash is required to overhaul power plants at the Sarir and Mesla fields. El Sharara was pumping around 160 kb/d at the time of writing. El Feel remained shut due to a PFG blockade. Apart from the southwestern fields of El Sharara and El Feel, the eastern Sirte Basin fields may be able to ramp up by around 100 kb/d in the short-term.

Saudi Arabia unveiled in 2016 its Vision 2030 strategy, designed to reduce dependence on oil and transform its economy. The year also saw the replacement of long-serving oil minister Ali al-Naimi. His successor, Khalid al-Falih, was a key player in OPEC's decision to return to active market management following two years of a hands-off market share policy.

On the domestic front, al-Falih has instructed Saudi Aramco to press on with upstream investment by taking advantage of cost reductions offered by service companies and suppliers. To that end, capacity is expected to be sustained at around 12.4 mb/d from 2019 to the end of the forecast. Saudi Arabia is the only producer in the world to hold substantial spare capacity: average output of 10.4 mb/d in 2016 allowed for a capacity cushion of some 1.8 mb/d.

New capacity additions will help compensate for natural decline rates and allow Saudi Aramco to reduce production at Ghawar, the world's biggest oil field. Ultimately this may allow for better reservoir management and recovery rates. Saudi Arabia's aim has been to stabilise, rather than increase, oil output capacity as it seeks to develop non-associated and unconventional gas reserves. The 250 kb/d Shaybah crude expansion, which lifted capacity of Arab Extra Light crude to 1 mb/d, came on line in June 2016. A natural gas liquids project started up alongside it, which, coupled with improvements in energy efficiency, has cut the amount of crude burned in power plants (previously up to 900 kb/d during peak summer air-conditioning use) and freed up more oil for export. Saudi Aramco is also continuing to fund the estimated USD 3 billion Khurais expansion project and is sustaining a robust drilling programme. Some 300 kb/d of additional Arab Light from Khurais is due to come online in 2018 and lift the field's total capacity to 1.5 mb/d.

A central plank of Vision 2030 is to sell a stake of up to 5% of Saudi Aramco by 2018. Deputy Crown Prince Mohammed bin Salman, who is driving the Kingdom's economic transformation plans, valued the company at around USD 2 trillion, although independent analysts suggest a much lower figure. In preparation for the anticipated listing, Saudi Arabia has allowed the first independent evaluation of its oil and gas reserves, usually assumed to be 260 billion barrels of proven oil reserves and 253 trillion cubic feet of gas.

Minister al-Falih says Saudi Arabia intends to uphold its long standing policy of maintaining idle capacity of around 1.5 mb/d - 2 mb/d to respond to supply outages even if potential investors might debate the policy's commercial merits. Saudi crude oil capacity could also be boosted from the offshore oil fields of Berri, Zuluf, Marjan and Safaniyah (the world's largest offshore field) – which could add more than 1.8 mb/d between them. Such a costly programme would, however, have to be launched in the early part of the forecast period in order to deliver oil by 2022.

Figure 2.37 Saudi sustains capacity

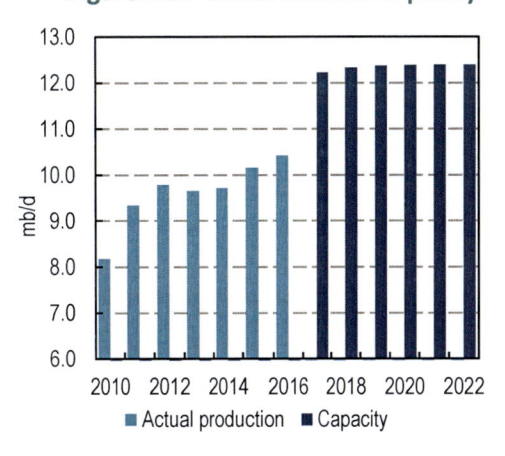

Given its ambitious plans for renewable energy, the Kingdom could have more crude to sell on international markets in the short-to-medium term. Saudi Arabia has invited international and domestic companies to bid for renewable projects, with deals expected to be awarded in September. The projects are part of a major renewable energy supply programme that is expected to involve investment of USD 30 billion to USD 50 billion by 2023.

Saudi Arabia and Kuwait are meanwhile taking steps to restart oil production from their shared fields in the Neutral Zone. Riyadh unilaterally shut the 300 kb/d offshore Khafji field in October 2014, ostensibly for environmental reasons. Another joint development, the 150 kb/d onshore Wafra field, has been closed since May 2015 due to a dispute over investment.

Kuwait is moving apace with its crude oil capacity expansion despite the extended closure of the Neutral Zone. For now, higher flows have been achieved by maximising output at the giant Burgan oil field and by lifting production at the northern fields. A further increase in capacity is expected in 2018, assuming a resolution to the Neutral Zone dispute. Growth of 160 kb/d during the forecast period is expected to lift capacity to 3.1 mb/d in 2022. Crucial to a further boost in capacity is the northern Ratqa oil field near the border with Iraq. Production of the field's heavy crude is expected to start by the end of 2018 and ramp up to 60 kb/d within six months. Kuwait awarded a USD 4 billion contract to a Petrofac-led consortium to build infrastructure to support the development. Initial production is expected to be delivered to domestic power plants and the planned al-Zour refinery.

Foreign technology and project management expertise are essential for tapping Kuwait's geologically complex reserves. To that end, Kuwait in 2016 signed enhanced technical service agreements (ETSAs) with Shell and BP. Shell secured a deal to help double output at Ratqa from 60 kb/d and then boost it to an eventual target of 270 kb/d. It also won a deal for a water management project at onshore oil fields, which is intended to lift production. BP won an ETSA for Burgan which may have the potential to produce as much as 2 mb/d from current levels of roughly 1.7 mb/d to 1.8 mb/d. For decades, Kuwait has struggled to develop upstream projects due to strenuous parliamentary opposition.

Qatari production capacity holds steady at 670 kb/d during the forecast period. Crude oil output has been in decline since hitting a peak of 860 kb/d in 2008 and sank as low as 610 kb/d in September 2016 - partly due to maintenance at the largest oil field, al-Shaheen. Though its crude output is slumping, natural gas is another story: Qatar is the world's largest LNG exporter. To better cope in a low oil price environment, Qatar Petroleum (QP) has cut spending and jobs and renegotiated production-sharing contracts. In 2016, it awarded Total a 30% stake in a new 25-year contract to run al-Shaheen. QP will hold the remaining 70% in the new joint venture. Total plans to invest more than USD 2 billion in developing the offshore field that now pumps around 300 kb/d, nearly half of Qatari crude production. The main focus of the deal is to stem natural declines and sustain output at around current levels. The new deal is a setback for Maersk, which operates the field under a 25-year production sharing contract that expires in mid-2017. They do not have a role in the new contract.

The terms of the new al-Shaheen contract will set the standard for the tender process for the 100 kb/d Idd al-Shargi, operated by Occidental, and due to expire in 2019. Total already operates the 25 kb/d offshore al-Khaleej field and Exxon, ConocoPhillips and Shell are also involved in Qatar. It can be very costly to develop Qatari oil fields due to their complex geology, yet a multi-billion dollar plan to double the 45 kb/d offshore Bul Hanine field is moving forward. QP is reportedly finalizing a list of selected contractors and is expected to issue tenders for the engineering, procurement and construction of new facilities in the first quarter of 2017.

Algeria, led by new minister of energy Nouredine Bouterfa, is working to manage a steep drop in energy earnings and to revive oil fields that have declined for nearly a decade. Although production capacity is expected to fall by 90 kb/d to 1.05 mb/d during the forecast period, the drop is not as severe as anticipated in previous years as Sonatrach takes steps to halt declines at oil fields such as Hassi Messaoud, its largest producer. Since peaking at 1.38 mb/d in 2007, crude output slumped to 1.11 mb/d in 2015. Production in 2016 held steady, reinforced by a stronger performance in the El Merk and Ourhoud fields.

Algeria's oil and gas earnings dropped to an estimated USD 18.3 billion in 2016 from the most recent peak of USD 51.4 billion in 2011 and it has been necessary to substantially draw down its foreign reserves in order to sustain welfare programmes. As a result, its financial cushion fell from USD 180 billion in 2014 to an estimated USD 114 billion at the end of 2016. Despite this daunting backdrop, Sonatrach insists it will carry out its USD 90 billion, 2015-19 oil and gas investment scheme. By drilling more wells and installing early production facilities and central processing facilities at fields such as Hassi Messaoud, Sonatrach is hoping at least to hold production steady. Algeria may also launch a new bid round for oil exploration in 2017 as well as negotiate upstream oil development deals directly with IOCs.

Production capacity in **Gabon,** which returned to OPEC in June 2016 more than two decades after it quit the group, is expected to ease to 210 kb/d by 2022. Output has declined steadily from a peak of 380 kb/d in 1997. It is set to slip further as the lower oil price environment leads firms to consider asset sales. Total agreed in February to sell interests in its mature oil fields (roughly 13 kb/d) to Perenco in a deal worth USD 350 million. Shell, which has operated in Gabon for more than five decades, is in talks to sell its onshore operations – including the Rabi and Gamba oil fields - as part of its divestment plan. US independent Harvest Natural Resources is due to withdraw from the country when it sells its Dussafu block to BW Offshore, which is based in Norway.

The lower oil price environment has hit **Angola** hard, with capacity in Africa's second largest producer expected to drop 40 kb/d to 1.77 mb/d over the forecast period. Ageing offshore oil fields need constant support from costly new projects to offset steep production declines. Since output peaked at nearly 1.9 mb/d in 2008, it has been a struggle to stave off further declines as prohibitively expensive projects are pushed back or abandoned.

After delays, a new oil field, Mafumeira Sul, operated by Chevron, finally started production in November 2016 with initial output of 10 kb/d. The USD 5.6 billion offshore project will eventually produce 150 kb/d. In early 2017, Eni started up the offshore East Hub project (in block 15/06) five months ahead of schedule. Eventual East Hub production of 80 kb/d is expected to raise overall block 15/06 output to 150 kb/d.

Sustaining production is critical for Angola as oil exports, half of which are shipped to China, account for around 80% of state revenues. Capacity should get a short-term boost in 2018 after the ramp up of Total's USD 16 billion Kaombo project, the biggest on the drawing board and the last to be sanctioned before the post-2014 price collapse. Sonangol has reportedly adjusted the terms of the production-sharing contract in response to lower oil prices and construction costs. First oil is expected this year and, at its peak, the ultra-deep water field is expected to pump 230 kb/d. Challenging market conditions have, however, led Maersk to further delay the 100 kb/d Chissonga deep water project.

Figure 2.38 Angola, Nigeria struggle

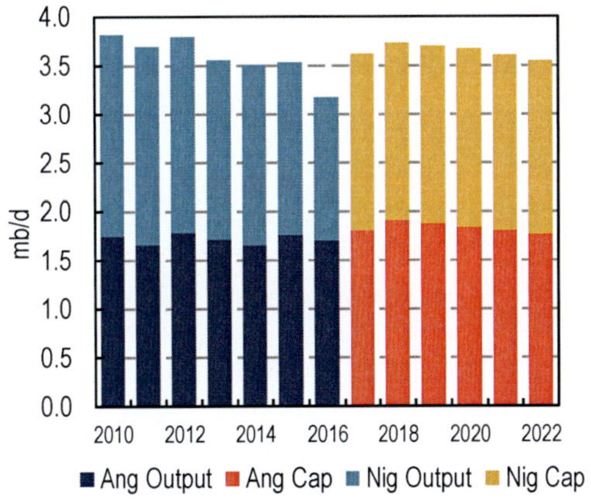

Nigerian President Muhammadu Buhari's first year in office was marked by a collapse in oil output and an economy sliding deeper into recession. Militant strikes and technical glitches disrupted four of the country's key export streams – Bonny Light, Forcados, Brass River and Qua Iboe. As a result, crude oil output in

SUPPLY

2016 fell by 300 kb/d to 1.47 mb/d – shutting in nearly 400 kb/d of capacity. The decline is disastrous for an economy that relies on oil exports for 60% of government revenues. In the short-term the Trans Forcados Pipeline, which has been shut for a year by militant attacks, is unlikely to restart before mid-2017. The line carries roughly 200 kb/d of Forcados crude.

Nigerian National Petroleum Company (NNPC) is meanwhile struggling to pay its foreign partners: joint ventures account for roughly 60% of crude oil production and NNPC is trying to boost production by renegotiating debt owed to partners including Exxon, Shell, Chevron and Total. Slowing investment in the capital intensive deep water projects is expected to cut crude oil production capacity by 50 kb/d over the forecast period to 1.78 mb/d.

Upstream spending had been falling in any case due to the long-running deadlock over the Petroleum Industry Bill (PIB), which aims to revamp fiscal terms. Nigeria's biggest project due online during the forecast period is the 220 kb/d offshore, deep water Egina, which Total is expected to start pumping at the end of 2017. Shell reportedly has scaled down its 225 kb/d Bonga Southwest-Aparo deep water field development to 150 kb/d, with a potential start-up unlikely before 2021. A Nigerian court has meanwhile ordered Shell and Eni to temporarily hand over deep water oil block OPL 245 – which contains the Zabazaba and Etan fields – to the government, pending the conclusion of a long-running corruption probe.

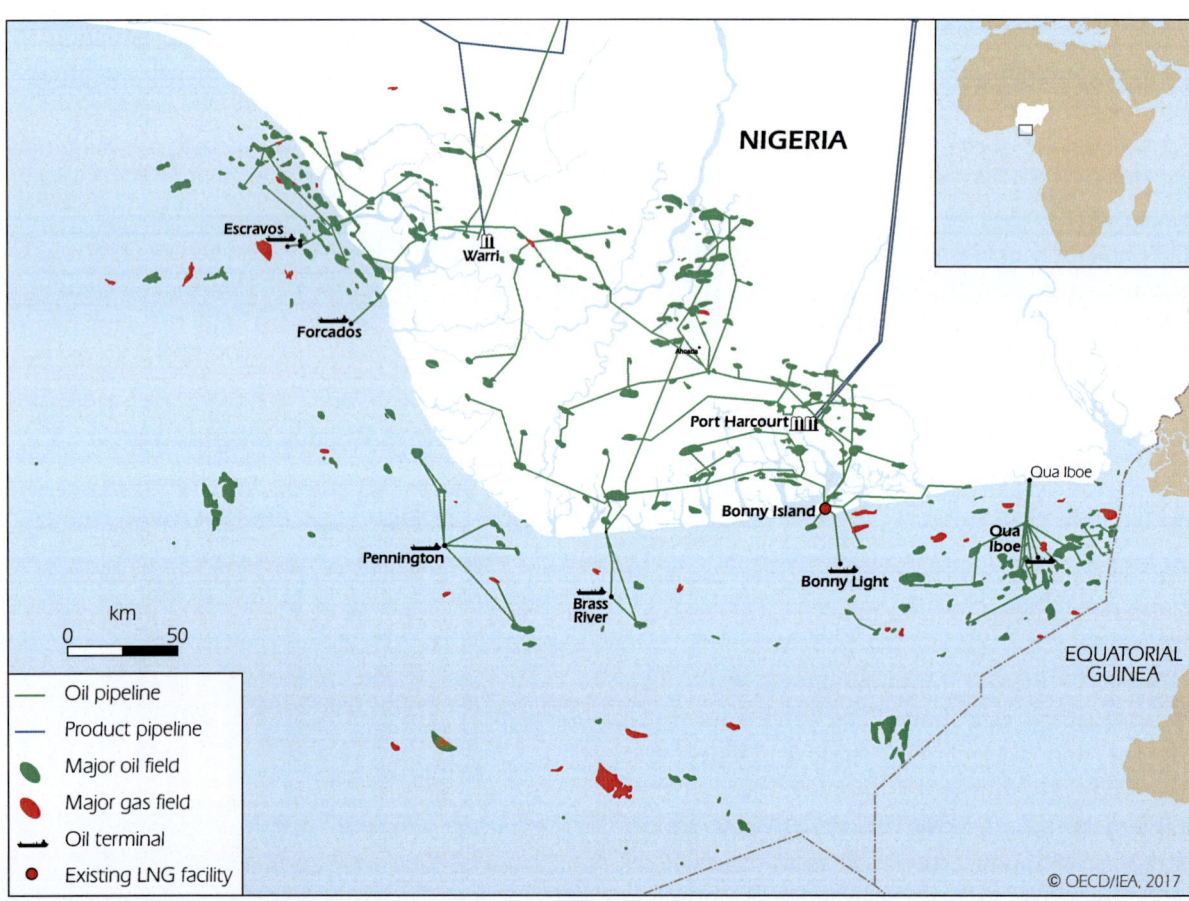

Map 2.4 Nigeria's oil infrastructure

This map is without prejudice to the status of or sovereignty over any territory, to the delimitation of international frontiers and boundaries and to the name of any territory, city or area.

Ecuador is expected to gain 80 kb/d of capacity during the forecast period, with crude production reaching 650 kb/d after the start-up of the Ishpingo-Tambococha-Tiputini (ITT) oil block in the Amazon rain forest. Output from ITT came on line in 2016 and reached 60 kb/d by the end of the year. Located within a UNESCO world biosphere reserve, ITT contains about a fifth of Ecuador's total reserves of 8 billion barrels and is crucial to boosting capacity. Some 19 wells have been drilled so far, many of which are horizontal to minimize the environmental impact. The field pumps heavy crude, with an API gravity of 13-15 degrees.

Overall output has been stuck around 500 kb/d to 600 kb/d after President Rafael Correa in 2010 tore up production-sharing-contracts, leading some foreign investors to flee, and forcing those who stayed to accept service deals that paid a per-barrel fee. When oil prices collapsed, these contracts became loss-makers and Petroamazonas, a unit of Ecuadoran state oil company Petroecuador, began to renegotiate. A Schlumberger-led consortium agreed to the new terms at the mature 70 kb/d Auca oil field and will invest an initial USD 1.1 billion, with total investment over the life of the contract pegged at around USD 5 billion. Petroamazonas says the deal will enable it to raise production by 20 kb/d to 85 kb/d. Ecuador plans to secure similar agreements with other companies.

A severe cash crunch is expected to take its toll on **Venezuelan** crude output, with capacity slipping by the end of the forecast period to 2.12 mb/d, the lowest level in three decades. A further 110 kb/d of capacity is expected to be lost by 2022 as foreign oil service companies reduce their activity and IOCs struggle with repayment issues and daily operational challenges. As budgetary pressure intensifies, there is growing concern that acute shortages of food and medicine could increasingly hamper industry operations. In turn, President Nicolas Maduro has leaned on state Petroleos de Venezuela (PDVSA) to cut costs, repair refineries and boost crude production immediately. Nearly all of Venezuela's foreign currency is generated via oil exports, but a lower oil price environment and mismanagement have left PDVSA short of money to pay suppliers or spend on upstream investment.

The mature fields in the east have suffered from deep output losses, but the fields in the west around Lake Maracaibo are also under pressure. Even when oil prices were close to USD 100/bbl from 2011-2014, these ageing fields were struggling from chronic under-investment and poor reservoir management. Natural declines accelerated during 2016 due to a severe electricity supply crisis. Even production in the hitherto relatively stable southeast Orinoco Belt has begun to slip due to a lack of light crude for blending and reduced investment from foreign partners. Venezuela hopes to increase output from the vast Orinoco Belt, which accounts for roughly half its output, to counter losses elsewhere. To that end, PDVSA announced a plan at the end of 2016 to drill 480 wells in the extra-heavy oil producing region. Schlumberger and other IOCs are reportedly expected to take part in the USD 3.2 billion effort to raise output by 250 kb/d over a 30-month period.

PDVSA is seeking financing to revive its output: CNPC plans to spend USD 2.2 billion to raise production of heavy and light oil and boost exports to China. Few details have been made public, but output could rise by roughly 160 kb/d from four projects. The Sinovensa joint venture would provide the biggest increase - with 70 kb/d - from a steam injection pilot project in the Orinoco Belt in north-eastern Venezuela. PDVSA supplies roughly 500 kb/d to China, which has loaned Venezuela more than USD 50 billion in exchange for future crude shipments. The problem is that the lower the oil price the greater the volume of oil that must be shipped. This is proving to be a major strain on PDVSA's system.

PDVSA has also signed financing deals worth nearly USD 1.45 billion with India's ONGC Videsh and a local firm. ONGC will provide USD 318 million to boost output at the San Cristobal field from 20 kb/d to 40 kb/d. DP Delta Finance will offer USD 1.13 billion in financing to raise supply at the Petrodelta joint venture from 40 kb/d to 110 kb/d over the next five years. Shell has agreed to provide USD 400 million in financing to boost output at Petroregional del Lago, a joint venture with PDVSA. Petroregional operates the 30 kb/d Urdaneta oilfield in western Maracaibo Lake.

OPEC gas liquids supply

Production of condensate, other natural gas liquids and non-conventional resources is forecast to rise by 350 kb/d to 7.03 mb/d by 2022 as many OPEC countries focus on natural gas developments. Iran leads the growth. Angola, Saudi Arabia and Qatar are also expected to show notable gains.

Iran continues to press ahead with development of the giant South Pars gas field as it seeks to meet rising domestic demand and eventually to become an exporter. The partial relief of international sanctions has already seen an initial deal with Total for phase 11 of the offshore field that is geologically linked to Qatar's North Field. Iranian NGL production is expected to reach 1 mb/d by 2022, equating to growth of 150 kb/d over the forecast period. As more access is gained to cash and technology, long delayed projects at South Pars are being fast-tracked, though a hefty chunk of the volume is likely to be earmarked for internal use, including petrochemicals.

The expansion of South Pars, which has 24 phases, had been set back by international sanctions. Iran is striving to catch up with Qatar, the world's largest LNG exporter, and last year saw the start-up of phases 15-16 and 19. Target condensate production from each project is around 75 kb/d, with an additional 30 kb/d of NGLs. Tehran hopes to bring on phases 17, 18, 20 and 21 in the near term.

Qatari condensate, natural gas liquids and non-conventional output - mostly from the North Field – is due to increase by 55 kb/d to just above 1.25 mb/d by 2022. The USD 10 billion offshore Barzan field, the last big project to come online since Doha's 2005 moratorium on further development of the North Field, is expected to add 50 kb/d. Much of the production from Barzan, owned 93% by QP and the remainder by Exxon, is to be routed to the power and water sectors.

Saudi Arabia, which holds OPEC's largest NGL capacity, is expected to boost output by 74 kb/d to 1.98 mb/d by 2022. Gas began to flow last spring from the 275 kb/d Shaybah NGL development, which includes 190 kb/d of ethane. The USD 3 billion-4 billion scheme, originally due to start up in mid-2014, will supply feedstock to the domestic market. Additional condensate output arrived from the start-up of the Wasit gas megaproject, which involves development of the Hasbah and Arabiyah fields. It, too, was hit with delays due to technical snags.

Angola is expected to raise gas liquids supply by 65 kb/d to 140 kb/d by 2022 following the long awaited re-start of Angola LNG. The USD 12 billion project had been beset with technical problems and was back on line at the end of December after a controlled shutdown at the 5.2 mt/y liquefaction plant, which accounts for 50 kb/d of NGL output.

Iraq plans to treble its exports of LPG and double shipments of condensates in 2017 as it gathers more of the fuels from its southern oil fields. Baghdad expects LPG exports to rise to 3 kb/d in 2017, with condensates expected to rise to 7 kb/d. Iraq shipped its first cargoes of condensate and LPG in

2016 as part of the Shell-led Basra Gas Co (BGC) project. BGC processes associated gas from the Rumaila, West Qurna-1 and Zubair oil fields, sells dry gas back to Iraq's South Gas Co and markets the liquids.

Table 2.4 Estimated OPEC condensate and NGL production (kb/d)

Country	2016	2017	2018	2019	2020	2021	2022	2016-22
Algeria	487	492	493	484	475	467	459	-28
Angola	75	98	105	108	117	135	140	65
Iran	848	912	932	960	977	994	999	151
Iraq	90	90	95	95	100	105	105	15
Kuwait	310	307	305	303	310	320	328	18
Libya	35	45	45	50	55	60	65	30
Nigeria	457	453	445	436	428	420	413	-44
Qatar	1 198	1 242	1 263	1 256	1 255	1 254	1 253	55
Saudi Arabia	1 909	1 942	1 950	1 968	1 976	1 980	1 983	74
UAE	838	843	868	870	872	877	872	34
Venezuela	190	180	175	175	170	160	160	-30
Total OPEC NGLs*	6 436	6 605	6 675	6 704	6 735	6 772	6 776	340
Non-Conventional**	251	224	253	256	257	257	257	7
Total OPEC	6 687	6 829	6 929	6 960	6 993	7 029	7 034	347

* Includes ethane.
** Includes gas-to-liquids (GTLs).

Biofuel supply

Global conventional biofuels production in 2016 was 2.35 mb/d, representing 2% growth on 2015 levels, and accounted for 4% of world road transport fuel. Our forecast is revised up versus last year due to a more optimistic outlook for both ethanol and biodiesel production. Over the medium term, average annual conventional biofuel production growth of 3% means output is forecast to reach 2.80 mb/d by 2022. However, this represents a slower rate of expansion compared to the 2010-16 period, when production increased at an average annual rate of 4%. Ongoing growth of gasoline and diesel demand limits the medium term increase in biofuels share of road transport to 4.5%.

Production growth of 20% over 2016-22 is primarily accounted for by non-OECD countries. Driven by security of supply considerations, enhanced policy support for the consumption of domestically produced biofuels is boosting Asian markets for ethanol (e.g. in China, India and Thailand) and biodiesel (e.g. in Indonesia and Malaysia). Furthermore, production of both fuels is anticipated to increase in Latin America, primarily driven by Brazil. Conversely, post-2020 growth prospects in the European Union (EU) are limited due to reduced policy support.

World ethanol production in 2016 was relatively stable versus 2015 levels at 1.73 mb/d and average annual growth of 2.5% will see output reach just under 2 mb/d by 2022. Biodiesel production recovered from a contraction in 2015 to reach 620 kb/d in 2016. Over the medium-term, we expect average annual growth of just over 4%, with production reaching just under 800 kb/d in 2022, an upward revision from the *MTOMR 2016*. For conventional biofuels production as a whole, in the period of our forecast 60% will come from ethanol and 40% from diesel.

SUPPLY

Mandates have proved effective in shielding biofuels from the low oil price environment that persisted through 2016. Oil prices, though, are only one determining factor in biofuel market prospects; policies, feedstock prices and fuel demand trends are also important. Mandates and supportive policies have been strengthened in many key countries since the downturn in crude oil prices starting in mid-2014, including in Argentina, Brazil, India, Indonesia and Spain. Consequently, medium-term production growth within the forecast period is anticipated regardless of the duration of lower oil prices. However, elsewhere lower prices did delay biofuel mandate increases in the Philippines and Malaysia.

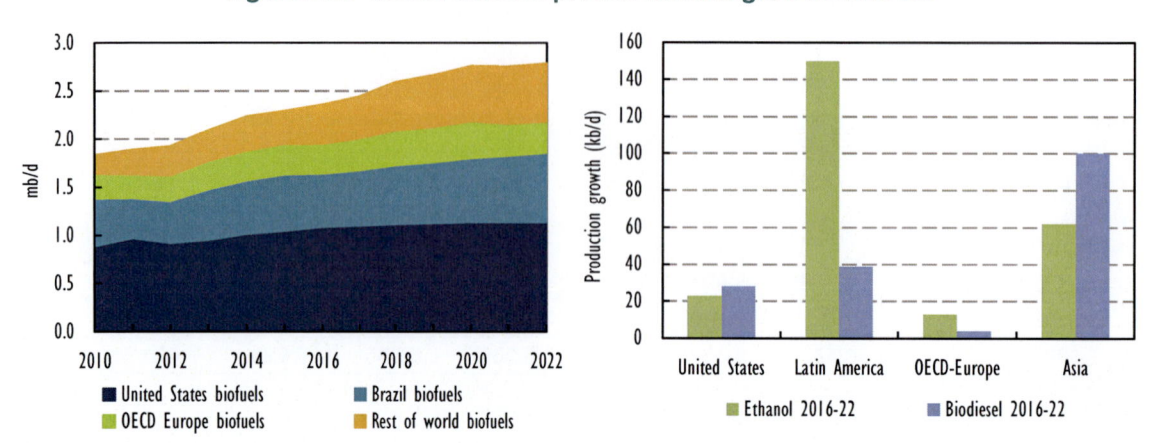

Figure 2.39 Global biofuels production and growth 2016-22

Sources: IEA (2016a), Oil Information (database), www.iea.org/statistics/; IEA (2016b), Monthly Oil Data Service (MODS) [December 2016], www.iea.org/statistics/; MAPA (2016), Ministério da Agricultura – Agroenergia; US EIA (2016), Petroleum & Other Liquids.

Where biofuel consumption is subsidised lower oil prices increase biofuel cost premiums over petroleum products and reduce the volume that can be subsidised for a given budget. This is the case in Indonesia for biodiesel and in Thailand for high ethanol blends. Another factor affecting the biofuels market is the limited opportunity for discretionary blending above mandated volumes, although this is a smaller share of biofuels demand compared to mandates. In addition, less favourable blending economics provide a greater incentive to minimise blend shares therefore highlighting the value of suitable governance arrangements to ensure compliance with mandated consumption. Last, and not least, there is overall economic uncertainty which provides a more challenging investment climate.

Ethanol markets regional outlook

In the **United States**, ethanol production rose by 2.5% y-o-y to around 990 kb/d in 2016. Growth was supported by another bumper corn crop in conjunction with very high capacity utilisation rates. For consumption, ethanol's share of overall gasoline demand occasionally rose above 10% during 2016 effectively crossing the "blend wall"[1]. Over the medium term, production is forecast to stabilise near this level with only slight growth to around 1,015 kb/d anticipated. This is due to limited investment in new capacity, a stabilisation of gasoline demand due to increasing vehicle fuel efficiency and 2017 Renewable Fuel Standard (RFS2) volumes for total renewable fuel volumes that indicate the limit for corn based ethanol will be reached.

1 The "blend wall" refers to the challenge of increasing biofuel consumption in the United States considering the suitability of the vehicle fleet and absence of widespread fuel distribution infrastructure for biofuel blends higher than E10 (gasoline with 10% ethanol by volume).

In order to grow production significantly further consumption of higher ethanol blends such as E15 and E85[2] will be needed. According to the US Environmental Protection Agency, light duty vehicles manufactured from 2001 onwards are approved for E15[3]; it has been indicated that there are nearly 20 million flexible fuel vehicles (FFVs) in the United States' passenger vehicle fleet (US Department of Energy, 2017). Therefore the key to unlocking market growth potential rests with scaling up fuel distribution infrastructure for these fuels. There are early indications of this occurring as the number of service stations offering E15 and E85 increased by more than 100 in 2016, and coverage is expected to expand faster in 2017 from its current low base. Also, growing ethanol exports would also support industry expansion.

Ethanol production in **Brazil** contracted 9% y-o-y in 2016 at 470 kb/d. Despite an early start to the harvest due to the availability of standover sugar cane from 2015, the rebound in international sugar prices resulted in a higher share of sugar production at the expense of fuel ethanol. However, higher sugar prices also helped improve the financial position for well diversified sugar mills. During 2016 price competitiveness generally tipped in favour of gasoline resulting in a reduction in hydrous ethanol consumption, only partially compensated by higher blended anhydrous ethanol. The expiry of the PIS/COFINS[4] tax exemption for hydrous ethanol at the end of 2016 is anticipated to further impact price competitiveness at the pump with gasoline-C[5] in 2017 unless reinstated.

The share of FFVs in the vehicle fleet, an anticipated increase in gasoline demand and strong policy commitment mean the long term drivers for fuel ethanol in Brazil remain strong. Consequently, a production increase of around 30% is anticipated by 2022 with output likely to reach 620 kb/d. The share of FFVs in the automobile and light vehicle fleet reached almost 72% FFVs in 2016, and it will continue to rise. In addition, gasoline demand is anticipated to grow 9% in the 2016-22 period, boosting prospects for hydrous and anhydrous ethanol.

The commitment within Brazil's Nationally Determined Contribution to increase the share of sustainable biofuels in its energy mix to approximately 18% would translate to in excess of 860 kb/d of fuel ethanol demand by 2030. Meeting this target will require further industry investment in new sugar mill capacity, which is in sharp contrast to the current fragile economic state of many sugar mills in the industry. Therefore, concrete measures to deliver further industry investment within the forthcoming federal RenovaBio 2030 plan would provide upside potential to our forecast.

In **China**, the world's third largest fuel ethanol producer, production increased to almost 50 kb/d in 2016 and is forecast to grow at an average annual rate of 5.5% to over 65 kb/d in 2022. While no mandate increases are expected in the provinces which have 10% ethanol blending in place, 6% average annual growth in gasoline demand is expected to boost ethanol demand. In addition, the 13th Five-Year Plan reaffirms the target of 4 million tonnes (around 85 kb/d) of fuel ethanol production by 2020. In the meantime, the stockpiling of corn for ethanol production has led to large quantities becoming unfit for human consumption. As a result, a number of provinces have introduced subsidies to encourage the production of ethanol from corn. This will improve capacity utilisation and reverse a trend which saw ethanol imports increase over 2015-16.

2 E85 equates to a blend of 85% ethanol by volume with gasoline, similarly references to E10, E15 and E20 refer to the volume share of ethanol blended with gasoline. Similarly references to B7, B10 and B15 etc. refer to the volume share of biodiesel blended with fossil diesel.
3 It should be noted that vehicle manufacturers also have to approve the use of E15 in their vehicles in order to provide consumers with the necessary confidence to use the blend without invalidating vehicle warranties.
4 Contribution for Intervention in Economic Domain, Contribution to the Social Integration Programme and Contribution for Financing Social Security.
5 A gasoline ethanol blend, the main alternative to hydrous ethanol at the pump.

OECD Europe fuel ethanol production reduced slightly to 80 kb/d in 2016. The main feedstocks used in 2015 were corn and wheat, with sugar beet making a lower contribution. However, the abolition of sugar production quotas in the EU in 2017 may reshuffle the feedstock landscape. A number of new national policy announcements indicate a scaling up of production towards 2020 in line with the European Union's (EU) Renewable Energy Directive and Fuel Quality Directive targets of 10% renewable energy in transport, and a 6% reduction in the greenhouse gas intensity of vehicle fuels. OECD Europe fuel ethanol production is expected to peak in 2020 at around 115 kb/d, with higher growth undermined by declining EU-28 gasoline demand. The lack of anticipated new ethanol production capacity means increased output is principally due to higher capacity utilisation at existing plants. However, production is anticipated to decline slightly post-2020 as EU policy support for conventional biofuels weakens.

Fuel ethanol production in **India** grew by almost 90% y-o-y to reach 19 kb/d in 2016, supported by a range of measures to strengthen the ethanol blending programme. As a result the best ever performance against the 5% blending mandate was achieved for the 2015/16 year, with, on average, 4.4% ethanol blending. Output in 2017 may be slightly lower, however, due to a reduction in regulated fuel ethanol procurement prices from sugar mills and the removal of a 12.5% excise duty exemption for ethanol blended with gasoline.

Long-term drivers for fuel ethanol industry expansion in India remain strong however, and over the medium-term production is anticipated to almost double to 36 kb/d. Average annual growth in gasoline demand is estimated at 10% and strong policy support is in place as domestically produced fuel ethanol is seen as a way to improve security of supply. Imports are prohibited under the fuel blending programme and while capacity is already in place to expand fuel ethanol production this would result in a diversion from industrial ethanol output. Therefore, meeting the more ambitious 10% ethanol blending target will require investment in new production capacity and actions to mitigate barriers relating to inter-state permits and taxes as well as constrained storage capacity at refineries. Broadening the feedstock base beyond the exclusive use of molasses may also be required to grow output. Growing ethanol consumption beyond the 10% target is considered challenging given the current market outlook.

Prospects for the ethanol industry in **Thailand** remain very positive. Production has grown steadily each year since 2010 and reached 21 kb/d in 2016, primarily from molasses. New production capacity is anticipated over 2017-18 and output is forecast to increase at an average annual rate of over 10% to reach 40 kb/d by 2022, with an increasing share from cassava. Multiple drivers are expected to support forecast growth. Over 2016-22 gasoline demand is anticipated to rise at an annual average rate of around 4.5%. In addition, E10 availability is widespread and coverage of subsidised E20 and E85 blends is rising with the number of service stations offering these increasing in 2016. Furthermore, the Alternative Energy Development Plan (AEDP) for 2015-36 establishes the long term target of an average of 32% ethanol blending.

Biodiesel markets regional outlook

Record biodiesel production of 98 kb/d was achieved in the **United States** during 2016, representing a 20% y-o-y increase on 2015 levels, as output was supported by a strong soybean harvest. Annually increasing biomass based diesel volumes required by the RFS2 have been established until 2018, and biodiesel is also eligible to contribute to the advanced biofuel and total renewable fuels categories within the scheme, providing demand certainty for the first half of the medium term. RFS2 demand also stimulated a step up in biodiesel imports in 2016, principally from Argentina. Due to this favourable policy environment the forecast has been revised up with biodiesel production forecast to reach 125 kb/d in 2022, an almost 30% increase over 2016 despite stagnant diesel demand.

The USD 1/gallon blenders' tax credit, which has supported profitability in the biodiesel supply chain and incentivised higher biodiesel blending, expired at the end of 2016. However, potential remains for this to be re-introduced as has occurred previously. Alternatively, should industry lobbying prove successful this could be altered to a producer's tax credit moving forward, potentially pushing domestic production higher than forecast levels and consequently reducing imports.

Biodiesel production in **Brazil** remained stable at 66 kb/d in 2016 aided by a high soybean harvest for the 2015/16 crop. To 2022, average annual production growth of around 6% is forecast with output scaling-up to over 90 kb/d. Demand is supported by a staged increase in the blending mandate from the current 7%, to 8% in March 2017, and then increasing by one percentage point annually to 10% in 2019. Higher production should go some way towards reducing current biodiesel plant overcapacity. While macro-economic factors in the Brazilian economy have dampened diesel demand a gradual recovery towards pre-economic downturn diesel demand is anticipated to slightly increase biodiesel volumes required to meet mandated requirements.

In 2016, **OECD Europe** biodiesel production remained stable at around 227 kb/d. France, Germany and the Netherlands remained key producer countries. The Hydrotreated Vegetable Oil (HVO) share of production was estimated at 20% in 2016 (F.O. Licht, 2016), an increase from around 2% in 2010. European HVO production will increase further in 2017 with the commissioning of a large plant in France. In early 2016, the World Trade Organization (WTO) ruled in Argentina's favour with regard to claims against EU anti-dumping duties imposed on Argentinian biodiesel imports. This raises the prospect of the recommencement of exports into the EU, not just from Argentina but also Indonesia. The anti-dumping rates are currently under review with finalised changes anticipated to be implemented in summer 2017.

In 2017, biofuels mandate increases in the Czech Republic, Italy, Netherlands and Spain, as well as an increase in Germany's Climate Protection Quota, should support higher demand. Over the medium-term, biodiesel and HVO production is anticipated to rise slowly to around 270 kb/d in 2020, in accordance with the need to satisfy the previously mentioned EU targets. Post 2020, production is anticipated to fall as no support is anticipated for conventional biofuels under European Commission state aid rules, while the proposals for a revised RED for the 2020-30 period include a reduction in the cap on the contribution of food-based biofuels towards the EU renewable energy target, from 7% (by energy) in 2021 scaling down to 3.8% in 2030. In this context prospects for new biodiesel capacity investment in OECD Europe during the medium term appear highly limited.

In **Indonesia**, biodiesel output increased in 2016 to reach 50 kb/d, levels broadly in line with the global high B20 mandate programme. The Indonesian biodiesel market is in transition from an export driven focus towards higher domestic usage. Biodiesel consumption premiums over fossil fuels are subsidised via a plantation fund using levies on crude palm oil and palm oil product exports. By 2022 a significant increase in production to around 110 kb/d is forecast. Growth is underpinned by steady gains in diesel consumption of around 3% per year, increased capacity due to a number of new plants coming online complementing existing underused capacity and new legislation to increase coverage of the B20 market segment eligible for subsidies and also subject to non-compliance penalties. Exports will remain an important part of Indonesia's biodiesel market structure.

Biodiesel output in **Malaysia**, predominantly from palm oil, declined slightly to 15 kb/d in 2016. The planned increase in the road transport blending mandate to B10, alongside a steady upward trend in diesel demand, should see production rise to around 24 kb/d by 2022. The aforementioned mandate increase is likely to be complemented by a B7 blending target for the industrial sector. However the timeline for the introduction of these higher mandates is currently unknown. Production output growth is achievable without additional new plants given current overcapacity in the industry. Higher production still could be achieved by the introduction of a nationwide B15 mandate, as outlined in the 11th Malaysia Plan for the 2015-20 period, although this is not included in the forecast.

Biodiesel production in **Argentina**, principally from soybean oil, rebounded to around 50 kb/d in 2016, with more than half destined for export. Despite slow diesel demand growth, by 2022 production is forecast to be around 17% higher at 60 kb/d, supported by excise duty waivers introduced for biodiesel used for electricity generation and a tax exemption on biodiesel production. In addition, underutilised capacity is available to increase output. However, prospects for the industry are principally shaped by export opportunities. Exports to the United States to serve RFS2 demand are anticipated to continue. Furthermore, the aforementioned WTO ruling in Argentina's favour reopens the prospect of biodiesel exports into the EU. Production could rise above the forecast should there be an increase in the current 10% blending mandate and as a result of discretionary blending opportunities opened up by higher crude oil prices over the medium term.

References:

US DOE (US Department of Energy) (2017), "Alternative Fuels Data Centre - Flexible fuel vehicles", http://www.afdc.energy.gov/vehicles/flexible_fuel_emissions.html.

F.O. Lichts (2016), "2017 world biodiesel demand may reach record level", https://www.agra-net.com/agra/world-ethanol-and-biofuels-report/features/2017-world-biodiesel-demand-may-reach-record-level-532781.htm.

IEA (International Energy Agency) (2016a), *Oil Information* (database), www.iea.org/statistics/ (accessed December 2016).

IEA (2016b), *Monthly Oil Data Service (MODS) [May 2016]*, www.iea.org/statistics/ (accessed December 2016).

MAPA (Ministry for Agriculture, Livestock and Supply) (2016), *Ministério da Agricultura – Agroenergia* [Ministry for Agro-energy], www.agricultura.gov.br/desenvolvimento-sustentavel/agroenergia.

US EIA (United States Energy Information Administration) (2016), *Petroleum & Other Liquids* (database), www.eia.gov/petroleum/data.cfm.

3. REFINING AND TRADE

Highlights

- After low crude oil prices lifted refining margins to impressive levels in 2015, earnings moderated in 2016. The oil industry started to trim their downstream capital expenditures after two consecutive years of upstream cuts, curbing forecasts of global refining capacity additions.

- The net 2016-22 capacity change is forecast at 7 mb/d, weighted towards the second half of the outlook. The Middle East countries collectively drive the new additions, closely followed by China. India, another major contributor, sees a more moderate expansion with only small extensions at existing refineries. Africa is expected to see its first mega-refinery come online in Nigeria while project cancellations in Brazil dramatically reduce Latin American additions.

- Underpinned by capacity expansions, global refinery throughput is forecast to grow by 6.5 mb/d. Total oil demand grows by 7.3 mb/d, but some 1.4 mb/d of incremental product supply will come from non-refining sources such as biofuels, gas-to-liquids, and natural gas fractionation plants.

- Global crude oil markets will see more volumes from non-OPEC exporters such as Brazil and Canada than from OPEC as the latter focuses on expanding refining capacity, consuming more of their crude oil at home. Assuming the US takes up most of the increase in Canadian volumes, US seaborne imports of crude oil will decline by 2 mb/d. Asian crude oil import requirements will grow by 3.6 mb/d to 24.6 mb/d. China's imports alone may reach 9.5 mb/d, while India will import 5 mb/d.

- Asia's few net crude oil exporting countries will all become net crude oil importers, resulting in a highly imbalanced Asian crude oil market. Some of the traditional Middle East crude oil export volumes to the west will be redirected to feed Asian refiners. Still, this will not be enough to satisfy Asian refiners' appetite, and they will have to import growing volumes from elsewhere, notably the FSU, Latin America and Africa.

- Already a large net importer of LPG and naphtha, Asia will add gasoline and diesel to its net product imports basket. While increased refinery throughput in the Middle East will cover some of this requirement, Asian importers will have to look to US and European markets to secure product flows.

- The global bunker fuel market is set to change as a new regulation caps sulphur emissions from maritime shipping to 0.5% from 2020. If the new global emissions standards are rigidly enforced, our forecast shows a lack of low-sulphur fuel options by 2020, possibly affecting fuel prices and effective compliance. The resulting price differential between low-sulphur and high-sulphur fuels will, however, create favourable conditions for wider-scale uptake of on-board abatement technologies, such as scrubbers.

Overview

Our medium-term forecast for the refining sector is set against a backdrop of unusual developments in 2016. While crude oil prices lost about USD 20/bbl over the course of 2015, in 2016 prices regained a similar amount, ending 2016 at exactly the same point as 2014, at USD 56/bbl. Lower crude prices boosted refinery margins in 2015, driving throughput up by 1.8 mb/d. Even though oil demand grew by a massive 2 mb/d in that year, incremental refined product demand lagged behind as more products were supplied from other sources, resulting in product oversupply and inflated inventories by the start of 2016.

Figure 3.1 Crude prices supported refinery margins in 2015 and constrained them in 2016

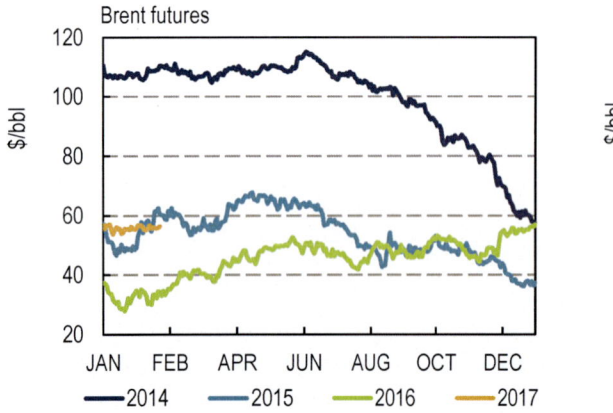

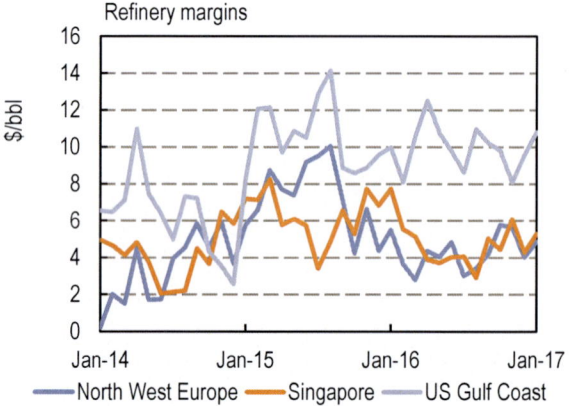

This, along with rising crude prices, created a major headwind for refinery margins in 2016, constraining global throughput growth to under 500 kb/d y-o-y, one of the lowest growth rates in a decade, despite solid 1.6 mb/d growth in demand. In addition, global refinery capacity fell in 2016 for the first time in at least a decade. Permanent refinery closures in Chinese Taipei, the UK and France were not fully offset by relatively small additions of new capacity in Qatar, US, China and elsewhere.

Figure 3.2 Refined product oversupply in 2014-15 resulted in refining slowdown in 2016

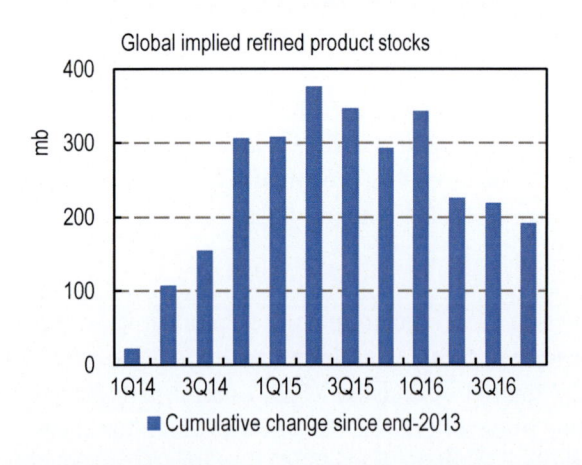

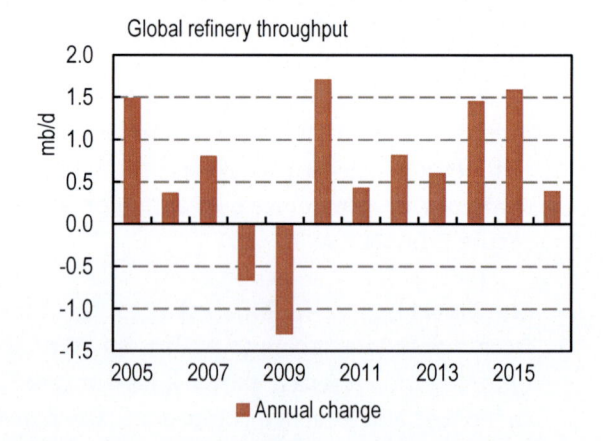

Another interesting feature of 2016 was the resurgence in stark differences between the Atlantic Basin and Asia. Runs in the Atlantic Basin were reduced by 800 kb/d vs 2015 –in a combined effort from North America, Latin America, Europe, FSU and Africa. East of Suez, by contrast, saw throughput grow by over 1.2 mb/d, with major contributions from China, India, Saudi Arabia and South Korea. After two years of growth, OECD refiners registered a collective annual decline in throughput.

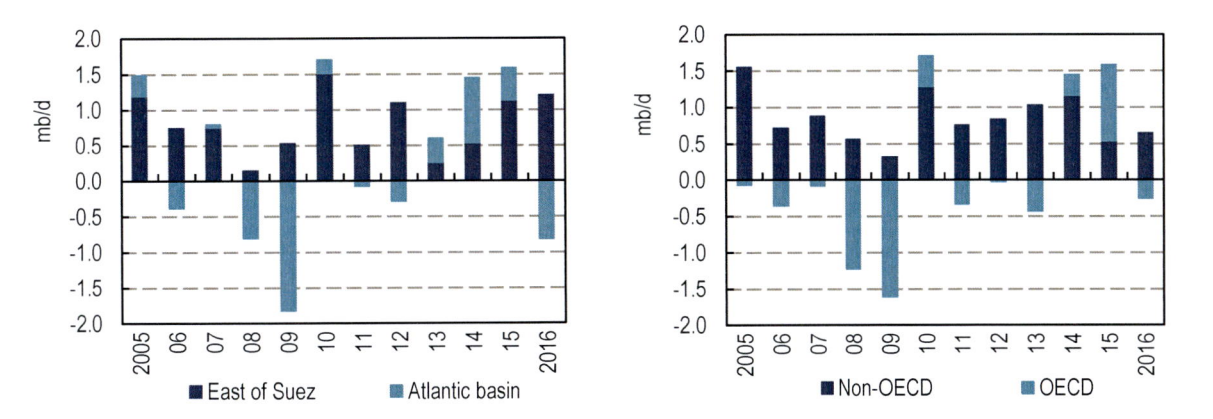

Figure 3.3 Annual refinery throughput changes

Refining sector outlook

The starting point for our medium-term forecast is a year (2016) when refiners were confronted with all possible types of heightened competition:

- From refining peers. Global spare capacity remained high at over 15 mb/d. This was best illustrated by China, where the liberalisation of the refining sector resulted in independent refiners squeezing the share of Chinese majors in refinery throughput.
- From non-refined products. Refiners currently supply only 85% of the global oil market, with biofuels, natural gas liquids, etc., supplying another 14 mb/d (Figure 3.4).
- From refined product inventories. The possibility to draw down from bloated inventories means refiners were not required to run as much crude.

While the global crude and products stock build of 0.9 mb/d seen in the 2014-16 period is cyclical and expected to go into reverse this year, the spare capacity and competition from non-refined products will persist throughout our forecast period. Refined products demand is forecast to grow by 6.1 mb/d over the forecast period, with increasing biofuels and NGLs supplying the remainder of 7.3 mb/d of total demand growth. Direct use of crude oil is the only category in the non-refined products market that will see volumes fall between now and 2022. This is mostly due to fuel switching in the power generation sector in the Middle East from oil to gas, rather than from crude oil to oil products. Coal-to-liquids and gas-to-liquids projects remain a niche industry for regions with abundant coal and gas reserves and companies with deep pockets to finance these projects that have high upfront costs. In an interesting move, last year Saudi Arabia's government-owned petrochemical giant SABIC announced a partnership with Chinese state-owned Shenhua group, the biggest coal producer in the world, to develop a coal-to-olefin projects.

Biofuels remain the fastest growing product category in our forecast, at a rate more than twice as fast as net oil demand (2.9% vs 1.2%). Among oil products, those supplied from natural gas fractionation (ethane, LPG and naphtha) see the fastest growth of 1.8% per annum, with refined product demand increasing by 1.2%.

REFINING AND TRADE

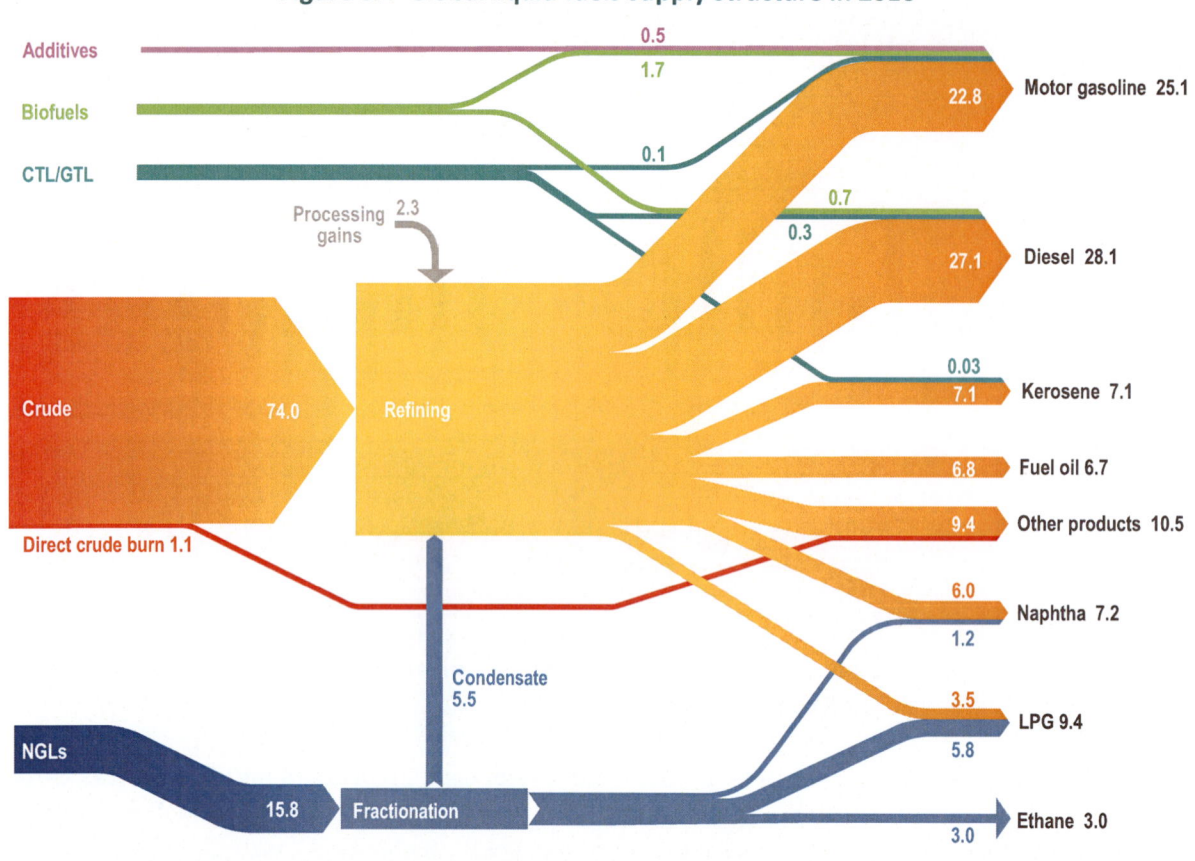

Figure 3.4 Global liquid fuels supply structure in 2016

Refining capacity additions, even though toned down from our previous forecast, are still expected at about 7 mb/d, some 0.9 mb/d above refined product demand growth. Nevertheless, with global throughput forecast to increase by 6.5 mb/d, average utilisation rates will improve by 2022. This is an unusual base year effect as utilisation rates in 2016 were lower than the implied call on refineries, with product inventories drawing to supply the market.

Table 3.1 Total oil demand and call on refineries

	2016	2017	2018	2019	2020	2021	2022
Total liquids demand	96.6	98.0	99.3	100.5	101.7	102.8	103.8
of which biofuels	2.3	2.5	2.6	2.7	2.8	2.8	2.8
Total oil demand	94.2	95.5	96.7	97.8	98.9	100.0	101.0
of which CTL/GTL and additives	0.8	0.8	0.8	0.8	0.8	0.9	0.9
direct use of crude oil	1.1	1.0	0.9	0.9	0.9	0.8	0.8
Total oil product demand	92.3	93.8	94.9	96.1	97.2	98.3	99.3
of which fractionation products	10.0	10.3	10.6	10.7	10.9	11.0	11.1
Refinery products demand	82.4	83.5	84.4	85.3	86.3	87.3	88.2
Refinery market share	85.3%	85.2%	85.0%	84.9%	84.9%	84.9%	85.0%

Our capacity forecast for 2022 is based on analysis of over 200 refinery and condensate splitter projects, including both greenfield projects and existing unit expansion plans. This was narrowed down to a final list of 70 projects, heavily weighted towards China, the Middle East and India, which account for more than half of the global total. The East of Suez total includes another eight projects elsewhere in Asia. North America, with the US driving the expansions, will see nine relatively small-scale additions, with the FSU's eight projects largely following the same pattern of capacity creep. Africa is expected to realise three small-scale projects in addition to a large new build in Nigeria. Meanwhile, only one capacity addition project will be completed in Europe and two capacity expansion projects in Latin America.

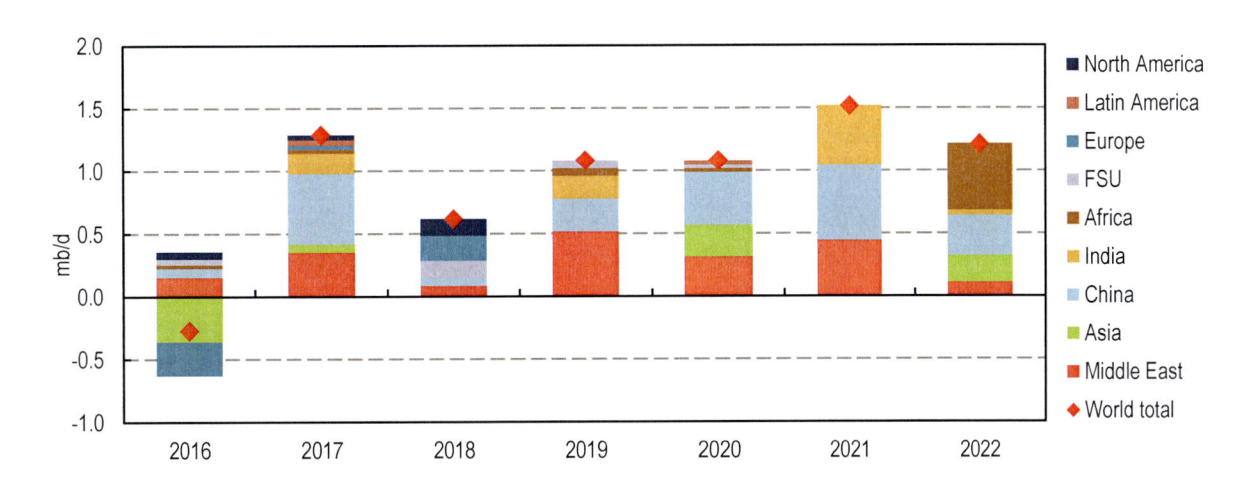

Figure 3.5 Global refinery capacity net additions by region

Box 3.1 Lock, stock and 15 million extra barrels

With the exception of illegal bush refineries found in Nigeria or China's very small "teapot" plants, refineries are usually complex installations that need to be well documented if only for industrial safety purposes given the nature of their operations. However, there is no single publicly available database with detailed information on global refining capacity by type. We periodically audit the IEA's in-house database to enhance its accuracy. The latest review saw downward adjustments to the baseline global crude distillation capacity (including condensate splitters) of about 1 mb/d.

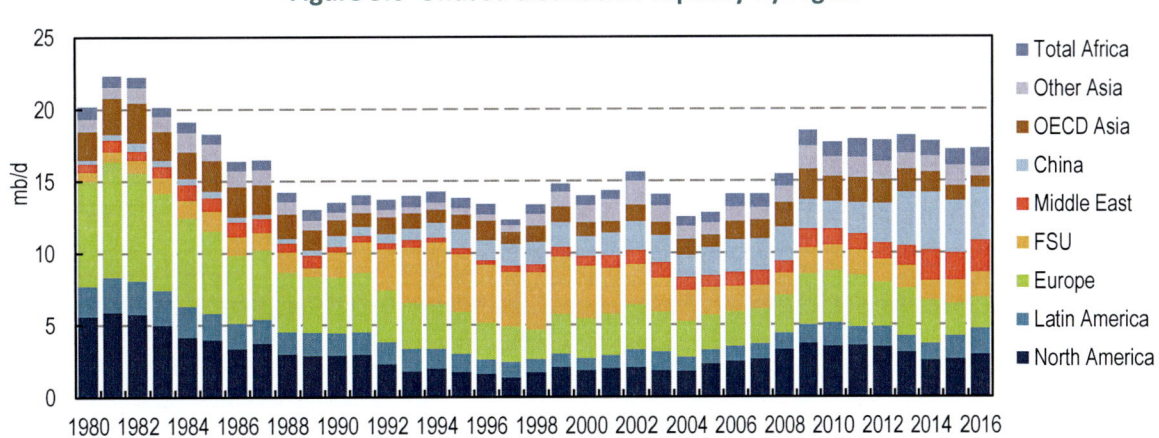

Figure 3.6 Unused distillation capacity by region

Sources: OMR refinery database and BP Statistical Review of World Energy 2016.

> **Box 3.1 Lock, stock and 15 million extra barrels (continued)**
>
> This still leaves about 15 mb/d of distillation capacity that remains currently unused. It may seem as if spare capacity of this magnitude is a recent phenomenon that has resulted from regional demand growth imbalances as developing countries have been building refineries to satisfy higher demand, while in the developed world, refiners have been running at lower rates due to a long-term structural decline in oil demand, and not shutting down excess capacity as fast as they might.
>
> However, as far back as the data go, we can see that unused capacity has been an integral part of the global refining industry. Economies of scale in construction of refining units are quite substantial, and this encourages higher nominal capacity of crude distillation units. Whole refining sites or distillation units are rarely idled temporarily, rather than permanently, unless it is for maintenance purposes. Thus, the extra barrels come largely from underutilised capacity at operating refineries. And the reason for underutilisation tends to be the bottlenecks in secondary units that turn straight-run products into finished fuels.
>
> In the early 1980s global unused capacity hit 22 mb/d as oil demand fell for three consecutive years and oil started to lose its position in the power generation sector. In Europe alone about 5 mb/d of capacity was closed down. In the 1990s, with accelerating Asian economic growth, spare capacity in refining fell to 12 mb/d. Since then, permanent shutdowns in Europe, North America, Japan and elsewhere have been more than offset by newbuilds in China, India and the Middle East, with unused capacity holding near 15 mb/d. Currently there is as much unused capacity in China as in Europe and North America combined. Will the Chinese finally start writing off these units en masse? If not, the global total of unused capacity will not change much, but the regional composition will.

Regional developments in refining

Table 3.2 Regional developments in refining capacity and throughput

	Total capacity			Runs			Utilisation rates	
	2016	2022	Change	2016	2022	Change	2016	2022
North America	21.7	21.9	0.2	18.8	18.9	0.1	86.6%	86.0%
Europe	15.1	15.3	0.2	12.9	12.4	-0.5	85.6%	81.2%
FSU	8.3	8.6	0.3	6.7	6.4	-0.3	79.8%	74.0%
China	14.4	16.6	2.2	11.0	13.0	2.0	76.2%	78.2%
India	4.7	5.5	0.9	4.9	5.7	0.7	105.4%	102.4%
Other Asia	13.8	14.4	0.6	12.1	12.3	0.2	87.7%	85.2%
Middle East	9.0	10.9	1.9	7.1	9.5	2.4	78.6%	87.3%
Latin America	6.2	6.3	0.1	4.2	4.9	0.7	68.4%	78.6%
Africa	3.3	3.9	0.7	2.0	3.1	1.1	61.9%	79.3%
World	**96.5**	**103.5**	**7.0**	**79.7**	**86.2**	**6.5**	**82.6%**	**83.3%**

North America

2016 was a tumultuous year for North American refiners, interrupting their five-year trend of throughput growth. The drop in throughput came largely from the deteriorating state in Mexican refining as multibillion dollar investments announced at the end of 2015 were effectively put on hold until private companies take on the upgrade projects. Wildfires in Canada temporarily affected refinery throughput. Refineries in the United States, having reached record throughput in 2015, seemed overwhelmed by reliability issues arising from intensive capacity utilisation and lower margins that forced import-crude dependent refiners in the north east to slow down activity. Nevertheless, capacity additions in the US and Canada underpin a 100 kb/d increase in North American runs by 2022.

The US will see net additions of 90 kb/d of crude distillation capacity at existing refineries owned by Valero, ExxonMobil and Flint Hills Resources to allow them to process more domestic light crude. In addition, two condensate splitters with combined capacity of 65 kb/d are expected to come online by end-2018. In 2016, the world's biggest refining sector was also busy with corporate M&A activity. Tesoro bought Western Refining in a USD 6.4 bn deal; Delek bought Alon USA Energy, while Shell and Saudi Aramco set out to split their Motiva joint venture refining assets.

Canada's sole project to come online in the next six-year period is North West Redwater Partnership's 80 kb/d Sturgeon refinery in Alberta, designed to process raw bitumen into finished oil products in a bid to extract more value from the province's heavily discounted bitumen crudes. The refinery's raw bitumen intake, though, will only account for 10% of Canada's incremental output of non-upgraded bitumen by 2022. Meanwhile, in Mexico, the forecast increase in refining throughput is based on utilisation rates improving from 2016's low of 56% to 71%, still low by recent historical standards.

Europe

European refiners, having enjoyed a phenomenal 2015, were confronted by an oversupplied market during most of 2016. In OECD Europe, 2015's 660 kb/d growth turned into a 160 kb/d decline in 2016. European runs would have declined more if not for the unexpectedly low refining throughput in Latin America that supported Atlantic Basin product markets. Total shut down 260 kb/d of capacity – half of its site in Killing Holme in the UK, and the La Mede refinery in France. Cepsa's Tenerife refinery in Spain is now also assumed to be permanently closed following the CEO's recent comment that the plant, which shut three years ago, is unlikely to restart. Shell sold its Danish refinery to a local firm, while Ireland's Whitegate changed hands among North American oil companies – from Phillips 66 to Canada's Irving Oil. Trading group Gunvor bought Kuwait Petroleum International's small Rotterdam refinery.

Only one new refinery is expected to be completed in the region – Turkey's 200 kb/d Aliaga project set to come on-stream in 2018. This will drop average utilisation rates even lower, with total runs in the region forecast to fall some 500 kb/d, unless more refineries are shut down in the region.

Former Soviet Union

Russian refinery throughput was widely expected to be affected by fiscal changes introduced to stimulate refinery upgrades to produce more premium fuels. Fuel oil's export duty advantage was removed, discouraging smaller and less sophisticated refineries. Annual decreases in refinery intake started in 2015, persisting until the last quarter of 2016. By then, higher than expected crude output in Russia, more solid domestic demand and better margins from upgraded capacity reversed the trend, driving up refinery throughput. Still, refinery runs are not expected ever again to reach the 2014 level. The energy ministry has repeatedly talked about expectations of lower refining activity in the medium-term. With combined additions of 150 kb/d at three existing refineries, throughput is forecast to decline by 350 kb/d, as utilisation rates drop from 88% to 81%. At this rate, in 2021 Russia will lose its top three refiner spot to India.

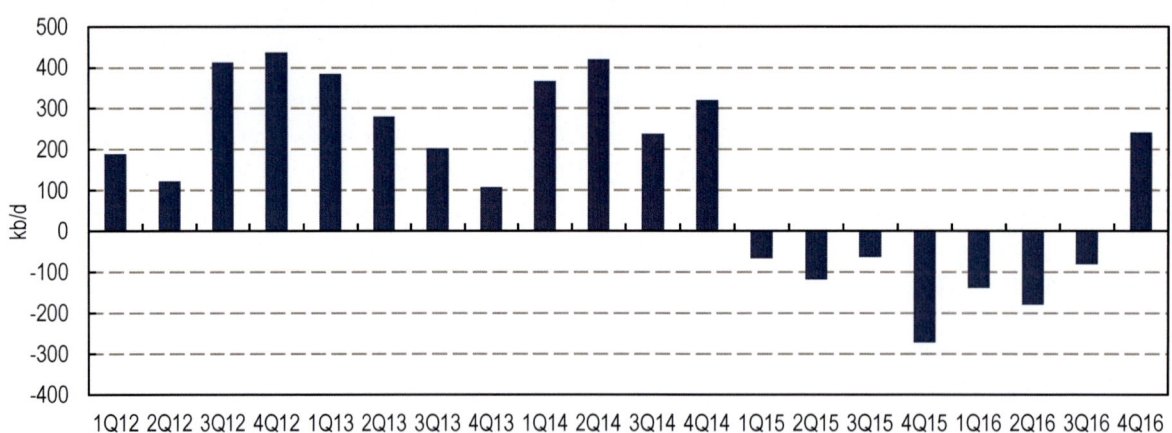

Figure 3.7 Russian refinery intake annual growth

Kazakhstan will focus on secondary units and product quality improvement, bringing in only a combined 45 kb/d of newly added capacity at its three main sites. In 2016, a 4 kb/d mini condensate splitter was launched to feed off Karachaganak gas field liquids. Azerbaijan and Belarus will each have net additions of 30 kb/d at existing refineries. Turkmenistan has plans to double throughput from current levels of 150 kb/d, but this is yet to be backed by concrete investment projects. Moreover, given the country's crude and condensate output forecast, higher throughput would result in Turkmenistan becoming a net crude oil importer.

Middle East

The region will see capacity additions of 2.8 mb/d, some 0.9 mb/d of which will be offset by closures of outdated units in Iran, Bahrain, Kuwait, Oman and Saudi Arabia. Kuwait's 615 kb/d Al-Zour refinery is the biggest new site expected to be commissioned, followed by Saudi Aramco's 400 kb/d Jizan and Bahrain's 355 kb/d Sitra refineries. Iran will bring online the 360 kb/d Persian Gulf Star condensate refinery and the first of the Siraf project's eight 40 kb/d splitters, while a new 200 kb/d crude distillation unit at Abadan refinery will replace an older one.

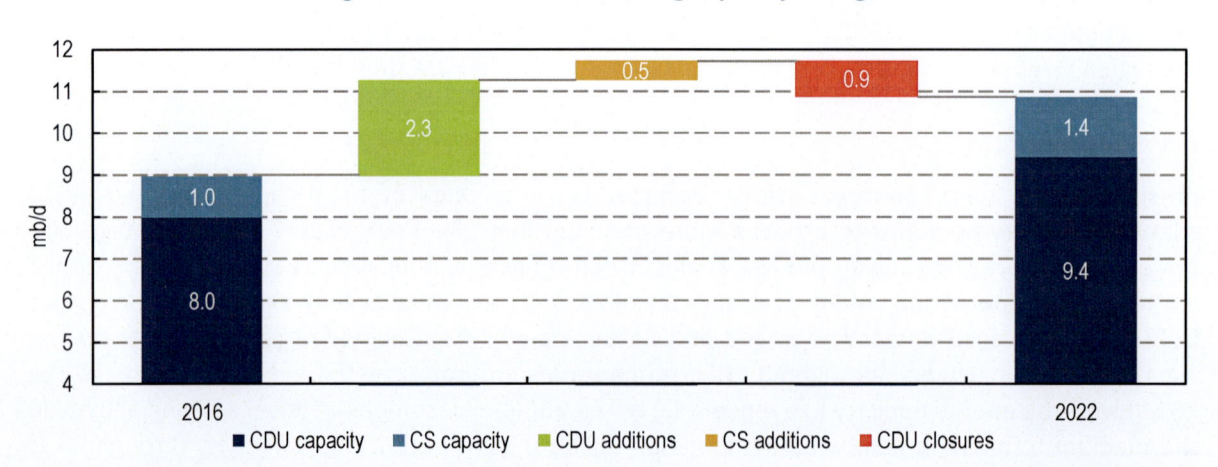

Figure 3.8 Middle East refining capacity changes

Iraq's Karbala project is assumed to be going ahead for commissioning in 2022, along with a 50 kb/d addition in the Kurdistan region. Oman's Sohar and Duqm projects, with a total capacity of 310 kb/d, will be completed by 2022. In the UAE, a 65 kb/d condensate splitter is the only unit to come online in our forecast period as Abu Dhabi National Oil Company focuses investment on improving gasoline yield and increasing petrochemical feedstocks output at its existing refineries.

Net capacity additions of 1.9 mb/d as well as demand growth of 1.3 mb/d are behind a forecast increase of 2.5 mb/d in refinery runs, including a 450 kb/d increase in condensate splitter throughput. Overall capacity utilisation rates will improve from an average 79% to 87%.

Africa

Dangote Group's 500 kb/d refinery project in Nigeria dwarfs all other developments on the continent. It is not exactly clear how construction has progressed so far, but the company has maintained its 2018 launch date. Nigeria's three existing refineries reportedly restarted last year after some essential repairs, but are still running at a fraction of their total capacity of 450 kb/d. Angola cancelled its long-planned 120 kb/d Lobito refinery due to capex pressures, even as some substantial work had already been done on the site. Uganda's first refinery project, a compact 60 kb/d facility, seems on track, as the project sponsors, including Total, recently reiterated their support. A 30 kb/d addition to Egypt's Alexandria refinery will be completed by 2019, while Cameroon is on track to expand its sole refinery by a similar amount in 2017.

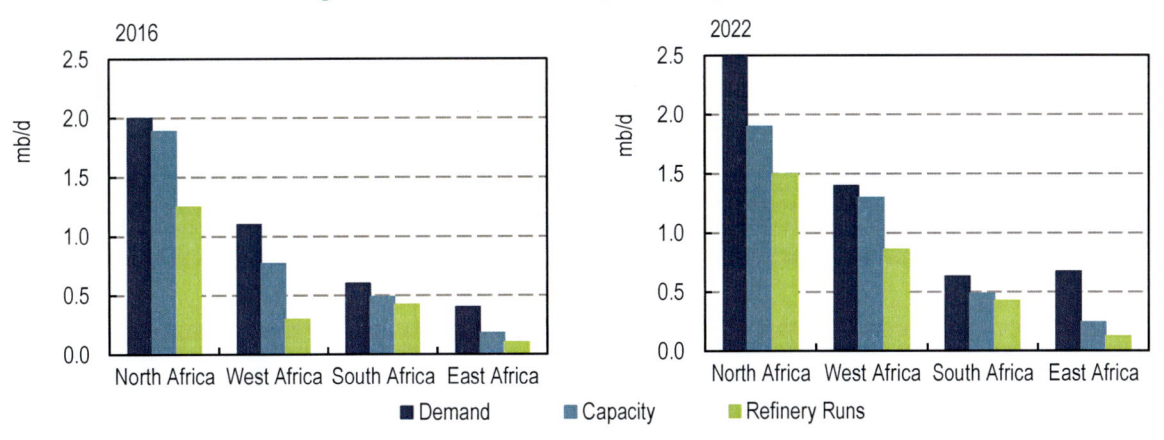

Figure 3.9 African developments by subcontinent

While Algeria contracted out front-end engineering and design for three new 100 kb/d refineries, we do not assume any will come online before 2022. A 20 kb/d refinery in Zambia was shut last year due to feedstock availability issues, while Morocco's sole refinery, Samir, did not restart after shutting down in August 2015 due to a legal proceeding. In our forecast, we assume this relatively modern refinery will eventually return to production, given the growing product imbalance in North Africa. Meanwhile, South Africa's PetroSA started converting its gas-to-liquids plant into a 20 kb/d condensate splitter due to lack of natural gas feedstock.

People's Republic of China

The partial liberalisation of the Chinese downstream industry, that started in mid-2015 by granting selected independent refiners crude oil import quotas, has challenged the positions of the state-owned majors and forced them to cut runs in an increasingly crowded internal market. CNPC and Sinopec reduced throughput by about 200 kb/d and 100 kb/d year-on-year respectively, while the independents increased their runs by 600 kb/d in aggregate, or by 30%. This coincided with a slowdown in Chinese refined product demand growth caused by structural changes in the economy. Gasoline demand growth of 8.5% was almost fully offset by declining diesel, fuel oil and other products demand, with the aggregate refined product demand growth averaging only 20 kb/d. At the same time, LPG growth was at 245 kb/d, with naphtha adding another 70 kb/d. In our discussion, we do not group LPG and naphtha in the refined product category even though refineries provide part of LPG and naphtha supplies to the market. The refining margins for these products are usually negative (i.e. their prices are lower than the crude oil price), which means that they do not drive refinery throughput, but, rather, are refinery by-products.

China's refining industry was traditionally geared towards diesel to fuel its domestic industrial growth, but a switch to consumption-driven growth saw the mainly gasoline-fuelled passenger vehicle fleet explode, driving gasoline demand. A strong petrochemical sector supported impressive growth in LPG and naphtha. Refiners tried to adjust to the new demand barrel by sourcing lighter crudes and increasing imports of gasoline blending components, but were still left with a diesel excess that was pushed on to international markets. Diesel exports amounted to 300 kb/d in 2016, reaching markets as far as Australia. This situation also explains the unusually high LPG yields in China, which, at close to 6-7%, are higher than the global average. Even so, about 400 kb/d was imported to fill the gap.

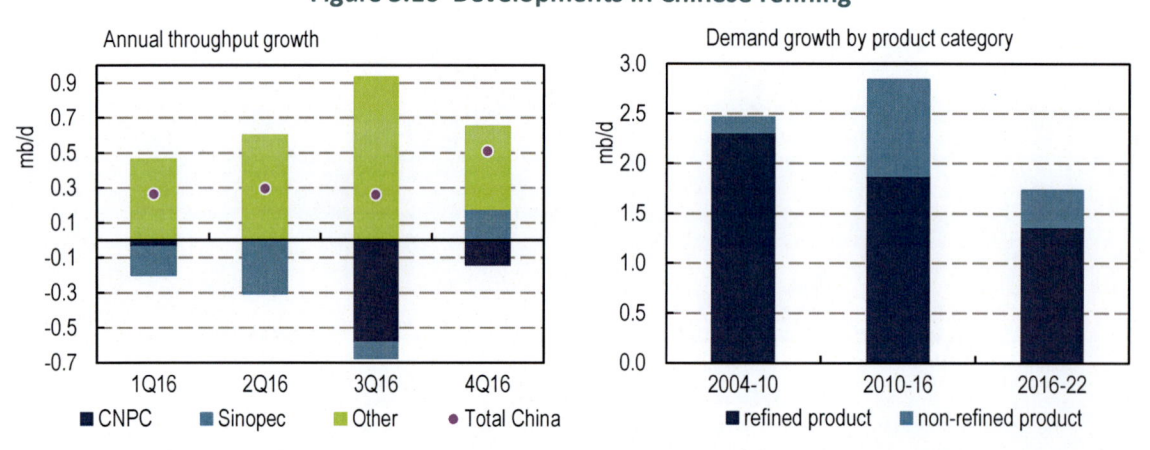

Figure 3.10 Developments in Chinese refining

In the next five years, this new demand growth pattern will largely persist. Of the forecast 1.8 mb/d demand growth, gasoline will account for the lion's share at 1.1 mb/d. Naphtha and LPG will add another 430 kb/d, with diesel and kerosene at just 630 kb/d, and fuel oil and other products declining by 400 kb/d. The challenge of increasing light product yields will remain, with possible increases in import requirements for gasoline components and light ends.

Despite the impressive demand growth of the last decade, China has too much refinery capacity. Since 2006, there has been a reasonably small gap between the 4 mb/d refined products demand growth and 4.6 mb/d capacity expansion. Most of the excess capacity dates back from earlier days (Figure 3.6) and is usually in the form of outdated facilities in logistically challenged locations. This is why, despite currently sitting on an estimated 3.5 mb/d of unused capacity, Chinese oil companies are still going ahead with plans to build new, more efficient facilities in better locations. Both CNPC and Sinopec have trimmed their plans, but the increasing role of independents with deep pockets has maintained our capacity growth forecast at 2.2 mb/d. Even though refinery throughput is forecast to increase by 2 mb/d, utilisation rates will only improve from 76% to 78%. At the same time, both majors and independents have been investing heavily into upgrading secondary units to meet the stricter China V pollutant emission standards. To encourage the upgrades, the Chinese government has subsidised interest payments on loans dedicated to refinery upgrades.

India

Indian refineries have some of the highest utilisation rates in the world, churning out products for both domestic and export markets. In the next five years, capacity additions totalling 860 kb/d will be made, but as a sign of the relative maturity of its downstream industry, all of these are expansion projects at existing refineries. Even so, the additions will lag behind refined product demand growth as export volumes will be halved. By the early 2020s India will replace Russia as the world's third largest refiner. This could explain the interest of Russian companies in the Indian downstream as Rosneft finalised the purchase of India's second-largest private refiner, Essar. Indian Oil Company floated its 1.2 mb/d mega-refinery project in Maharashtra, but we do not assume it will be constructed and launched before 2022.

Other Asia

In Japan, another 230 kb/d of planned closures by March 2017 will have completed Phase two of the Ministry of Economy, Trade and Industry's plan to rationalise the refining industry in light of falling domestic demand and competition in export markets. It is not clear yet whether a Phase three will be issued. In the ten years to 2017, the Japanese refining industry shed some 1.1 mb/d of its capacity, a quarter of the original level. Korea, meanwhile, will complete its expansion spree with the addition of another 100 kb/d condensate splitting unit in 2017. The country added some 500 kb/d capacity in recent years, of which 400 kb/d were condensate splitters aimed at producing petrochemical feedstocks.

In Chinese Taipei, CPC will launch a 150 kb/d CDU at Ta-Lin refinery to replace an older unit. A 50 kb/d condensate splitter unit is also planned to start in 2017. Indonesia announced the liberalisation of the refining industry late last year, allowing non-state companies to own and operate refineries, import crude oil and export oil products. Mini-refinery projects in oil production areas for supplying local markets will be proposed to potential bidders. For the larger projects, we assume a 100 kb/d addition to the Balikpapan refinery will be ready by 2020, while Cilacap's capacity will be expanded by 52 kb/d in a partnership with Saudi Aramco. The latter was reported first pulling out of a partnership with Petronas to build a 300 kb/d refinery in Malaysia, but at the time of writing the two companies were reportedly going to finalise the agreement. We assume a 150 kb/d unit will be operational by 2022. Viet Nam's second refinery, the 200 kb/d Nghi Son project, will come online in 2017, with no new additions expected in the next five years. A new project in the region, a 160 kb/d refinery in Brunei proposed by Chinese petrochemical company Zhejiang Hengyi has been included in our list for a 2022 startup.

Latin America

For Latin America 2016 was a highly inauspicious year, with refinery runs down. Problems in the Venezuelan downstream sector (with refinery utilisation rates down to 50%) were the major reason for a 250 kb/d annual decline in regional throughput, while relatively new units in Brazil did not manage to ramp-up due to the delay in the installation of pollution abatement units. Moreover, Petrobras put all of its remaining capacity expansion projects on hold due to capex pressures. A small, 50 kb/d refinery project in Costa Rica that was revived in 2014 after being cancelled earlier, was shelved again last year, due to lack of interest from potential investors. The only expansion plans we assume will go ahead on the continent are additional units at Peru's Talara (+30 kb/d) and Argentina's Campana (+40 kb/d) refineries.

Aruba's Hovensa refinery, shut by Valero in 2012, was formally transferred to Petroleos de Venezuela's US subsidiary Citgo, which plans to convert its crude distillation units to upgraders for Venezuelan extra-heavy oil. The upgraded crude will then be delivered to Citgo's Gulf Coast refineries while naphtha recovered from the diluents will be sold by PDVSA. The latter will also need the extensive tank farm at Hovensa if it loses the 330 kb/d Curacao plant that it currently operates under a lease agreement until 2019. A Chinese commodity trader recently signed a memorandum of understanding with the government of the island regarding the refinery and its infrastructure. The Aruba upgrader is projected to start in 2018, but we have not reinstated it in our database because it will not function as a refining unit with finished products output.

Crude oil trade

In a change to our previous methodology, for the purposes of crude oil trade developments we look at the supply of refinable liquids only, i.e. crude oil of all grades (including both non-upgraded and diluted bitumen), synthetic crude oil and condensate. For simplicity, we will refer to this group as crude oil. Natural gas liquids such as ethane, LPG and pentanes plus (light naphtha) from fractionation plants are accounted for in the product supply balances. On the demand side, refinery and condensate splitter intake, as well as crude oil direct use in power plants and petrochemical facilities are included.

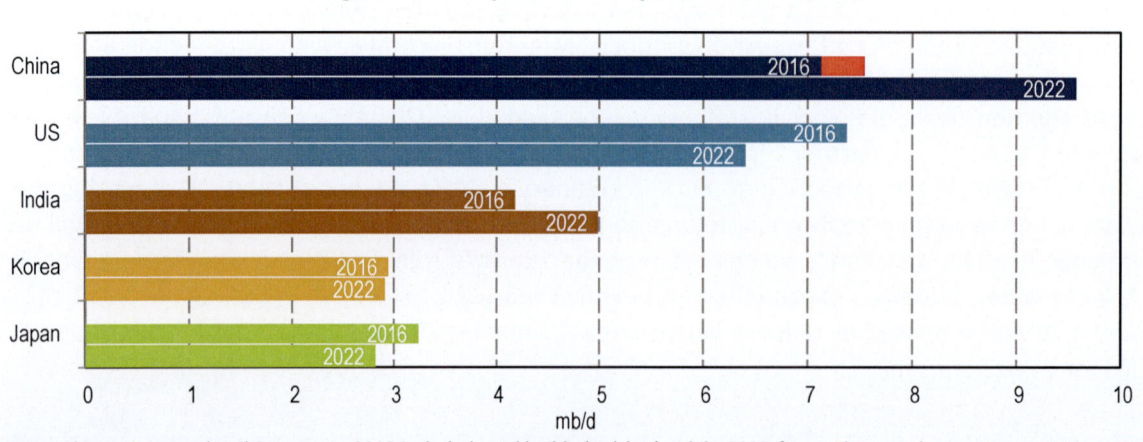

Figure 3.11 Top five net importers of crude oil

Note: Chinese net crude oil imports in 2016 included stockbuilds (red bar), while 2022 figure shows only net import requirement for refining.

Between 2016 and 2022 net importers will collectively increase their crude oil import requirements by 1.5 mb/d. While western refining centres will see decreasing dependence on imported crude (the US will see higher domestic production, Europe's refinery runs will decline), most Asian countries where refining activity increases, will see local production either flat or lower. This is why Asia will see its net crude oil import requirement grow by 3.6 mb/d.

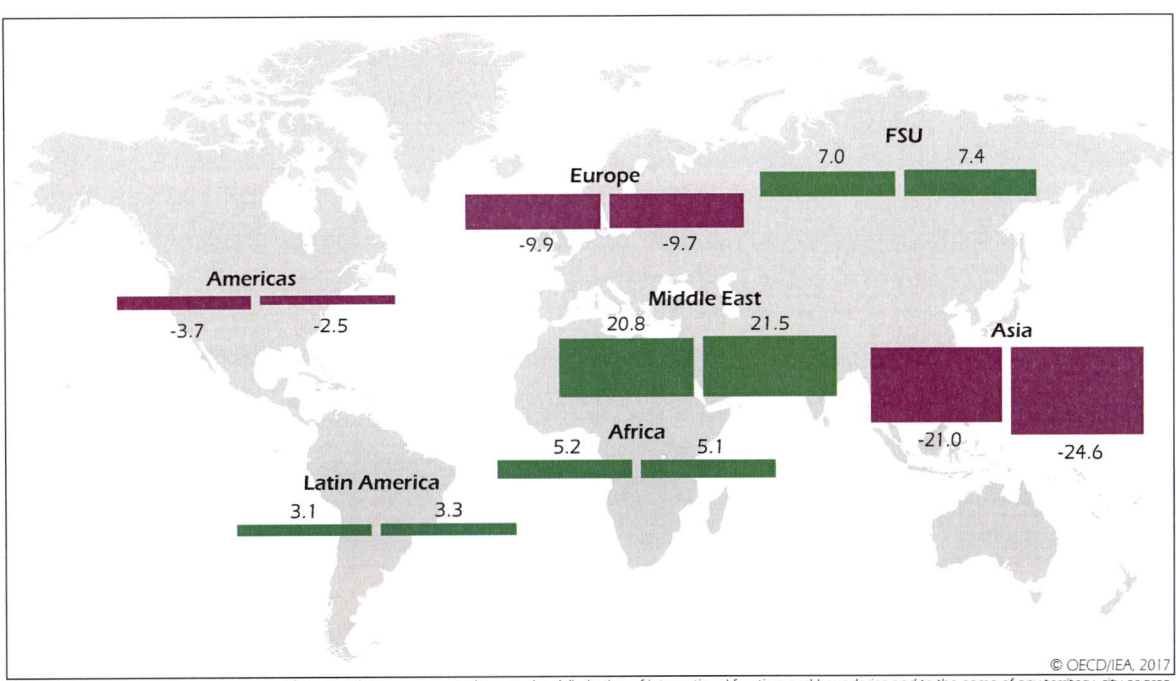

Map 3.1 Regional crude oil balances in 2016 and 2022 (mb/d)

Region	2016	2022
FSU	7.0	7.4
Europe	-9.9	-9.7
Americas	-3.7	-2.5
Middle East	20.8	21.5
Asia	-21.0	-24.6
Africa	5.2	5.1
Latin America	3.1	3.3

Notes: Positive numbers indicate export availability (green columns). Negative numbers indicate import requirement (purple columns).

On the crude oil export side, some of the forecast developments are less intuitive. While OPEC as a group sees a net increase in crude oil exports, thanks to a higher share in global crude oil output (from 47% to 51%), two non-OPEC countries, Canada and Brazil, send substantially more crude to global markets. OPEC's biggest Middle Eastern producers, plus Libya, will see an increase in net exports, but lower exports from Nigeria and Venezuela will partially offset this (Figure 3.12). In both of these countries output is projected to stay relatively steady versus 2016, but crude volumes available for exports are lowered by the start-up of a new large refinery in Nigeria and the recovery of refining volumes in Venezuela from the 40-year lows in 2016. As a result, net 500 kb/d of OPEC export growth will be lower than the 850 kb/d forecast for both Brazil and Canada. Lower Russian refinery runs and steadier output also help increase Russian crude oil export availability.

REFINING AND TRADE

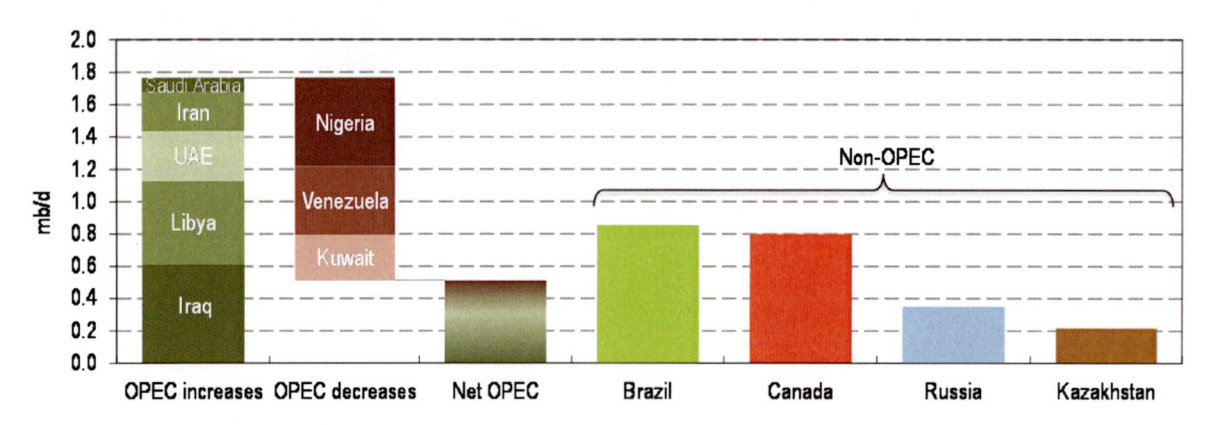

Figure 3.12 Changes in net crude oil exports

Despite a forecast increase in Middle Eastern oil output, the crude oil balance East of Suez will swing further into the red. Growing refinery runs in Asia (+3 mb/d) combined with lower output (-0.7 mb/d) result in a 3.6 mb/d increase in the net import requirement of the region. The Middle East is the natural supply source for Asia, given its geographic proximity. However, the growth of refining activity there constrains crude oil export growth. Of 2.8 mb/d of incremental output of crude and condensate, some 2.5 mb/d will be used by new refineries and condensate splitters, leaving only 500 kb/d to be supplied to global markets (taking into account lower crude burn). Even with such an impressive growth in refining volumes, the Middle East in aggregate will still export more than half of its crude oil output, as the proportion of crude refined at home will increase from 34% to only 43%.

The growing net short position of the Asian crude oil balance poses interesting questions about future crude trade flows and the security of supply in the region (Box 3.2). In 2016, of the 21 mb/d net crude oil import requirement in Asia, some 1.5 mb/d was a direct flow from Russia/Kazakhstan. The remaining 19.5 mb/d could have been fully covered by the Middle East's export availability of over 20 mb/d. However, 4.5 mb/d of Middle Eastern crude oil went westward, to American and European refiners. The reverse flow from West Africa, Venezuela, seaborne FSU exports from western ports and even the occasional North Sea cargoes to Asia filled the gap.

Russia is expanding the capacity of East Siberia Pacific Ocean (ESPO) pipeline by 400 kb/d by 2020. But, despite the discussions of Russia's geopolitical shift to the east, infrastructure constraints mean that Russia's natural markets are still in the west. By 2022 Russia will be able to directly supply Asian markets, via the ESPO spur to China, or from its Kozmino port in the Far East, some 2.1 mb/d of crude oil, which is less than 40% of total exports.

By 2022, net import requirements in Asia reach almost 25 mb/d. Direct supplies by FSU pipelines and the Far East will account for only 2.5 mb/d. The remaining 22.5 mb/d gap is higher than the 21.2 mb/d availability from the Middle East. At the same time, North American and European net import requirements decline by 2.2 mb/d in total. Assuming no substantial export outlets for Canadian diluted bitumen outside the US within the next five years, the US may see their crude oil imports from the Middle East halve to 1 mb/d as the coking capacity dealing with heavy crudes will get increasingly utilised for Canadian bitumen. The efforts of Middle Eastern exporters to increase their market share in Europe at the expense of Russian and other suppliers made many headlines last year, but in five years' time those European refiners that prefer the Middle Eastern crude diet will potentially find themselves in a seller's market, having to compete with Asian importers for available Middle Eastern cargoes.

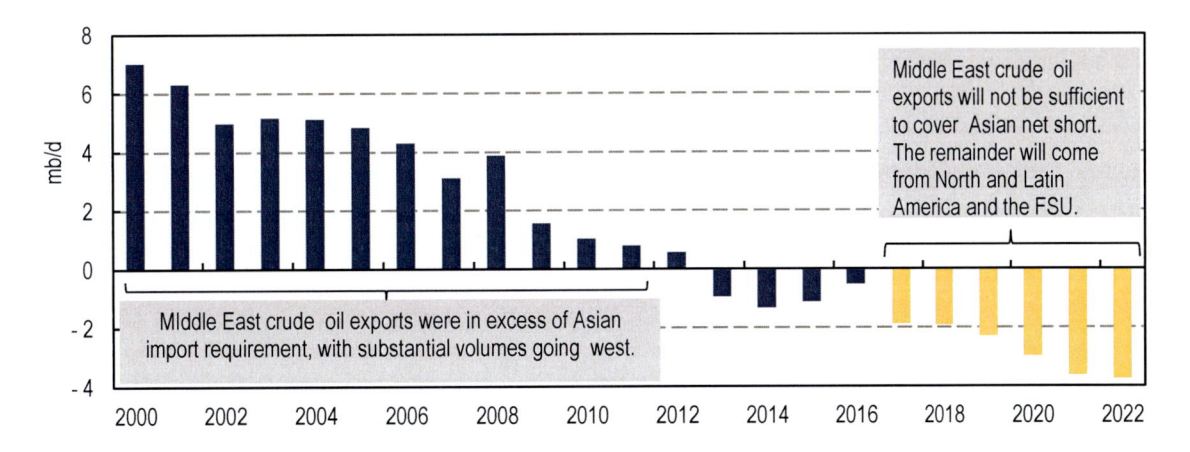

> **Box 3.2 Security of oil supply: implications for Asian importers**
>
> Chinese stockpiling was a big driver in global crude oil markets in 2016, helping to absorb part of the significant excess of crude oil supply. Data are not sufficiently transparent to estimate strategic storage fill as opposed to commercial crude oil inventories, but what is certain is that China needed to build a cushion against any supply disruption.
>
> **Figure 3.13 Geographical structure of US imports** 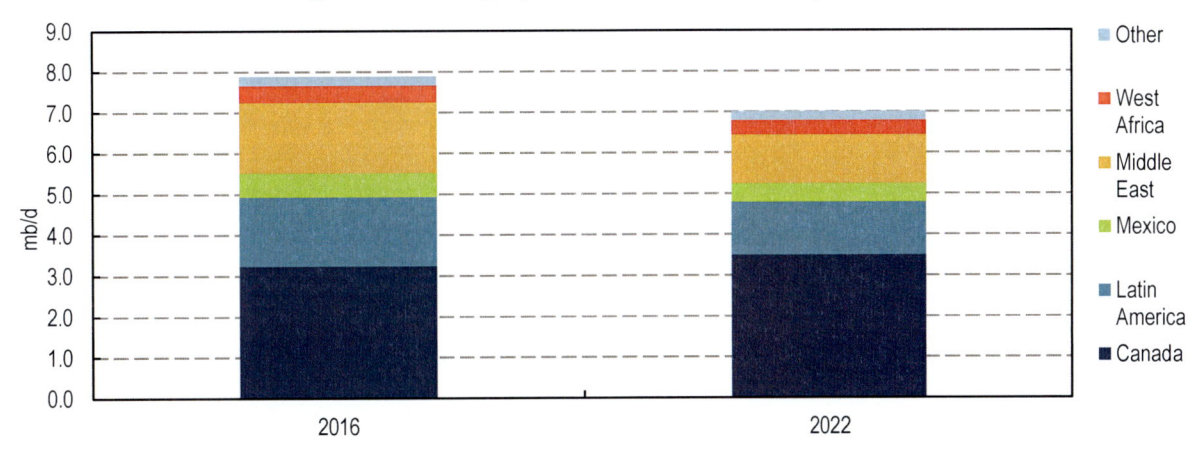
>
> The oil market in Asia is quite different from the west. In the Atlantic Basin, the big net importers, such as the US and Europe, are literally surrounded by exporters. The US gets half its imports from Canada and Mexico. Latin America contributes another 22%. Long-haul crudes from Africa and the Middle East account for just 27% of imports into the US.
>
> **Figure 3.14 East of Suez crude oil balances**

> **Box 3.2 Security of oil supply: implications for Asian importers (Continued)**
>
> European importers receive half their crude oil from their FSU neighbours. Another 15% comes from relatively close African exporters, with further-flung Middle East and Latin American producers accounting for the rest. In our forecast, the US and Europe will further lessen their dependence on long-haul crude imports. With increased US LTO and Canadian output, the US reliance on seaborne exports will decline by over 2 mb/d.
>
> Most Asian countries are net crude oil importers with only exceptions being Brunei, Malaysia, Viet Nam and Papua New Guinea that export a combined 400 kb/d crude oil (with Australian condensate exports adding another 130 kb/d to the regional market). By 2022 all of these countries will become net importers, due to increased refinery throughput or lower domestic output, while Indonesia will see imports tripling to almost 500 kb/d.
>
> This in turn results in a market heavily reliant on long-haul crude imports. Most of the crude cargoes, from origin to destination, travel further to reach Asian ports relative to Europe or North America. Moreover, the greater part of eastward traffic passes through the Malacca straits, which are becoming increasingly congested. Security of supply issues usually have a geopolitical dimension, but for Asian importers future logistical challenges are enough to justify paying more attention to emergency response mechanisms.

Product trade

In 2016 we saw an interesting year in product markets as refinery runs lagged behind demand growth, particularly in the developing world. Part of the market was supplied from inventory draws, which explains some unusual developments in trade flows. These could also be the start of a long-term trend. For example, in our modelled 2016 regional product balances, based on our latest estimate for demand and refinery activity (as we do not have yet full data for global trade data by product), for the first time, East of Suez (Middle East plus Asia) was a net importer of LPG and gasoline. In this *Report*, for the first time, we have included a forecast for LPG/ethane regional balances.

LPG/ethane

LPG and ethane are mainly supplied from outside the refining sector, by natural gas liquids fractionation plants (Figure 3.4). LPG is used mostly in residential and petrochemical sectors, while ethane is almost exclusively used in petrochemicals production. Both of these products require special tankers – pressurised gas carriers – as they are gaseous under standard atmospheric pressure. Seaborne trade of ethane is a recent phenomenon, enabled by cheap supplies of US shale liquids. The first seaborne cargo travelled from the Marcus Hook terminal in the US Northeast in March last year, arriving at an INEOS cracker in Norway. In September, a second terminal started up in the US, this time on the Gulf Coast, sending cargoes to Europe and Reliance's facilities in India. Reliance has ordered a fleet of six VLEC (very large ethane carrier) ships each with a capacity of 87 000 deadweight tonnes, to serve its supply contract out of the US.

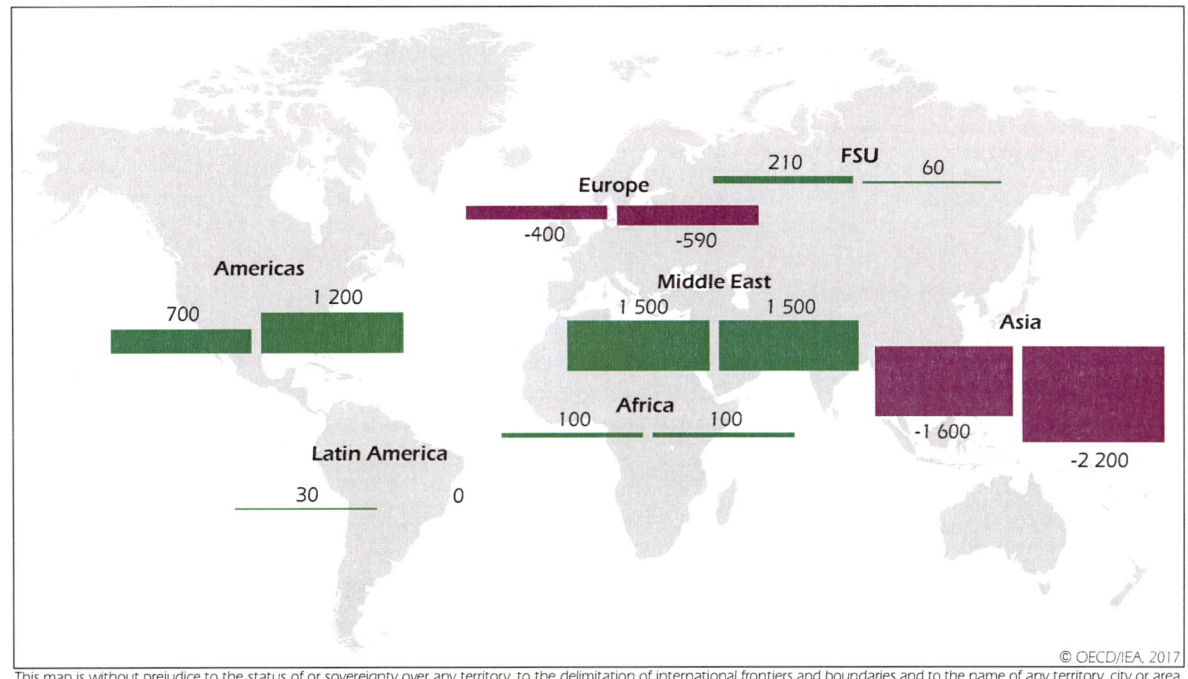

Map 3.2 Regional LPG/ethane balances in 2016 and 2022 (kb/d)

Region	2016	2022
Americas	700	1 200
Latin America	30	0
Europe	-400	-590
FSU	210	60
Middle East	1 500	1 500
Africa	100	100
Asia	-1 600	-2 200

Notes: Positive numbers indicate export availability (green columns). Negative numbers indicate import requirement (purple columns).

Growth in US ethane exports may be restricted by the start-up of new ethane crackers in the US. In contrast, US LPG exports are likely to expand significantly, reaching 1 mb/d in 2022. Already a net importer of almost 1.6 mb/d, Asian markets will be short of 2.2 mb/d of LPG/ethane in 2022. This is the largest product deficit among all products and regions in our forecast. The Middle East is able to supply only 1.5 mb/d, meaning that the rest will have to come from the US. The expanded Panama Canal can accommodate VLGC (Very Large Gas Carriers) and may get substantial interest from LPG shippers. India will become the largest LPG importer in the world, doubling its imports to almost 600 kb/d, with China not far behind.

Gasoline/naphtha

Trade in the Atlantic Basin is dominated by gasoline, while Asian flows are mostly naphtha. In the west, gasoline flows from Europe to the US Northeast and Africa, and, out of the US Gulf Coast to Latin America. Two major defining factors here are the European structural length in gasoline as the demand barrel in Europe is heavily skewed towards middle distillates; and, the Jones Act in the US that allows European refiners to deliver gasoline to fill the deficit in the US Northeast at a lower cost than seaborne cargoes from the US Gulf Coast. This situation has come in handy for Mexico where troubled refineries under produced last year, and imports, especially from US Gulf Coast refineries, accounted for over half of local demand.

European refiners will find it harder to reduce their already low gasoline yields even further, and the problem is not helped by declining demand. Even with lower refinery runs forecast for Europe by 2022, gasoline length actually increases, offset slightly by naphtha. African total gasoline/naphtha balances are virtually unchanged as higher local refining throughput offsets product demand growth. Increased supplies from Middle Eastern refineries will mostly flow to cover Asia's growing demand.

REFINING AND TRADE

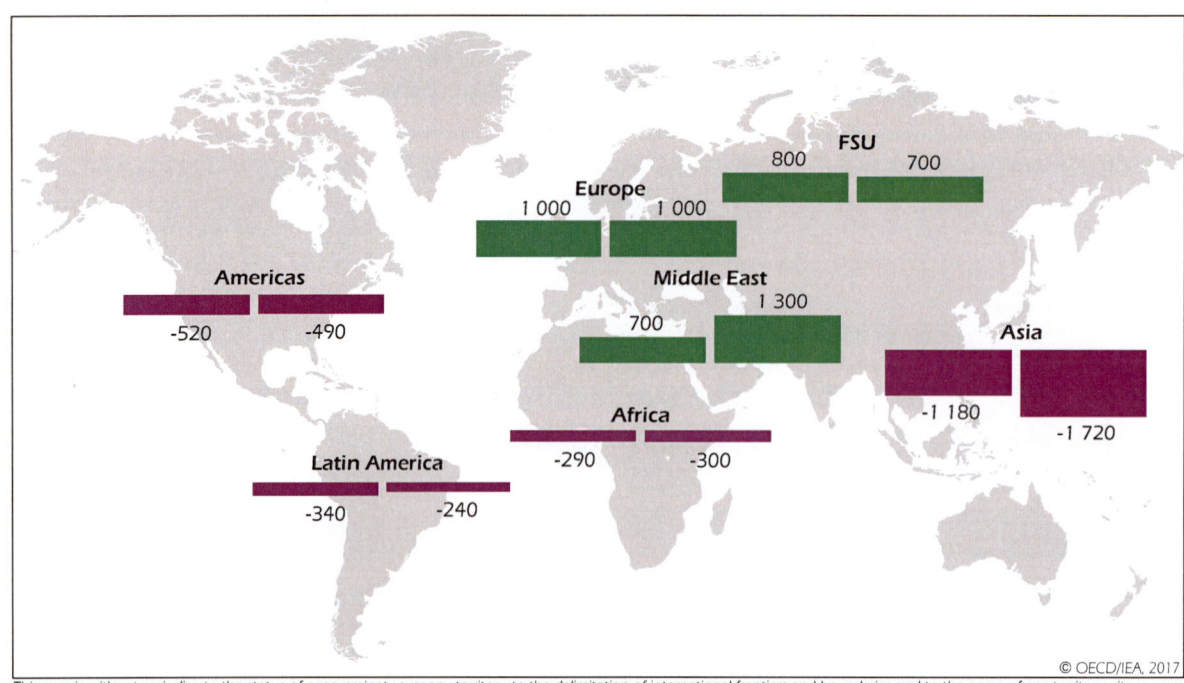

Map 3.3 Regional gasoline/naphtha balances in 2016 and 2022 (kb/d)

Region	2016	2022
Americas	-520	-490
Europe	1 000	1 000
FSU	800	700
Middle East	700	1 300
Asia	-1 180	-1 720
Latin America	-340	-240
Africa	-290	-300

© OECD/IEA, 2017

This map is without prejudice to the status of or sovereignty over any territory, to the delimitation of international frontiers and boundaries and to the name of any territory, city or area.

Notes: Positive numbers indicate export availability (green columns). Negative numbers indicate import requirement (purple columns).

Diesel/kerosene

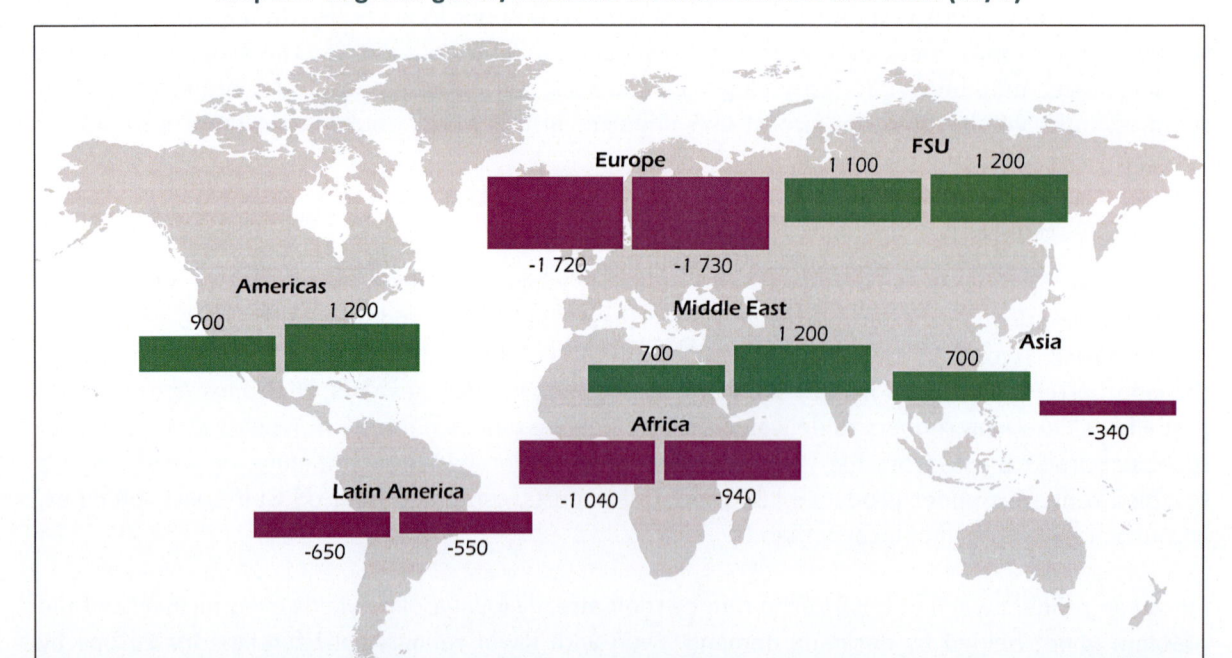

Map 3.4 Regional gasoil/kerosene balances in 2016 and 2022 (kb/d)

Region	2016	2022
Americas	900	1 200
Europe	-1 720	-1 730
FSU	1 100	1 200
Middle East	700	1 200
Asia	700	-340
Latin America	-650	-550
Africa	-1 040	-940

© OECD/IEA, 2017

This map is without prejudice to the status of or sovereignty over any territory, to the delimitation of international frontiers and boundaries and to the name of any territory, city or area.

Notes: Positive numbers indicate export availability (green columns). Negative numbers indicate import requirement (purple columns).

Middle distillates are the only product category in which the Atlantic Basin is still a net importer from Asian and Middle Eastern refineries. While the FSU and the US both export significant volumes (over 2 mb/d combined), Europe remains in a very large deficit. Latin America and Africa are also substantial net importers. Future flows will be greatly influenced by developments in marine bunkers after the 2020 sulphur cap limit comes into force. In our forecast, the switch to diesel is restricted by the fuel's availability (*Developments in marine bunkers*). The 1 mb/d swing in Asian balances from net exporter to net importer is the most interesting development. Export availability from the Middle East can comfortably cover this shortage, leaving extra volumes to go to other deficit regions, for example, East Africa.

Fuel oil

The global fuel oil market in 2016 was undersupplied due to lower exports from Russia and higher imports by some Asian countries and the Middle East for peak summer power generation. Future developments in interregional flows, again, are intertwined with what happens with marine bunkers as the latter accounts for over half of total fuel oil demand globally. Overall interregional trade in fuel oil will decline slightly, as the Middle East and Asia will import less. There will be a smaller flow from the FSU countries, while the increase in North American exports is a result of the bunker fuel switch to diesel, and in Latin America, it is the result of higher refinery runs.

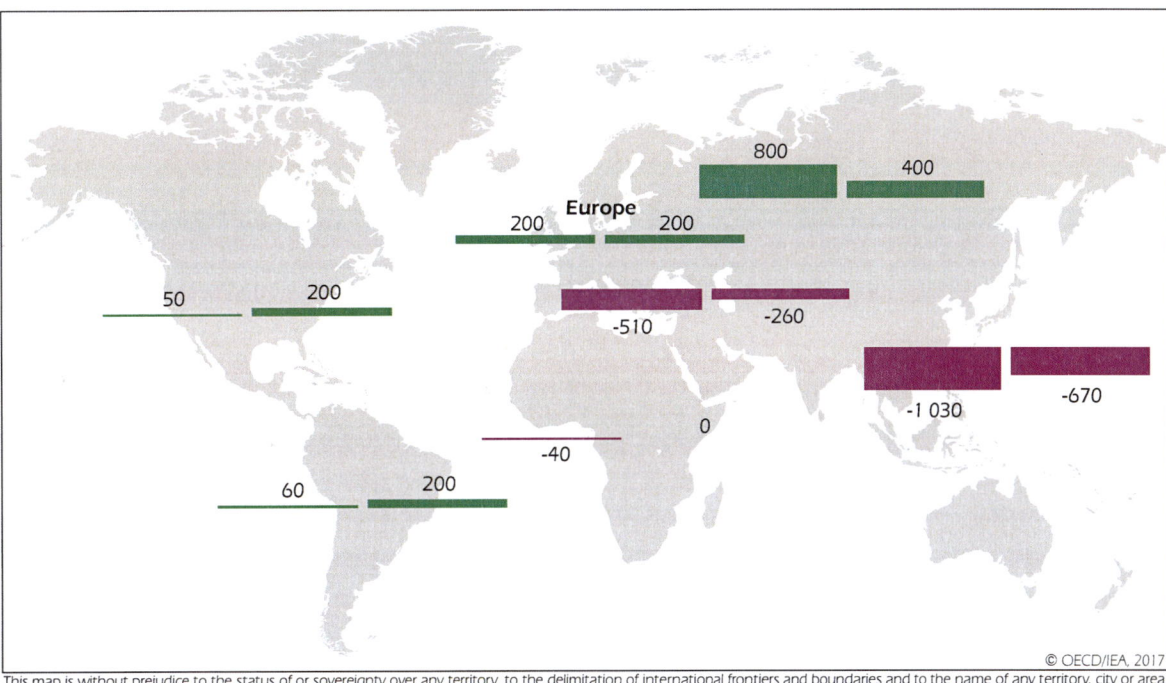

Map 3.5 Regional fuel oil balances in 2016 and 2022 (kb/d)

Notes: Positive numbers indicate export availability (green columns). Negative numbers indicate import requirement (purple columns).

Physical flows: implications for shipping

The expected development of oil movements will have an impact on global oil tanker traffic. The inbound clean product flow (naphtha, gasoline, kerosene and gasoil combined) into North and Latin America will shrink, while the outbound gas carrier (LPG/ethane) requirement will increase. In

Europe and FSU, the main changes will be reduced tonnage requirements for dirty (fuel oil) outbound vessels, and an increase in inbound gas carrier traffic. Outbound clean exports from the Middle East will see a significant increase, while no extra gas carrier requirement is seen in our forecast. There will be increased inbound clean traffic in East Africa, and a decrease in movements to West Africa.

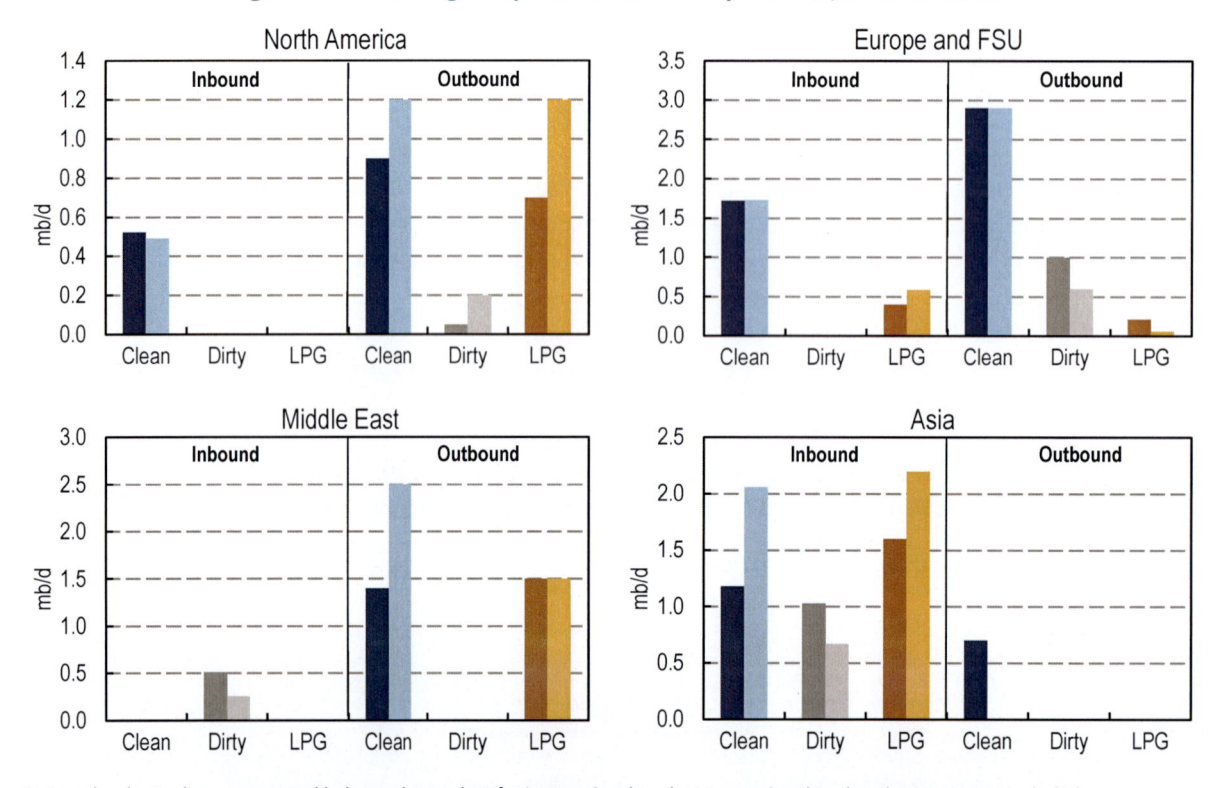

Figure 3.15 Tonnage requirements for oil products, 2016 vs 2022

Notes: the charts show aggregated balances by product for interregional trade. Intra-regional trade volumes are not included.

Asian product balances imply no outbound tonnage requirement for clean products in 2022 as the region will turn into a net importer for all products, and the dirty tankage requirement will subside. Clean product inflows from either the Middle East or the Atlantic Basin will double, and an additional 700 kb/d of LPG/ethane will have to come from the Americas, as the Middle East will not be able to increase its supplies (Figure 3.15).

Developments in marine bunkers

It has become a tradition in recent issues of this *Report* to have a detailed discussion of global marine bunkers. This sector accounts for only 4% of global oil demand, but it deserves a closer look for two reasons. First, it has traditionally been an important outlet for the refining industry, absorbing unwanted refining by-products, e.g. residual fuel oils, as onshore oil use has gradually moved to higher-priced cleaner products. Second, global maritime transport accounts for 80% of global trade in physical goods, including both high value and low-value items, variously sensitive to freight costs. A third of seaborne traffic is dedicated to energy (oil, gas and coal) transportation.

In October 2016, the International Maritime Organisation (IMO), the UN agency responsible for standards in international shipping, lowered the sulphur emissions cap from marine bunkers, from 3.5% to 0.5%, effective 1 January 2020. Despite their 4% share in global oil demand, marine bunkers account for 40% of sulphur emissions from the use of oil, or about 8-9 mt annually. About 80% of global bunker fuel comes from residual fuel oil blends with weighted average sulphur content of 2.5%. This is 2 500 times higher than the sulphur content of road diesel in the OECD and China. Marine gasoil blends, with sulphur content of 0.1%, account for the remaining 20%, or some 800 kb/d. This leaves a high-sulphur pool of about 3.4 mb/d in 2020 to be adapted to the new regulation. By setting the limit on emissions, rather than on the sulphur content of the fuel burnt, the IMO has allowed for a number of approaches to comply with the new limits. We will discuss each of these options below.

Switch to low sulphur fuel oil

Sulphur is heavier than most of the oil products, therefore during the distillation process it tends to accumulate in heavier fractions. Thus, the average sulphur content of straight-run fuel oil or cracked fuel oil will always be at least twice as high as that of the original crude oil. We estimate the global average sulphur content in crude oils at about 1.42%, which means that the average straight-run fuel oil sulphur content before any treatment is about 3-4%. High sulphur, or sour crudes, e.g. Iraq's Basra grade with 2.85% sulphur yields residual fractions with sulphur content above 6%.

Figure 3.16 Sulphur content in straight-run products

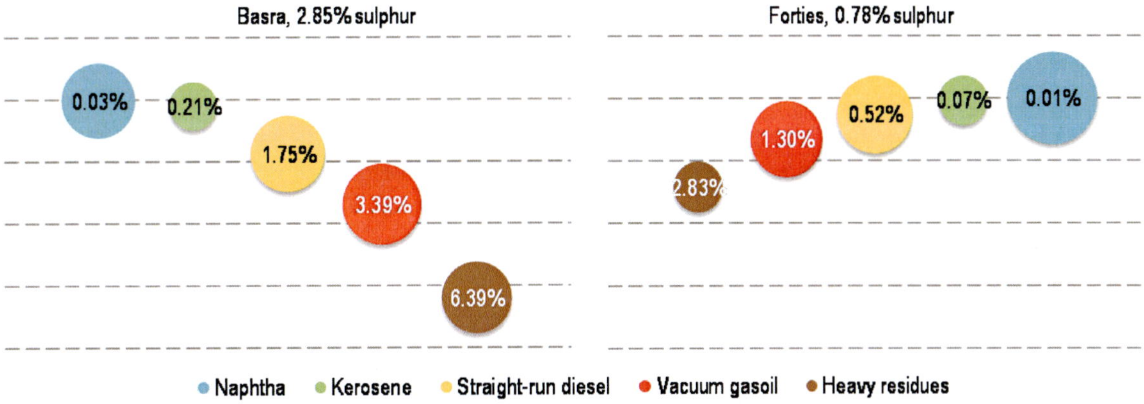

Basra, 2.85% sulphur: Naphtha 0.03%, Kerosene 0.21%, Straight-run diesel 1.75%, Vacuum gasoil 3.39%, Heavy residues 6.39%

Forties, 0.78% sulphur: Heavy residues 2.83%, Vacuum gasoil 1.30%, Straight-run diesel 0.52%, Kerosene 0.07%, Naphtha 0.01%

• Naphtha   • Kerosene   • Straight-run diesel   • Vacuum gasoil   • Heavy residues

Note: bubble size reflects the product yield.
Source: product yields and sulphur content are based on BP crude assays from www.bp.com.

Only very low sulphur crudes, up to 0.25% sulphur, will be able to yield residual fuel oil with a sulphur content under 0.5%. Based on global volumes of such low sulphur crude oil production, we estimate total compliant fuel oil output at about 500-600 kb/d. In regions where fuel oil is used for power generation, the preference is for straight-run low sulphur fuel oils to meet industrial emission restrictions. However, even if all of the low sulphur residual fuel oil were to flow to the marine bunker pool, it would not be enough to meet the demand for low-sulphur bunkers.

Refiners could apply the same hydrotreatment technology to fuel oil as they do with gasoil, kerosene and naphtha, to meet specifications for road diesel and gasoline. However, this requires costly investments and energy-intensive processes which refiners conduct for premium products to support their margins. Since hydrotreatment of residual oil requires the same scale of capital and operating expenditure as upgrading units such as hydrocrackers, we discuss this option further below.

Switch to diesel

Currently about 800 kb/d of bunker fuel is marine gasoil (MGO), essentially a diesel-based blend with 0.1% sulphur content. This is mostly used in Emission Control Areas (ECA) – designated coastal regions in Europe, North America and the Caribbean where sulphur emissions are restricted to only 0.1%. How much more diesel can be used in the bunker sector will depend on the availability of diesel at prices that will still look attractive to ship owners and charterers compared to historical bunker prices. The current diesel oversupply has resulted in a very narrow discount of marine gasoil to 10 ppm diesel (i.e. road fuel that meets stringent European specifications). Prices for marine gasoil for delivery in Rotterdam mid-February 2017 were at about USD 480/t, just USD 20/t lower than 10ppm diesel. At the same time, diesel cracks (i.e. the difference between the diesel price and the crude oil price) are closer to the lows of their historical range at just over USD 10/bbl. The differential between 10 ppm diesel and high sulphur fuel oil is at the lowest level since 2009 at about USD 200/tonne.

The development of diesel prices and cracks will depend on future supply-demand balances. In our forecast, combined middle distillates demand (kerosene and diesel), excluding additional requirements from the marine bunker sector, will grow by about 1.9 mb/d to 2020. At the same time, refinery runs will increase by 3.9 mb/d, meaning that in aggregate, with higher middle distillate yields from the new refineries, the demand for non-bunker diesel will be adequately met. However, in our forecast, it will not be possible to meet incremental diesel bunker demand, without causing a significant rise in diesel prices. Onshore uses of diesel, such as road freight and passenger vehicles, off-grid power generation and agriculture, are insensitive in the short term to higher prices and will not significantly lower consumption. Road freight in particular is highly reliant on diesel and will see demand growing by almost 1.5 mb/d. Adding gasoline and naphtha to our middle distillates demand forecast, we see a total of 3.4 mb/d growth for light product demand by 2022.

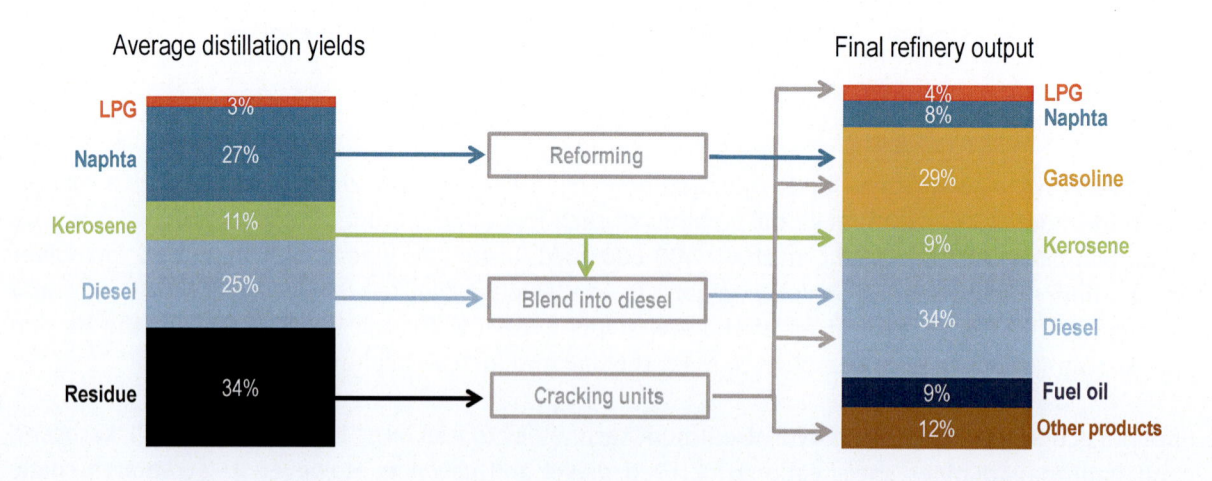

Figure 3.17 How refiners meet final oil product demand

Refiners rely heavily on secondary upgrading units such as hydrocrackers, cokers, etc., to produce the required slate of products out of straight-run material. Why would they not build more upgraders to turn the unwanted residual fuel oil into diesel? The simple answer is that, with only three years to the IMO's 2020 deadline, it is not possible to plan and build any more units than what already is planned. Moreover, with road fuel specifications tightening globally, including in many Asian countries and Africa, there is no certainty there will be enough hydro-desulphurisation capacity able to work at sufficient intensity to meet all of the incremental demand. In addition to this, refineries face restrictions concerning their own emissions of pollutants, hazardous substances and CO_2, which are closely linked to operating deep conversion units. This also explains the lack of appetite among refiners to rise to the challenge of low-sulphur marine fuels.

Box 3.3 Will French dentists come to the rescue of the global shipping industry?

Veteran observers will remember how the 2008 oil price spike to USD 147/bbl was partially attributed to Europe's then seemingly insatiable appetite for ultra-low sulphur diesel, driven by the growing dieselisation of the European passenger fleet. Diesel fuelled-cars had significant tax advantages compared to gasoline, and, alongside rising global oil prices, the euro strengthened against the dollar, making dollar price increases less visible to European consumers. The term "French dentists" was coined to refer to the French middle class, the most enthusiastic buyers of diesel cars in Europe.

The link between European ultra-low sulphur diesel demand and the crude oil price spike of 2008 is not as far-fetched as it appears. The tightening of European road fuel specifications in the early to mid-2000s, which required large investments into hydrocracking and hydro-desulphurisation units, also coincided with declining output of low-sulphur crude oil. Between 2000 and 2008, Europe and North America together lost about 5 mb/d of low-sulphur crude oil output, with little offsetting increases in crude output of similar quality from elsewhere. Those refiners that did not manage to bring online secondary upgrading units, had to source low-sulphur crude oil at almost any cost. This resulted in significant upward pressure on crude prices.

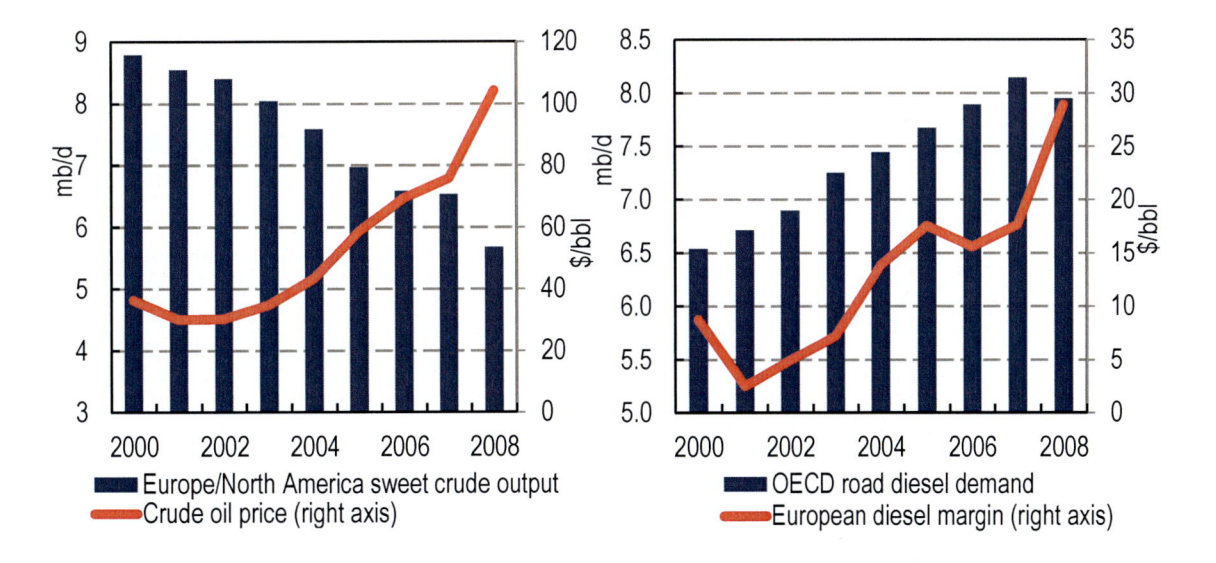

Figure 3.18 Crude oil and diesel market drivers

> **Box 3.3 Will French dentists come to the rescue of the global shipping industry? (Continued)**
>
> Subsequently, diesel cracks fell due to demand slowdown in the global recession 2008-09, which coincided with a few major diesel-focused refineries and long-planned upgrading units coming online, increasing low-sulphur diesel supply.
>
> The Volkswagen diesel engine emissions scandal sparked a discussion about a possible reversal of Europe's heavily dieselised passenger vehicle fleet back into gasoline or alternative fuels. European passenger cars consume about 1.9 mb/d of diesel, so a decline in this volume could free up diesel for other uses. Even before the scandal, diesel car sales started slowing down.
>
> Recently, in some countries, the tax advantage of diesel relative to gasoline at the pump has narrowed. Concerns about particulate matter pollution in Europe's big cities have initiated calls to ban diesel vehicles from urban areas. However, reversing dieselisation will not be an easy task.
>
> The chief executive of BMW said in a 2016 interview that European automakers rely heavily on diesel car sales to fulfil their obligations under the EU regulations concerning CO_2 emissions reduction targets. The model line-up of car manufacturers takes years of research and development to change dramatically. A quick shift away from diesel in Europe would put in danger the health of an industry that is a major player in two of Europe's largest economies, Germany and France.

On-board scrubbers

The use of scrubbers allows vessels to continue using high-sulphur fuel as the engine exhaust gases are treated to remove the pollutants. Scrubbers can be retrofitted on vessels, but a minimum period of one month in dock is required to perform the installation. During operations, extra servicing for maintenance and training for crew members may be necessary. Wastewater regulations concerning the disposal of washwater effluent from scrubbers with open loop design that uses seawater are not finalised yet and may have an impact on scrubber uptake. Of a global merchant shipping fleet of about 90 000 vessels totalling 1.75 billion deadweight tonnes, only about 500 are fitted with scrubbers. Industry experts suggest that about 2 000 scrubbers are likely to be installed by 2020, leaving the majority of the fleet unconverted. Even so, a comparative analysis of low-sulphur fuel economics based on scrubber use and refinery production indicates that the use of scrubbers requires lower investments and operating costs.

Table 3.3 To scrub or to refine – comparative economics

	Onboard scrubber	Secondary upgrading units at the refinery
Capacity	100 kb/d scrubbed ≈ 1100 scrubbers	150 kb/d upgrading unit for a final yield of 100 kb/d diesel
Capex (USD Bn)	3.9	5.3
Opex (USD/bbl)	≈1	≈5
Estimated fuel cost at USD 60/bbl oil	USD 300/tonne (heavy fuel oil)	USD 600/tonne (diesel)

We estimated the payback period for a hypothetical average vessel, assuming it spends a third of its time in ECA zones, which requires even lower sulphur content at 0.1%. We looked at a number of values for the price differential between marine gasoil and heavy fuel oil, to determine savings from using the cheaper fuel oil with scrubbers compared to burning 0.5% sulphur marine gasoil. The longest payback period is just under eight years, at a price differential of USD 150/tonne, which is close to February 2017 levels of USD 180/tonne. Using the largest differential observed historically (2Q08), the payback period shrinks to around two years. It is thus likely that scrubber uptake will intensify from 2020 when the price differential is likely to surge, supporting the economics and facilitating capex loans from banks.

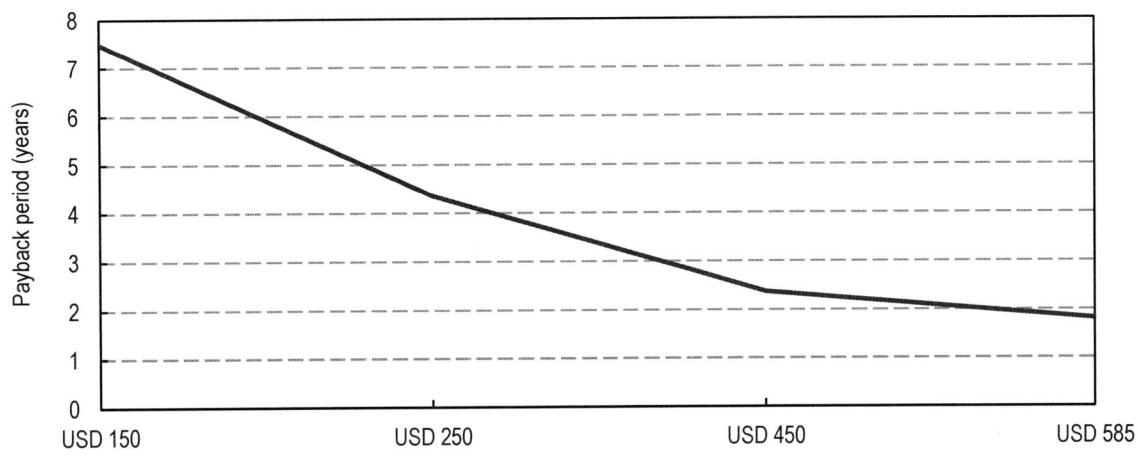

Figure 3.19 Scrubber payback periods

Notes: The following assumptions for MGO vs HFO price differentials were used in the calculations. USD 150/tonne is based on 2020 forward curve as of January 2017. USD 250/tonne is the average value observed in 2016. USD 450/tonne is the highest historical value observed in 2Q08 (quarterly average). USD 585/tonne assumes a 30% wider spread than the historical max described above.

Switch to alternative fuels

LNG and methanol have been discussed as alternatives to oil use in bunkers for pollution abatement purposes. There are significant challenges for both of them, first and foremost logistics. The European Union (EU) has launched several initiatives encouraging LNG use in coastal traffic. Korea has announced plans for financial incentives for LNG-fuelled vessels visiting the country's ports. It is also seriously looking to re-orient its shipbuilding industry towards LNG-fuelled ships to move ahead of rivals in this increasingly competitive industry. Methanol is further away from large-scale practical application and may not play a visible role in the medium term.

Conclusion

Lowering the bunker fuel emissions cap from 3.5% to 0.5% is easily the most dramatic change in fuel specifications in any oil product market on such a large scale. In the EU, it took over a decade of gradual changes to lower road fuel sulphur limits from 500 ppm (0.050%) to 10 ppm (0.001%). Countries in Southern Europe were allowed to delay the implementation of the directive due to a lack of on-spec fuel availability.

REFINING AND TRADE

Each of the options discussed above has its limitations when it comes to wide-scale use as early as 2020. Directing all available low-sulphur fuel oil use to marine bunkers, chipping away at the least important diesel use segments, installing scrubbers, using LNG-powered vessels that will come online in the next three years, will be part of the solution. If demand for light products grows less strongly than in our forecast, there will be more compliant fuel available for marine bunkers, but the opposite could also be true.

The IMO may also decide to grant waivers to allow the continued use of heavy fuel oil to vessels that pledge to install scrubbers in their next dry dock period scheduled after 2020. It is also not clear how compliance will be monitored. Currently, it is the flag state that has to ensure the vessel's compliance, but it is not clear that the main registry states (e.g. Panama and Liberia) will have enough resources to control their vast fleets. Pending further rulings by the IMO, port states may be entrusted to make sure vessels leaving the port are compliant with the directive.

The IMO has prepared draft mandatory data collection requirements to collect detailed fuel consumption data from ships. If these are approved, vessels with 5 000 gross tonnage or above will be required to report the data at the end of each calendar year to the flag state, which would then transfer the data to the IMO. This would help to monitor compliance. However, the nature of statistical data gathering suggests that 2020 data may not reach the IMO earlier than 2022.

With our forecast of crude oil supply, refining capacity additions and light product demand growth, we do not see availability of low-sulphur bunkers in the required volumes (Figure 3.20). The shipping industry would need to bid accordingly high prices to draw more diesel away from other uses, which would mean that in aggregate global oil demand growth would be lower than in our forecast. Last-minute waivers and lack of compliance could also extend the use of high-sulphur fuel oil.

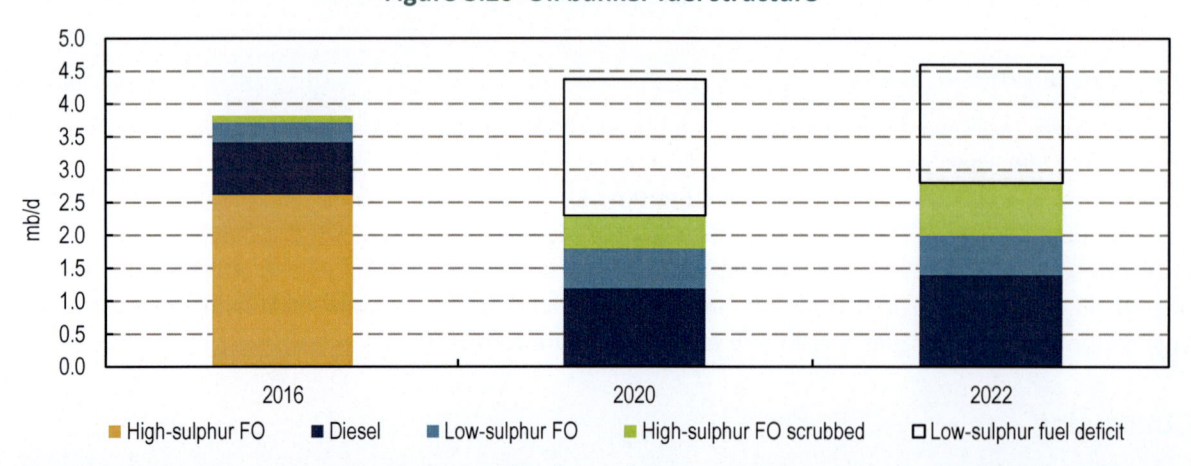

Figure 3.20 Oil bunker fuel structure

■ High-sulphur FO ■ Diesel ■ Low-sulphur FO ■ High-sulphur FO scrubbed □ Low-sulphur fuel deficit

The IMO has made it clear that limits on NO_x emissions may follow. Even if the shipping sector was excluded from the landmark COP21 agreement, a future measure constraining greenhouse gas emissions from the shipping industry cannot be ruled out. In the last three centuries the global maritime industry underwent several major fuel switches: from wind and muscular force to coal, and later to oil. Perhaps the time is coming for another major revolution in shipping fuels. Given the size of the modern global fleet though, this will be an issue well beyond the medium term.

4. TRENDS IN GLOBAL OIL STORAGE

Highlights

- **OECD total oil stocks were 2 986 mb at end-2016, up 427 mb from the end of 2013.** Global storage capacity is forecast to continue to grow rapidly over the next few years with a total of 226 mb under construction or expansion, of which only 40% is situated in the OECD. Oil stocks in the OECD started drawing in 2H16 on the back of tighter supplies.

- **Growth in global storage capacity over the medium term will be led by Asia Oceania, followed by North America, then the Middle East.** In Asia, capacity will continue to build in line with higher demand and expanding petrochemical production, while in North America rising LTO and oil sands output will drive growth in crude storage.

- **Asia Oceania has 120 mb of new tanks under construction with a further 141 mb planned. China is focused on building oil products and chemicals storage** in coastal regions. In India announced projects fall short of forecast demand increases. Malaysia and South Korea are both busy building tanks in the hope of becoming significant oil trading hubs. Australian refinery closures have led to investments in new oil product storage and this will continue.

- **A total of 70 mb of crude and oil products storage is being built, expanded or planned in the US, only second in volume behind China.** US crude inventories rose nowhere near as fast in 2016 as they did in previous years due to slowing and then falling LTO production. In this Report we expect a return to growth for LTO production to 2022.

- **The Middle East has 17 mb of storage under construction or expansion, almost all of it situated in the UAE.** Fujairah is the largest bunkering hub in the region thanks to its strategic location and has plans to become a new pricing and storage location.

- **Libya lost 7 mb of crude storage capacity due to attacks on the Ras Lanuf and Es Sider terminals during the civil war.** There are few prospects in the short term to add infrastructure due to the security situation and lack of funds.

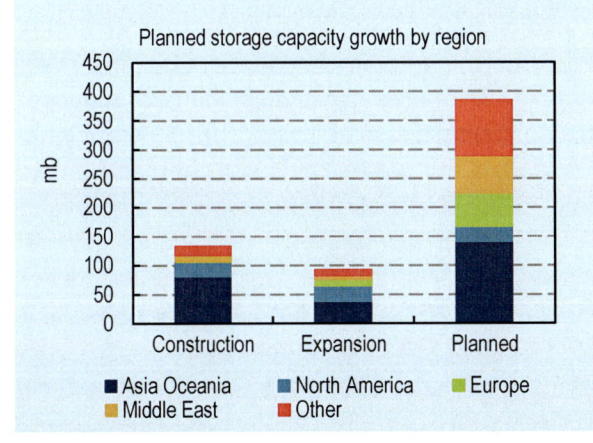

Figure 4.1 Planned storage capacity growth by region and country

Global overview

Global oil inventories increased by approximately 900 kb/d during 2014-16 due to persistent oversupply. At the end of 2016 total OECD oil inventories stood at 2 986 mb, up by 427 mb from the end of 2013. Over the period, oil stocks built at an average rate of 390 kb/d. They reached a historical peak of 3 101 mb in July 2016, before falling by 23 mb per month over July-December 2016 (approximately 755 kb/d) on the back of winter demand in the northern hemisphere. There were draws for crude and middle distillate stocks in Europe and 'other products' (mainly LPG and naphtha) in North America and Asia during 2H16. It is important to remember that recent stock falls remain modest relative to the recent builds and that inventories outside the OECD are likely to have increased all the way to the end of 2016. The key question now is whether inventories will fall more steeply in 2017 and over the medium term. The task of tracking stock movements outside the OECD remains fiendishly difficult. There have been few advances in data collection since countries such as Saudi Arabia and South Africa were included in the Joint Organisations Data Initiative (JODI) and the emergence of third party datasets for China, Singapore and Europe. Advances in technology, including developments in ship-tracking software, have helped track flows and likely stock movements more accurately, but the picture is still far from complete.

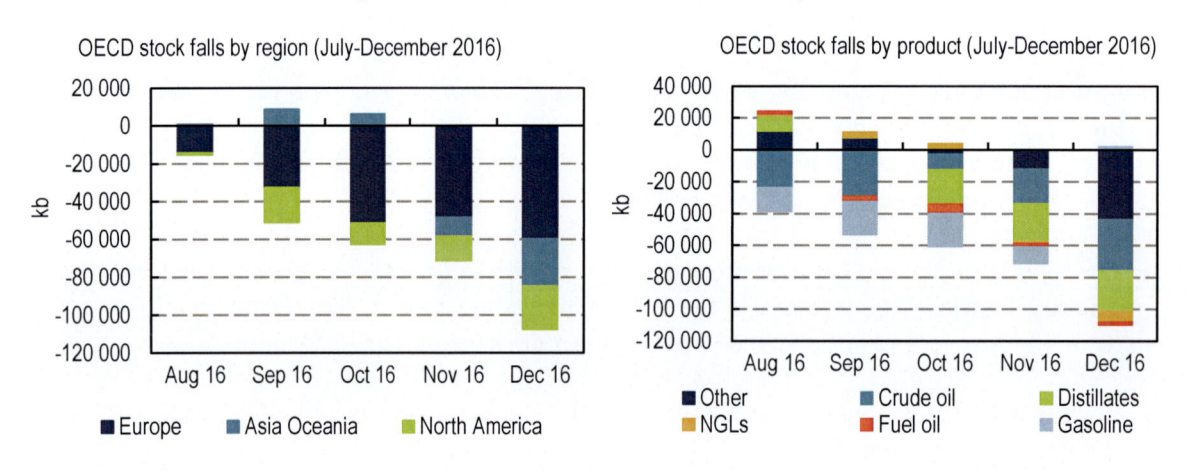

Figure 4.2 OECD oil stock falls since July 2016

This, in turn, often leaves analysts to guess stock levels based on the interaction between supply and demand, rather than actual figures. In Table 1 of the IEA's monthly *Oil Market Report*, stock changes outside the OECD implicitly fall under the *Miscellaneous to Balance* line item, along with the possibility that supply was overstated or demand understated. China, India and other emerging economies have over the last few years acted as a key balancing point for oil markets, absorbing unwanted volumes into strategic and commercial storage. As oil prices rise and supplies are reduced, this trend might be about to change. Non-OECD countries are forecast to account for 55% of global demand in the 2018-22 period, but storage capacity, including for strategic purposes, remains below that of OECD countries even if it is nearly impossible to know exactly by how much. Land-based storage capacity has been tested at times of high imports or low seasonal demand in key oil-consuming countries, such as at the end of 2015 when diesel and jet fuel cargoes queued up for discharge at European ports, or in late 2016 in the Singapore LPG market. But generally speaking it has remained just about adequate.

Figure 4.3 OECD oil stocks vs North Sea Dated price

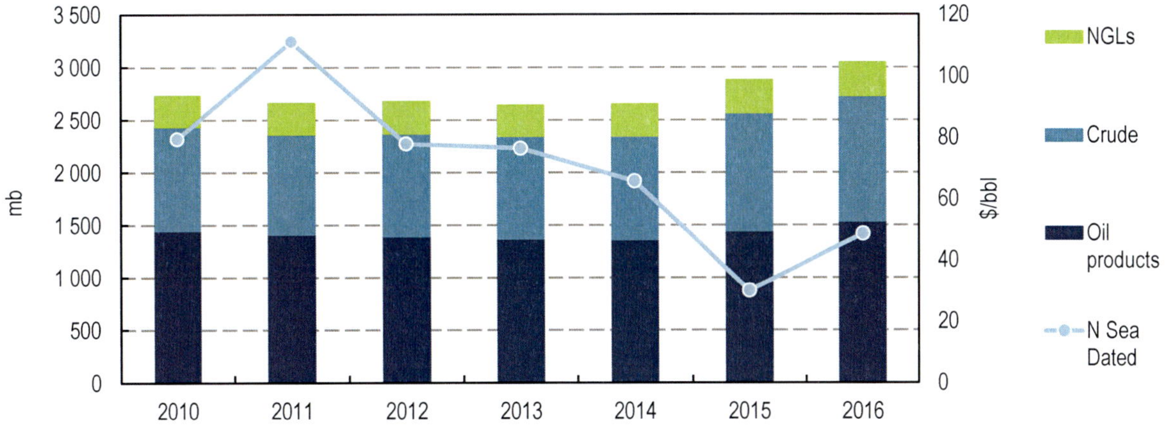

Sources: Argus; IEA.

Short-term storage on ships, a clear sign that onshore tank farms are reaching their maximum capacity, rose steadily from the end of 2014 onwards to levels last seen during the immediate aftermath of the financial and economic crisis in 2009. It reached a near-record of 111 mb in May 2016, but has since fallen back to around 83 mb, according to figures from shipbroker *E.A. Gibson Ltd*. The futures curve and our forecast demand/supply balances suggest floating storage could continue to fall. Benchmark ICE Brent futures have traded in an almost continuous state of contango – where prompt contracts are priced lower than further forward on the curve – since July 2014, highlighting the oversupply in Atlantic Basin crude markets. The Month 1-Month 2 spread, where the bulk of market activity takes place, traded between minus USD 0.15-1.00/bbl during most of the period. Long-dated Brent inter-month spreads narrowed after OPEC and non-OPEC producers agreed to cut output. Brent spreads for 4Q17 delivery have been in backwardation since early December 2016, signaling that traders expect stock draws in the second half of 2017. Backwardation steepened further at the time of writing as output cuts by OPEC members impacted physical markets.

Table 4.1 Storage capacity under construction, expansion and planned globally (mb)

Country	Under Construction	Under Expansion	Planned
Asia Oceania	82	38	141
North America	24	27	26
Africa	12	3	40
Middle East	11	7	65
FSU	3	5	4
Europe	1	11	58
Latin America	1	2	53
Total	134	93	386

Sources: TankTerminals.com; IEA.

Our analysis of oil inventories in this *Report* includes figures for tank farms being built or planned over the next few years, based on project-by-project data from industry provider *Tankterminals.com* and the IEA's own analysis. Capacity under construction represents new tank farms being built, while expansions are taking place at existing facilities. Finally, planned projects have yet to be sanctioned and remain speculative at the time of writing. Our analysis shows that storage investments are continuing across the world due to the ongoing oversupply in oil markets and the increase in demand expected over the next few years. A total of 226 mb of capacity is under construction or expansion globally, enough to service 2.3 additional days of global consumption. A further 386 mb of capacity could be built, based on existing plans, although not all of it will be. Of the capacity currently under construction or expansion, only 90 mb, or 40%, is taking place in the OECD and the rest outside it.

Asia Oceania – including countries within the OECD and outside it – has long been a hot spot in global stock building and is expected to remain so over the forecast period to cater for its growing oil consumption. A total of 82 mb of new tank capacity is under construction and 38 mb is being built at existing facilities, the largest of any region and more than twice as much as the second largest contributor, North America. A further 141 mb of capacity is planned. In OECD Asia Oceania, storage developments are being driven by South Korea, which is positioning itself as a logistically important oil hub able to welcome crude from the Middle East and to supply the region's growing oil products demand. There are also significant developments afoot in Australia, where the closure of several refineries over the last few years has boosted products imports.

Table 4.2 The 10 largest tank farms under construction/expansion globally

Project	Country	Capacity (mb)	Timeline
Pengerang	Malaysia	13.2	1H19
Sabah	Malaysia	11.3	-
Fairway Energy Houston Salt Cavern	US	11.0	1H17
Pin Oak Holdings New Orleans	US	10.0	1H17
Ulsan South Port	South Korea	9.9	1H19
Ulsan North Port	South Korea	9.9	1H19
TAG Marine	Malaysia	9.4	-
Zhejiang Tyloo Energy	China	7.5	-
Huizhou Daya Bay	China	7.2	2H17
Wanxiang Zhoushan	China	6.9	-

Sources: TankTerminals.com; IEA.

Outside the OECD, China leads with 40 mb of capacity under construction, while India is a notable laggard. In China, most of the capacity is being built in industrial coastal provinces and is focused on oil products and petrochemicals rather than crude. Impressively, for a country many times smaller than China, Malaysia has almost as much capacity under construction, 34 mb, and a further 18 mb at the planning stage. Capacity growth is driven by lack of available storage space in neighbouring Singapore and the continued development of regional oil trade.

North America has 51 mb of additional tanks under construction at new or existing facilities with a large focus on the US and Canada where LTO production and bitumen sands output will continue to grow. In the US, the largest investments are taking place in Texas with 13 mb of capacity currently under construction and 13 mb added at existing facilities, followed by Louisiana with 10 mb under construction and 4 mb under expansion. Crude storage dominates, with projects focused on areas close to Gulf Coast refineries and export terminals in order to alleviate existing bottlenecks. Mexico is also expected to see a boom in oil storage infrastructure after the government decided to open the sector to competition from the private sector, and as demand continues to grow (Box 4.1).

In the Middle East, 17 mb is under construction or expansion, almost all of it situated in the UAE. Fujairah has established itself as the largest bunkering centre in the region thanks to its strategic location outside the Strait of Hormuz. It has bigger ambitions as a pricing hub independent from Singapore and started releasing more inventory data at the start of 2017 (Box 4.2). Europe has 12 mb of extra storage capacity being built or expanded, with the largest investments focused on the Amsterdam-Rotterdam-Antwerp area, Croatia, Turkey and Spain. This makes it the second smallest capacity builder in the world. Finally, the Former Soviet Union, Africa and Latin America all have plans for more storage capacity over the medium term, but investments do not always appear to grow as fast as demand.

OECD Americas

Storage levels in the OECD Americas – comprising Canada, Chile, Mexico and the US – have been for many years the most transparent in the world due to the weekly provision of data by the *Energy Information Administration* (EIA) for the US and, secondly, the focus on projects aimed at expanding storage and transport infrastructure for the LTO and oil sands revolution. US crude inventories rose nowhere near as fast in 2016 as they did in previous years due to falling LTO production, reducing the need for new projects aimed at storing oil. Now, our forecast is for resurgent LTO production over the next five years, meaning that more storage projects are likely to be agreed over the coming years. A total of 70 mb of crude and oil products storage is being built, commissioned or planned in the US. In Canada, storage concerns have focused for many years on the ability of Albertan producers to store their output in the event of disruption to exports. Investments in major storage hubs with important pipeline connections, such as Hardisty and Edmonton, are continuing. Finally, Mexico is a case apart in that crude production has fallen in recent years, but a strong economy and the liberalisation of the energy market are reinforcing the need for products storage and strategic stocks (*Box 4.*).

Figure 4.4 Mexico's industry product stocks

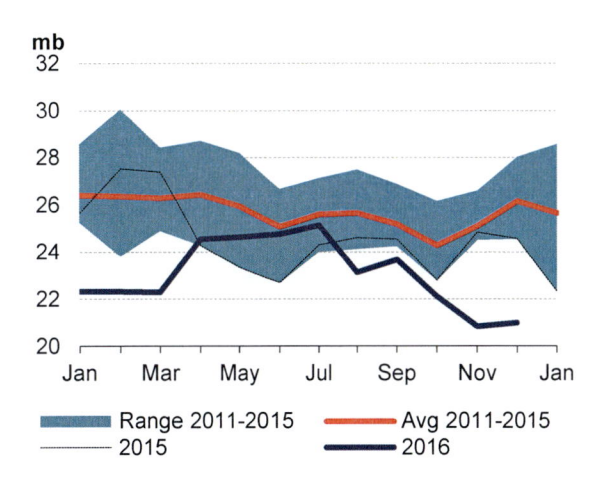

At end-2016, crude and oil product inventories in the OECD Americas stood at 1 613 mb, up 236 mb (or 17%) from the 2011-2015 average. The build was largely driven by higher production of LTO in the US and the associated rise in refinery throughputs. Crude stocks were up 143 mb versus the five-year average to 646 mb by end-2016, followed by oil products (+66 mb) and NGLs (+27 mb). Inventories of crude in the OECD Americas reached a historical peak in April 2016, before falling on the back of output cuts by US producers. US crude exports to countries other than Canada became possible at the end of 2015. Ongoing infrastructure bottlenecks meant they remained restricted, even if this started to change in late 2016 with the commissioning of a new export terminal at Ingleside, near Corpus Christi on the US Gulf Coast. The US exported 490 kb/d of crude oil on average in 2016, up from 35 kb/d in 2010. Even with higher exports the US has plentiful stocks going into 2017, and with higher forecast US LTO production (See Supply Section) it is likely to benefit from higher crude inventories than Europe and Asia over the forecast period.

TRENDS IN GLOBAL OIL STORAGE

Oil product stocks, by contrast, continued to rise through most of 2016 as US refiners offset lower domestic crude supply with higher imports and maintained strong runs. Oil product exports from the US rose throughout 2011-2015 as leading refiners and exporters developed infrastructure for product exports, including for diesel, LPG and NGLs. US oil product exports averaged 4 130 kb/d in 2016, up from 1 920 kb/d in 2010 and more than eight times higher than for crude. All in all, crude stocks accounted for 40% of all commercial oil stocks in the OECD Americas at end-2016, up from 35% at end-2010, whereas oil product and NGL stocks both fell in relative terms.

In Mexico, oil stocks fell to 40 mb in November 2016, their lowest level since 2005, due to the shutdown of two of the country's refineries for unplanned maintenance and strong growth in consumption. Stocks had recovered to 47 mb by end-December 2016. There is a plan to build more storage space for security of supply reasons (Box 4.1). In Canada, oil stocks were at 190 mb at end-2016, up 9 mb from the average in 2011-2015, with a general increase in crude stockpiles prompted by growing production.

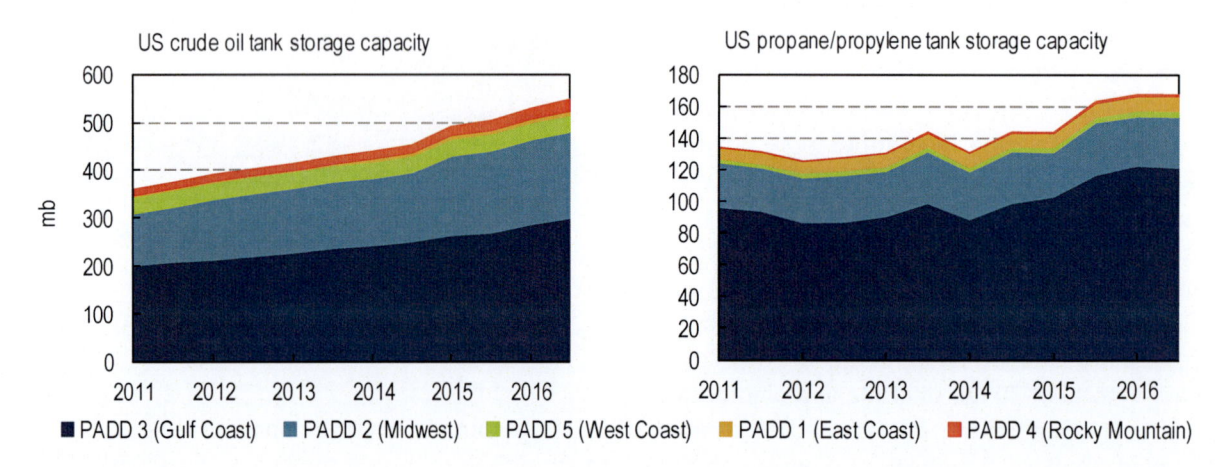

Figure 4.5 US tank storage capacity growth by PADD

Source: EIA.

The US is the only country to publish twice-yearly statistics on storage capacity at tank terminals and refineries. The latest data available for the end of September 2016 shows net shell storage capacity in the commercial sector at 1 666 mb, up 22% from 1 362 mb in September 2010. Independent (i.e., non-refinery) crude storage capacity expanded strongly in response to the boom in LTO production, growing by 202 mb (or 61%) and accounting for two-thirds of the overall increase in oil storage capacity during the period. The bulk of the increase took place in the Gulf Coast (+101 mb) and Midwest (+84 mb) regions, where LTO is either produced or refined. There was also strong growth in propane and propylene storage capacity (+34 mb to 167 mb at end-September 2016) and NGLs (+54 mb to 466 mb) as they are closely associated with shale oil and gas activity. Gasoline (+31 mb to 252 mb) also saw capacity growth in the Northeast and Gulf Coast regions in line with higher consumption. By contrast, storage capacity for distillate fuel oil (-3 mb to 192 mb) and fuel oil (+4 mb to 69 mb) fell or grew moderately. On top of these figures, available capacity for the US Strategic Petroleum Reserve (SPR) and tank storage at refineries must be added.

TRENDS IN GLOBAL OIL STORAGE

The SPR has 727 mb of capacity at underground caverns in Texas and Louisiana, unchanged over 2010-2016, whereas tank capacity at refineries fell by 18 mb to 620 mb by end-September 2016. The SPR currently holds 697 mb of crude – not including the latest sales – and the figure has remained in a narrow range of 690-697 mb since mid-2011. The Department of Energy announced in early 2017 the sale of up to 18 mb of crude from the SPR to pay for repairs and refurbishment to the tanks and medical research. Congress has scheduled 156 mb of crude sales by 2025 and further drawdowns are thus possible.

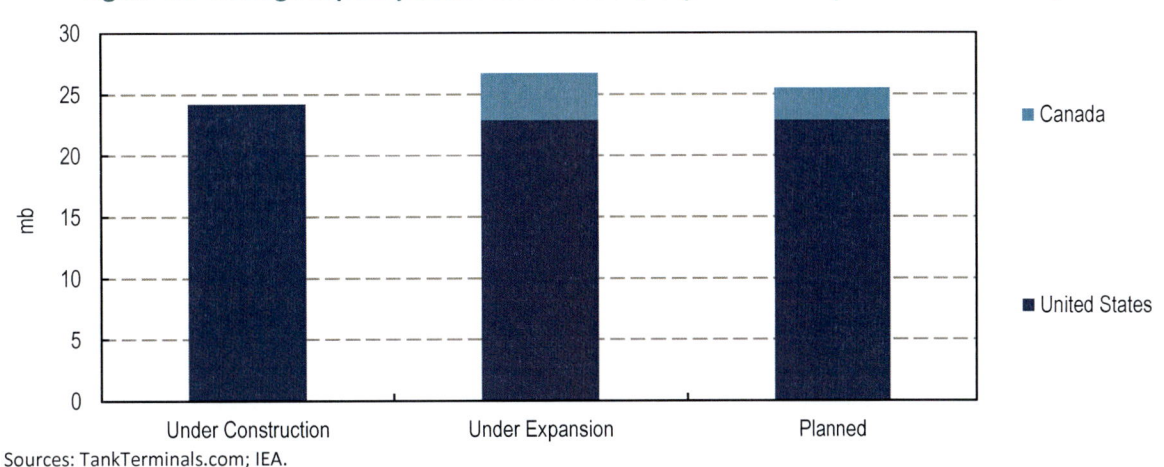

Figure 4.6 Storage capacity under construction, expansion and planned in Canada, US

Sources: TankTerminals.com; IEA.

North America currently has 51 mb of storage capacity being built or expanded, of which the majority is focused on the US and Canada where oil production is forecast to grow. In the US, the largest investments are taking place in Texas with 12.7 mb currently under construction and 13.3 mb being expanded, followed by Louisiana with 10 mb under construction and 4.4 mb under expansion. Crude dominates with projects focused on storage in areas close to Gulf Coast refineries and export terminals in order to alleviate existing infrastructure bottlenecks.

Table 4.3 The 10 largest planned storage additions in the US and Canada (mb)

Project	Country	Construction / Expansion	Planned	Timeline
Fairway Energy Houston Cavern	US	11.0	9.0	1Q17
Pin Oak Holdings Garyville	US	10.0	-	1H17
TDWP Terminals Houston	US	-	10.0	-
Enterprise Products Beaumont	US	6.2	-	-
Buckeye Perth Amboy	US	5.0	-	-
Magellan Corpus Christi	US	4.0	-	1H17
TransCanada Keystone Hardisty	Canada	-	2.6	-
Gibson Energy Hardisty	Canada	2.1	-	1H17
Kinder Morgan Galena Park	US	1.9	-	-
Gibson Energy Edmonton	Canada	1.7	-	1H18

Sources: TankTerminals.com; IEA.

The largest projects due to be commissioned over the next 18 months include the 11 mb Fairway Energy salt cavern crude project near Houston, the 10 mb Pin Oak Holdings Garyville oil and chemicals storage terminal along the Mississippi River in Louisiana, and the 1.4 mb Marathon butane cavern under the existing 212 kb/d Robinson refinery in Illinois. There are also longer-term projects still at the planning stage, such as the 10 mb TDWP Galena Park expansion on the Houston Ship Channel, and Phase 2 of the Fairway Energy salt cavern. In Canada, the key projects are Gibson Energy's 2.1 mb expansion of its Hardisty terminal and its 1.7 mb expansion at Edmonton. Hardisty started operations in 2014 as a gathering point for Western Canada Select crude, while Edmonton is situated further north. There is also the possible construction of a terminal by TransCanada linked to the Keystone pipeline. It was shelved in 2015 following the Obama Administration's veto of the project but may be built after President Trump announced his support for the project.

Box 4.1 Mexico energy liberalisation to boost private oil storage

Mexico's energy sector is in a period of profound change, following the launch of the comprehensive Energy Reform in 2013. The Reform seeks to bring new investment into the energy industry by ending the monopoly of Petróleos Mexicanos (Pemex) and by attracting new players into the oil, gas and power sectors. Investment is critical to revitalise the downstream sector, which is beset by such poor performance that gasoline imports exceeded 50% of total demand in 2016. The liberalisation of the diesel and gasoline markets is one of the most complex aspects of the Reform. It started in January 2017, a year earlier than planned, with the relaxation of retail price ceilings based on a formula taking into account wholesale prices in the US Gulf Coast – the source of most of Mexico's gasoline imports – logistical costs and retail margins. The reform, along with the depreciation of the peso against the dollar, saw retail prices rise by 14-20% on 1 January. Prices will then be progressively set free on a region by region basis from March, starting with northern states and ending with the southern province of Yucatan in December 2018. Previously, maximum fuel prices had been set by the finance ministry.

Figure 4.7 Mexico's net oil exports

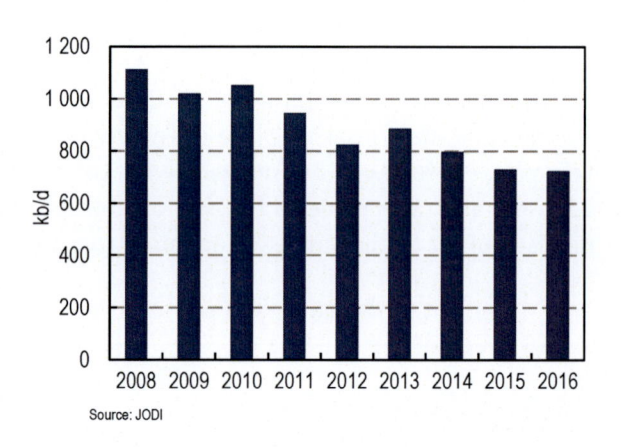

Source: JODI

Mexico applied in November 2015 to join the IEA and is close to completing the process. IEA members are obliged to store 90 days' worth of combined net imports, but, as a net exporter Mexico is a special case. In 2016, net exports of crude were 1 275 kb/d and net imports of oil products were of 555 kb/d, with a net export balance of 720 kb/d, albeit down from 1 110 kb/d in 2008. Taking into account Mexico's gasoline import dependency, the government has released a draft policy asking distributors to build a mandatory stockpile covering 30 days of sales by 2025. The latest draft shows the policy is likely to be staggered on a regional basis, possibly with delayed implementation, but we await more details. At end-2016, Mexico operated 14.6 mb of storage capacity at 73 terminals across the country, of which 6.8 mb was in in the north, 5.8 mb in central states and 2 mb in the south. Of the country's 117 ports, 15 can accommodate oil trade and there was 8.6 mb of storage capacity. Mexican refineries held 24.5 mb of storage capacity for crude and oil products, while an additional 7 mb was available in salt caverns. Only 37% of working capacity was used at storage and dispatch terminals at end-September 2016 amid high demand and refinery works that resulted in a faster turnover of products.

Box 4.1 Mexico energy liberalisation to boost private oil storage (continued)

Through the January-October 2016 period, inventories covered 14.7 days of demand for gasoline, 16.5 days for diesel and 14 days for jet fuel, according to Pemex. Energy liberalisation, the government's mandated storage levels and rising oil demand are likely to boost the construction of storage capacity over the next few years. Even if they were cautious initially, several companies have revealed projects in the last few months.

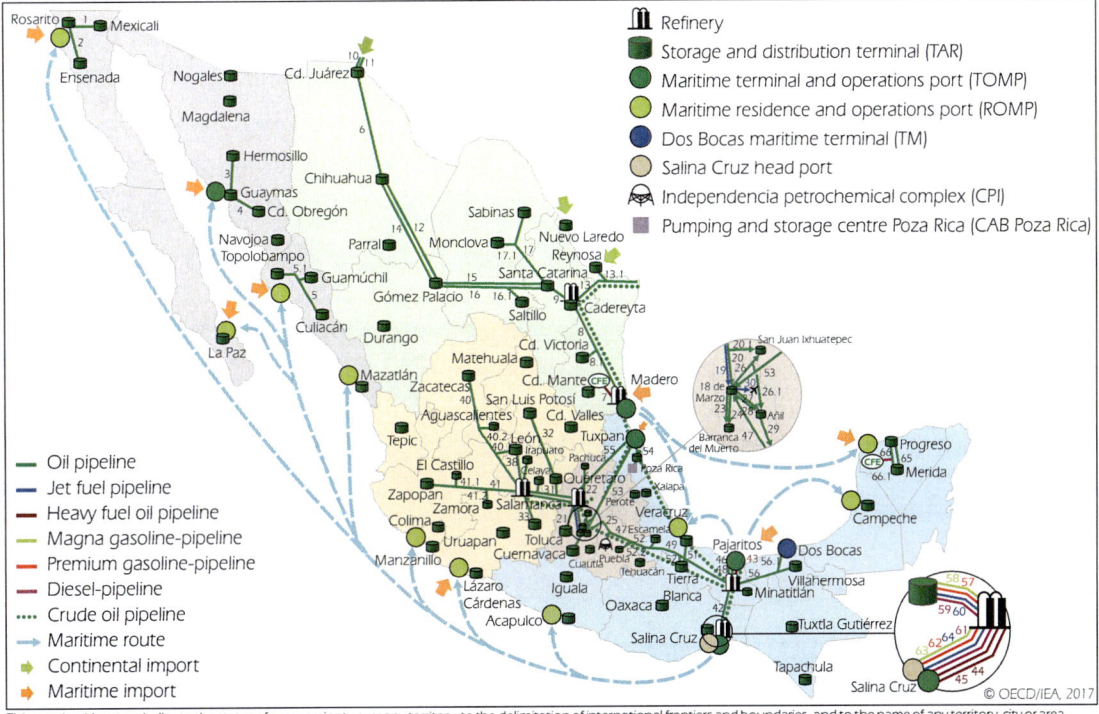

Map 4.1 Mexico's oil infrastructure

Those interested in accessing Pemex's pipelines and storage sites have been invited to bid in an open tender. Several US and Canadian companies, including Howard Partners, TransCanada and T&R Terminals, have expressed interest. TransCanada proposed in August 2016 to build a marine terminal near Tuxpan in the east of the country, along with a 265 kilometre oil products pipeline from the US Gulf Coast to Mexico, and a storage hub in central Mexico for a total cost of USD 800 million. In January 2017, Zenith Energy reached an agreement with cement producer Cemex to store LPG and other oil products at several of Cemex's sites, while in the same month Kansas City Southern and Watco WTC Industrial announced a joint venture to build a USD 45 million import and storage terminal in San Luis Potosi, in central Mexico. In April 2017, Ferropuerto Midstream will start building a terminal in Aguascalientes linked by rail to Houston, TX. It could be operational by the end of the year and be focused largely on gasoline, diesel and LPG. Additionally, Pemex began receiving diesel by rail from Port Arthur, TX, into a new private terminal at San Jose Iturbide at the start of 2017. Finally, Mexico is currently reconditioning storage sites at decommissioned power stations for a total capacity of 5.1 mb, of which 2.6 mb is expected to be ready by the end of 2017, with a further 1.3 mb in later years.

OECD Europe

The downstream sector in Europe saw a significant change in 2008-14 when up to 3 mb/d of refining capacity closed, mainly in Western Europe, due to poor margins and intense competition from the US, the Middle East and Asia. But the considerable fall in oil prices since the middle of 2014 and the resulting boost in global oil consumption threw the industry a lifeline. The fall in refining capacity has largely stopped, with only two closures recorded in 2016, both of which were planned several years ago (the UK's Lindsey and France's La Mede plants). Meanwhile, demand for oil product storage has continued to rise, and Northwest Europe remains a global storage hub supporting long-haul trade. Europe acts as the global barometer for crude oil prices – via the Brent benchmark – and for diesel and jet fuel markets. It is also a key export hub for gasoline, fuel oil and naphtha, and is likely to remain so over the forecast period. Looking ahead, most investments in additional storage capacity are being directed into areas that have seen quick demand growth over the last few years such as parts of Eastern Europe, the Balkans and Turkey rather than the more mature markets of Western Europe (even if Spain is an exception).

At end-2016, OECD Europe commercial stocks of crude oil, NGLs and oil products stood at 958 mb, up 42 mb from the 2011-2015 average. Stocks rose to a six-year high in the middle of 2016 on the back of higher crude and middle distillate imports linked to oversupply for both products. On the contrary, gasoline inventories have been largely stable in the 2011-2015 period and fuel oil stocks fell with reduced imports from Russia and despite lower demand from the European shipping sector. Stocks appear to have largely responded to growing supplies of crude and middle distillates globally rather than higher demand. Crude and product inventories covered 72 days of forward demand at end-2016, four more days than at end-2013. All in all, crude stocks accounted for 34% of all oil stocks at end-2016, unchanged since end-2010, whereas oil products were 58% of stocks and NGLs 8%. Since July 2016, European commercial inventories have fallen in line with other regions.

Table 4.4 The 10 largest planned storage additions in OECD Europe (mb)

Project	Country	Construction/ Expansion	Planned	Timeline
Horizon Enerji Ceyhan	Turkey	-	12.6	2H17
La Coruña	Spain	-	9.0	-
Hartel Oil	Netherlands	-	7.5	-
Norterminal Kirkenes	Norway	-	4.4	1H18
Thames Oilport	UK	0.4	3.1	-
Baltic Oil Terminal	Latvia	-	3.0	-
Vopak Lonessa	Estonia	-	2.9	-
PERN Gdansk	Poland	-	2.0	2H17
Starpet	Turkey	-	1.9	-
Botlek	Netherlands	1.7	-	-

Sources: TankTerminals.com; IEA.

Several European refineries have been converted into import and storage terminals with their deep-water jetties often used for larger tankers, which have increasingly become the norm in oil product trading as they bring significant economies of scale. For example, TotalERG's former Fiumicino refinery near Rome was converted into a jet fuel and diesel terminal following its closure in 2012. It is one of a few product terminals in the Mediterranean region now able to handle 80,000 tonnes DWT vessels from Asia and the Middle East through its offshore single buoy mooring that had previously been used for crude oil imports to the refinery. A less happy story is that of the former Coryton refinery in the UK, which closed in 2012 following the bankruptcy of its owner Petroplus. The site was bought by a consortium comprising Greenergy, Vopak and Shell to be transformed into a diesel terminal able to handle Long-Range vessels, and meant to open at the end of 2013. After many delays, cost overruns, and the withdrawal of Vopak, a scaled-back terminal was finally opened in mid-2016, highlighting the possible complications with such projects.

Europe currently has 12.3 mb of extra storage capacity being built or expanded, with the largest investments focused on the Amsterdam-Rotterdam-Antwerp area, Croatia, Turkey and Spain. This makes Europe one of the smallest capacity builders in the world, behind Asia Oceania, North America, Central and Latin America, the Middle East and Africa, and only just in front of the FSU countries. Significant investments are underway in the Netherlands, at Botlek near ExxonMobil's Rotterdam refinery, and Koole Tankstorage near Shell's Pernis refinery. In Turkey, three terminals were being expanded or had been recently commissioned at the time of writing, including the 1.2 mb Yeniyurt project and the 0.8 mb Delta Rubis project in the Bay of Iskenderun, southern Turkey, and the 0.6 mb Arkem Kimya Sanayi project for oil products and chemicals near Mersin. Outside the OECD, capacity expansions are being led by the 2.5 mb storage project at Omisalj in Croatia, the starting point of the JANAF pipeline that carries crude to refineries in Central Europe.

Table 4.5 Storage capacity under construction, expansion and planned in Europe (mb)

Country	Under Construction	Under Expansion	Planned
Turkey	0.6	2.0	15.0
Spain		0.8	9.8
Netherlands		3.3	8.5
Norway			4.4
Estonia			3.7
Latvia		0.1	3.6
United Kingdom		0.4	3.5
Croatia	0.4	2.5	2.6
France		0.2	2.3
Poland			2.2
Cyprus*			1.9
Albania	0.2		0.2
Belgium	0.1	1.0	0.2
Germany		0.1	0.1
Italy			
Slovenia		0.4	
Serbia		0.3	
Portugal		0.1	
Total	**1.3**	**11.0**	**58.0**

Sources: TankTerminals.com; IEA.

*Note by Turkey. The information in this document with reference to "Cyprus" relates to the southern part of the Island. There is no single authority representing both Turkish and Greek Cypriot people on the Island. Turkey recognises the Turkish Republic of Northern Cyprus (TRNC). Until a lasting and equitable solution is found within the context of the United Nations, Turkey shall preserve its position concerning the "Cyprus issue".

*Note by all the European Union Member States of the OECD and the European Union The Republic of Cyprus is recognised by all members of the United Nations with the exception of Turkey. The information in this document relates to the area under the effective control.

Several storage expansion projects with overall capacity of 58 mb are also at the planning stage. Turkey will contribute a significant share with 15 mb, followed by Spain, the Netherlands and Norway. Turkey's projects include the 12.6 mb Horizon Enerji crude storage project in Ceyhan, where Kirkuk blend crude oil from northern Iraq is stored and exported, the 1.9 mb Starpet crude storage project near Mersin and the 0.5 mb Yilport storage expansion in Gebze, in northern Turkey. There are also large facilities planned in northern Spain, such as the 9 mb oil products storage project in La Coruna, where product demand has outpaced refinery output over the last few years, raising imports of diesel. Amsterdam-Rotterdam-Antwerp is likely to continue seeing large investments in new capacity over the next few years as, despite a lack of space for new construction, there remains significant demand from refiners, importers and traders. The new 7.5 mb Hartel oil terminal in Rotterdam and the 1 mb expansion of the Rubis terminal are currently at the planning stage. Refining capacity in ARA has been largely maintained over the last few years due to its logistical advantages over other European refining centres, such as the ability to handle the largest oil tankers, good pipeline interconnection, existing storage capacity as well as the possibility to supply oil products by barge to Germany, France, Switzerland and Central Europe.

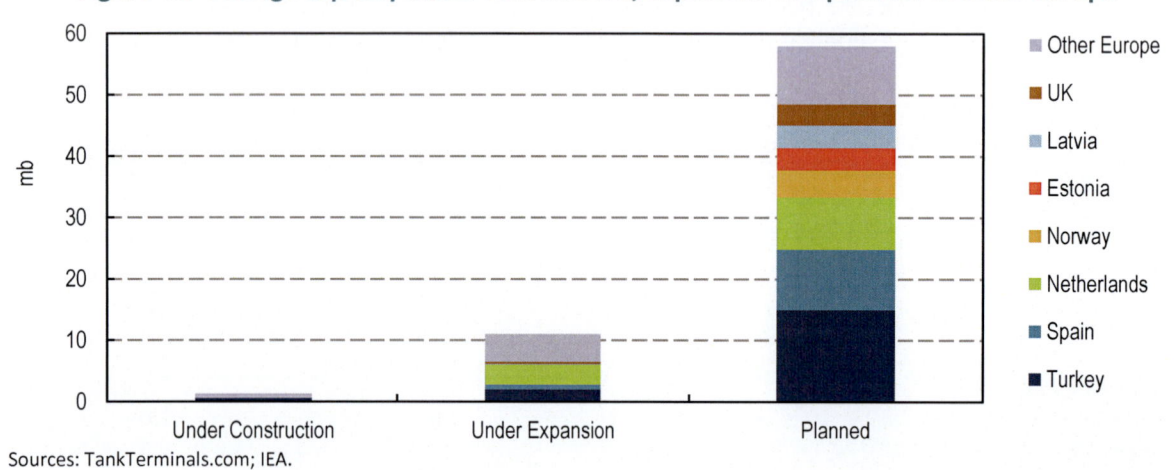

Figure 4.8 Storage capacity under construction, expansion and planned in OECD Europe

Sources: TankTerminals.com; IEA.

OECD Asia Oceania

Storage developments in this region are driven largely by South Korea, which is positioning itself as an important oil hub able to handle crude and condensate from the Middle East and cater to the region's growing oil products demand. It is also situated in a strategic location between some of the world's largest consumers (China and Japan) and the world's biggest producer, Russia. There are also significant developments afoot in Australia, where the closure of four refineries with total crude throughput capacity of 415 kb/d over the last few years has boosted oil product imports. Australia is now the largest ultra-low sulfur diesel importer in Asia Pacific. By contrast, Japan holds the largest commercial inventories in the region, with 238 mb at end-2016, and the world's second largest SPR, with 328 mb, but has few storage developments planned over the next few years.

At end-2016, OECD Asia Oceania industry inventories of crude oil, NGLs and oil products stood at 415 mb, up 8 mb from the 2011-2015 average. Following patterns seen in other regions, stocks rose to their highest in nearly 10 years at the end of September with higher cargo arrivals and steady refinery output. However, it was also noticeable that stocks did not exceed the five-year average in

OECD Asia Oceania as much as in other regions. In addition, stocks in the region remain small relative to demand compared with Europe and North America, a fact that can be attributed to lack of gasoline and distillates storage capacity. Commercial crude and product inventories covered 49 days of forward demand at end-2016, five more days than at end-2013. This compares with 72 days of forward demand coverage in OECD Europe and 66 days in OECD North America. Crude stockpiles accounted for 47% of all oil stocks at end-2016, up from 41% at end-2010, and NGLs fell four percentage points to 14%. By contrast, product stocks fell by 2 points to 39% of oil stocks.

Table 4.6 The 10 largest planned storage additions in OECD Asia Oceania (mb)

Project	Country	Construction /Expansion	Planned	Timeline
Ulsan South port	South Korea	9.9	18.5	1H19 (construction), 2025 (extension)
Ulsan North Port	South Korea	9.9	9.9	1H19 (construction)
Caltex Kurnell	Australia	4.7	-	1Q17
Okinawa Oil Base	Japan	-	1.9	2H21
Busan Marine & Oil	South Korea	-	1.4	-
TQ Port Kembla	Australia	1.4	-	2H17
Geelong Terminals	Australia	1.3	-	2H18
Stolthaven Newcastle	Australia	-	1.3	-
Onsan Terminal	South Korea	-	0.7	-
United Pet. Hastings	Australia	0.3	-	-

Sources: TankTerminals.com; IEA.

OECD Asia Oceania currently has 30.4 mb of storage capacity being built or expanded, with a further 36.7 mb at the planning stage. South Korea has by far the most projects on the table. Korea National Oil Corp announced in 2015 plans to transform Ulsan, where SK Energy operates the third largest refinery in the world with crude throughput of 840 kb/d, into a major storage and trading hub for the North Asia region. Other North Asian ports have failed to achieve such status in the last few years, despite superior demand. Two 9.9 mb storage projects for crude and oil products, due to be commissioned in 2019, are currently being built in Ulsan. A further 28.4 mb could be in place by 2025, according to current plans. While the projects certainly have the potential to turn Ulsan into one of the world's largest storage hubs, high concentration in the Korean downstream industry could hamper the development of a fully-fledged trading hub similar to ARA, Singapore or the Gulf Coast. In those regions, multiple actors were key to boost trade volumes.

Figure 4.9 Storage capacity under construction, expansion and planned in OECD Asia Oceania

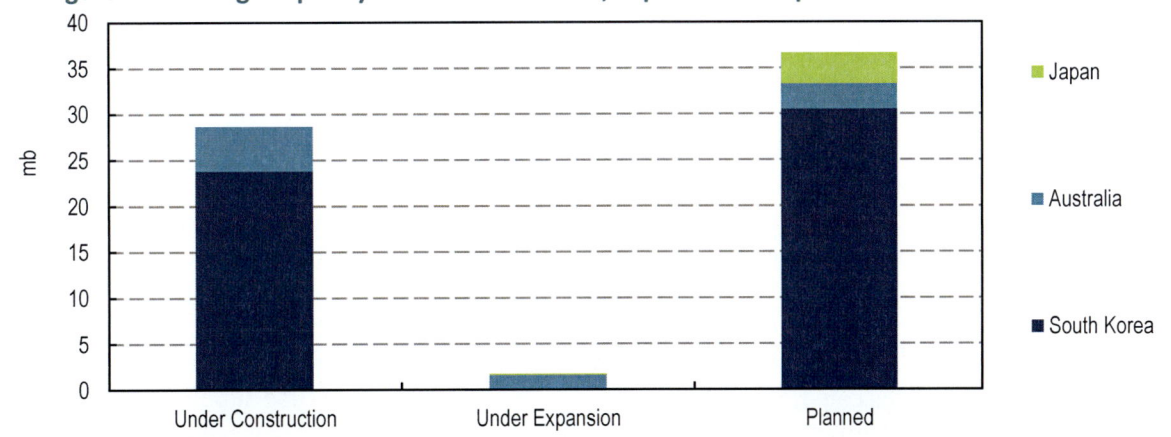

Sources: TankTerminals.com; IEA.

Other projects in OECD Asia Oceania include the 1.9 mb plan to add crude storage at Okinawa in Japan by 2021, the 1.5 mb Busan bunker fuel storage terminal in South Korea and other smaller projects. The region is also expected to see an increasing number of LNG terminals over the next few years in line with higher natural gas consumption, some of which plan to store oil products and LPG. Australia will see the second largest additions over the forecast period with oil product storage projects aimed at replacing refining capacity lost to economic closures. At the time of writing, Caltex was putting the finishing touches to a project to convert its former Kurnell refinery in New South Wales into a 4.7 mb storage site, while a 1.3 mb oil products terminal in Geelong, Victoria state, is being built and could be operational by the end of 2018. There are at least two other projects in New South Wales with respective capacities of 1.5 mb and 1.3 mb.

Non-OECD Asia

Storage levels in the rest of Asia are notoriously more difficult to understand given the paucity of data published. The region's largest consumer, China, does not report stocks to the JODI database. Some estimates for the commercial sector are available from *China Oil, Gas and Petrochemicals* (*China OGP*) on a monthly basis, but only published as a percentage change from the previous month rather than outright stock figures. Using base data for outright stocks from July 2010, the figures show moderate growth in total oil stocks of 14 mb to 356 mb by end-2016. Since November 2014 the *National Bureau of Statistics* has released annual updates on the status of the Strategic Petroleum Reserve, but the figures are not timely.

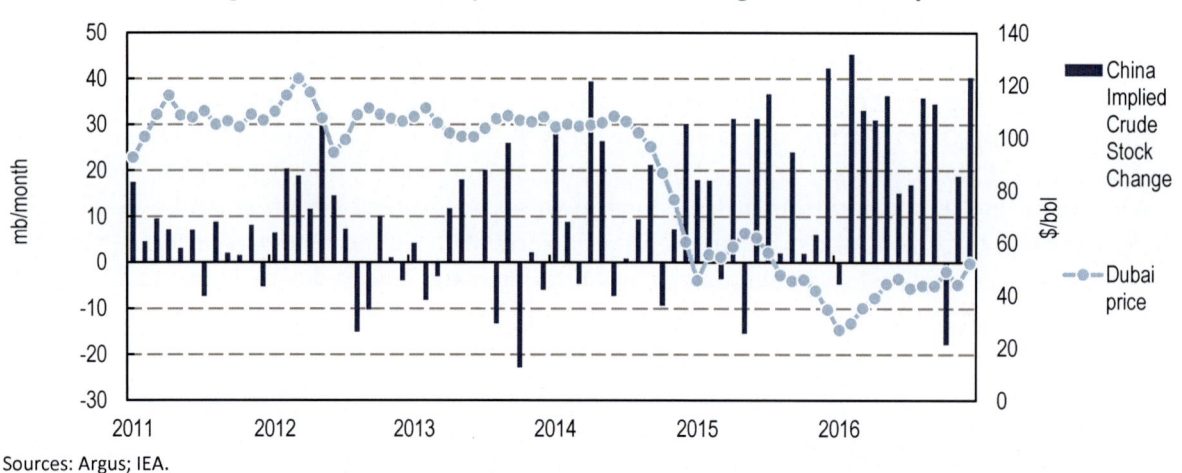

Figure 4.10 China's implied crude stock change vs Dubai oil price

Sources: Argus; IEA.

Analysts typically estimate China's crude stock changes using their forecasts for crude production and refining throughput, as well as customs data. The wider availability of ship-tracking software also makes it easier to track oil flows to/from China ahead of official customs releases. Using this methodology, implied data show that in 2011-2016 total crude stocks are likely to have built strongly given that supplies (Chinese crude production plus net imports) outpaced refinery runs by around 802 mb, or approximately 370 kb/d. The build gathered pace in 2015 as lower oil prices boosted runs at Chinese refineries and stockpiling. Between one third and a half of this amount went into the strategic reserves, with the rest likely allocated to commercial storage facilities. Higher than estimated runs at refineries could be partly to blame for the gap between crude supplies and runs, as this period also coincided with the rise of independent refineries for which data is harder to obtain.

TRENDS IN GLOBAL OIL STORAGE

The *National Bureau of Statistics* estimates China's SPR amounted to 233 mb at end-2015, equivalent to more than 70% of Japan's SPR and one third of the United States'. The volume is more than the stated capacity of the eight sites mentioned by the government (Zhoushan 1, Zhennai, Dalian, Huangdao 1, Dushanzi 1, Lanzhou, Tianjin 1, Huangdao 2), meaning that around 50 mb was likely to be stored in the commercial petroleum reserve (CPR) or at other SPR facilities at that time. Since then, several SPR sites have continued to build stocks or commissioned new storage units, including at Huangdao, Tianjin, Zhoushan, Jinzhou and Huizhou (See Table). Phase one of the programme was completed at the end of 2008 with 103 mb of crude imported mainly from the Middle East and West Africa, while phase two was estimated to be full at end-2016 with crudes from the Middle East and Kazakhstan. A further eight locations are either filling, under construction or planned over the next few years. Several sites were delayed (Jinzhou, Zhanjiang) for technical reasons. Phase three of the SPR is unlikely to be finished before 2020 at the earliest, perhaps later as some facilities have not begun construction yet.

Table 4.7 China's Strategic Petroleum Reserve

	Operator	Location	Capacity (mb)	Status	Completion	Type
Phase 1	Sinopec	Zhenhai	32.7	Filled	3Q06	Above ground
	Sinochem	Zhoushan 1	31.4	Filled	4Q07	Above ground
	Sinopec	Huangdao 1	20.1	Filled	4Q07	Above ground
	CNPC	Dalian	18.9	Filled	4Q08	Above ground
Phase 2	CNPC	Lanzhou	18.9	Filled	4Q11	Above ground
	CNPC	Dushanzi 1	18.9	Filled	4Q11	Above ground
	Sinopec	Tianjin 1	20.1	Filled	4Q14	Above ground
	Sinopec	Huangdao 2	18.9	Filled	3Q16	Rock cavern
Phase 3	Sinopec	Tianjin 2	20.1	Filled	2H16	Above ground
	Sinochem	Zhoushan 2	19.0	Filling	1Q17	Above ground
	CNPC	Jinzhou	18.9	Filling	1H17	Rock cavern
	CNOOC	Huizhou	31.4	Filling/being built	2018	Rock cavern
	Sinopec	Zhanjiang	44.0	Being built	2018	Rock cavern
	CNPC	Jintan	15.7	Planned	-	Salt cavern
	Sinopec	Yangpu	18.0	Planned	-	-
	CNPC	Shanshan	39.0	Planned	-	-

India, with its booming consumption growth, is also busy building sizeable reserves. The statistical office published stocks data in the JODI database for the first time in March 2011 and since then its crude stocks have risen strongly, from 33.2 mb to 43.1 mb at end-2016. Oil product stocks also gained over the period and were assessed at 64.9 mb at the end of 2016. As is the case for China, the best method for estimating Indian crude and product stocks in real time is to use estimates for refinery activity, crude production and import/export data, leaving considerable room for uncertainty. India's SPR has been relatively slow to build due to technical problems with pipelines at the 18.4 mb Padur facility. Padur was finally commissioned late in 2016 and is due to fill over 1Q17. The 9.8 mb Vishakhapatnam SPR was filled in June 2015 with crude from Iraq. Hindustan Petroleum Corp is using 2.2 mb of capacity at the site for commercial purposes and has agreed to set aside those volumes in case of emergency.

The 11 mb Mangalore site was half filled with Iranian crude in 2016. The UAE's Adnoc will fill the rest of the facility before the end of 2017 and will use 5.5 mb of capacity at Mangalore for commercial purposes and has agreed to supply India in case of emergency. This is similar to the deal between the Indian government and Hindustan Petroleum Corp at Vishakhapatnam. Such agreements have also been made in the past between Japan and Saudi Aramco to reduce the overall costs of holding strategic reserves. A total of 91.6 mb of capacity is scheduled to be built under phase two of the Indian SPR programme across four sites. A provisional start-up date of 2020 has been set, but this may well prove optimistic given that work has not yet started. As a result, its impact on overall demand over the forecast period is likely to be minimal.

Table 4.8 India's Strategic Petroleum Reserve

	Location	Capacity (mb)	Status	Completion	Type
Phase 1	Vishakhapatnam	9.8	Filled	Jun 2015	Rock cavern
	Padur 1	18.4	Filling	1Q17	Rock cavern
	Mangalore	11.0	Half filled	4Q17	Rock cavern
Phase 2	Chandikhol	27.5	Planned		Rock cavern
	Bikaner	27.5	Planned		Salt cavern
	Rajkot	18.3	Planned		Underground tanks
	Padur 2	18.3	Planned		Rock cavern

In other Asian countries, storage data is regularly available for Brunei Darussalam, Chinese Taipei, Hong Kong, Papua New Guinea, the Philippines and Thailand in the JODI database. The figures highlight continued economic growth and the associated rise in oil demand, as stocks have generally expanded in the 2010-16 period. In 2012, Myanmar also resumed publishing data for its crude and oil product stocks as part of the opening up of its economy. It held 3.9 mb of crude and oil products at end-September 2016, up from 0.6 mb in September 2012. Singapore is the world's largest bunkering hub and publishes, via *International Enterprise,* weekly statistics on oil product stocks covering all terminals, even if crude storage is not covered. Over the 2010-16 period overall stocks have remained broadly stable, rising and falling in line with seasonal patterns. They were 43 mb at end-2016, down 1 mb from the end of 2010. Storage capacity has little room to grow due to lack of space in the densely populated country.

Non-OECD Asia currently has 89.3 mb of commercial storage capacity being built or expanded, with a further 104.1 mb planned. China leads the amount of capacity currently under construction or expansion with 40.2 mb. In China, most of the capacity is being built in the coastal provinces of Zhejiang, Jiangsu, Tianjin, Shandong, Fujian and Guangdong where the bulk of industrial activity takes place. Whereas China has often focused in the past on crude storage, the largest commercial projects likely to come online over the forecast period focus on oil products and petrochemicals due to strong growth in those sectors over the last few years and rising output from independent refiners. Of the projects being built or at the planning stage, the largest include Sinopec's 10.4 mb Yangpu terminal in Hainan, Tyloo Energy's 7.5 mb expansion in Zhejiang, the construction of a new 7.2 mb facility at the Daya Bay petrochemical cluster and the 6.9 mb Wanxiang storage expansion in Zhejiang.

For a country many times smaller than China, Malaysia has almost as much commercial capacity under construction with 34 mb, and a further 18.1 mb at the planning stage. Capacity growth is driven by lack of available storage space in neighbouring Singapore and the continued development of regional oil trade. The new 13.2 mb terminal in Pengerang is the largest storage project being built in Malaysia and, indeed, the largest globally. It is due online in 2019, followed by the 11.3 mb Sabah oil project. Construction of the 9.4 mb TAG Marine project in Malacca is due to start in 2017.

Indonesia, Asia's third most populous country, has 2.2 mb of capacity under expansion and 44.5 mb of projects at the planning stage. Its proximity to Singapore and fast developing oil demand help justify new storage facilities, but few projects appear ready to move to the construction stage, suggesting that this capacity will take many years to build and some may never be commissioned. Other projects in Asia include Vopak's 6.2 mb Banyan cavern storage project in Singapore and several smaller facilities in Viet Nam. We have tracked very few commercial storage projects in India. While this could be due to lack of publicity for new projects, this is surprising given the rapidly growing oil consumption, and suggests more investments are required in order to develop the oil infrastructure. This is likely to cause logistical problems in the medium term as oil storage is key to smooth operations across the supply chain.

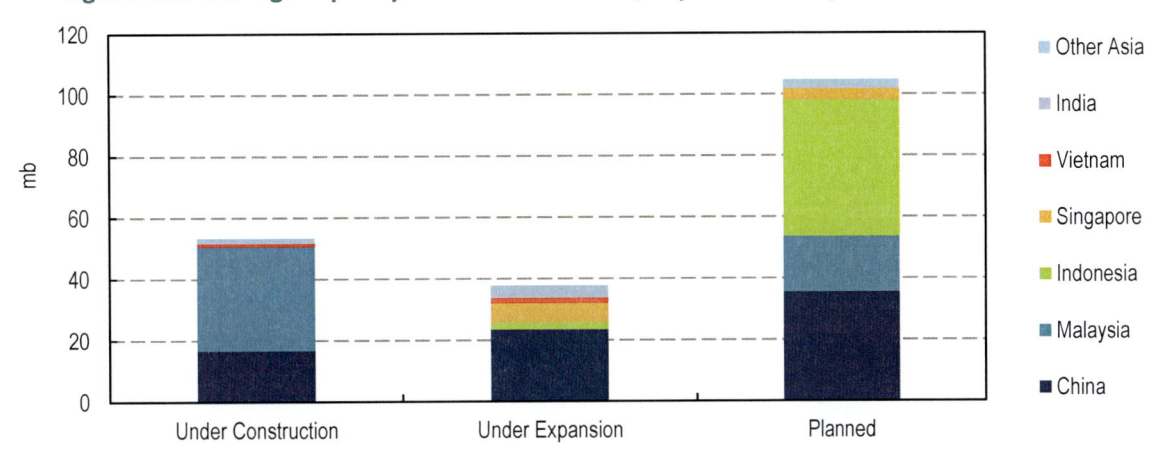

Figure 4.11 Storage capacity under construction, expansion and planned in non OECD Asia

Sources: TankTerminals.com; IEA.

Middle East

Saudi Arabia, unsurprisingly, has the largest crude oil storage capacity in the Middle East, mainly at its export terminals, including the 33 mb tank farm at Ras Tanura, the largest facility, and 22.6 mb at Yanbu on the Red Sea. Growth in recent years has been focused on oil products storage for the new refineries commissioned by Saudi Aramco and its partners in Jubail and Yanbu. According to JODI, oil stockpiles in Saudi Arabia grew from 299 mb at the end of 2010 to 365 mb at the end of 2016, largely because of a 64 mb build in oil products, whereas crude oil grew by 2 mb. But crude still accounted for three quarters of all oil stored in the country at the end of 2016. In terms of new projects, a 2.6 mb facility for oil products and chemicals at Jubail will be commissioned by Vopak in 2017, and a 1.5 mb storage site at Yanbu, also for oil products and chemicals, is planned. Elsewhere, the UAE, Iraq and Iran have ambitious plans for commercial storage expansions over the next few years.

Bahrain, Iraq and Qatar also submit storage data to JODI on a regular basis. Oil stocks grew exponentially in Qatar over 2010-2016, from 16 mb to 64 mb, boosted by growing demand for fuels amid an economic boom and construction work linked to the 2022 FIFA World Cup. Oil products accounted for 34 mb of capacity at end-2016, or 53%. Crude stocks also grew in the period, from 6 mb to 30 mb, despite stable and, lately, falling production. Oil stocks also grew in Bahrain and Iraq, in both cases to accompany rising products demand.

The Middle East currently has 17.3 mb of commercial storage under construction or expansion, almost all of it situated in the UAE. There are 11 projects underway in Fujairah and Sharjah with a combined capacity of 13.4 mb. Fujairah has established itself as the largest bunkering hub in the region – and the second largest globally – for ships travelling between Europe, Africa and Asia, thanks to its strategic location outside the Strait of Hormuz. There is also storage for gasoline, with ships coming from Europe or Asia to discharge their cargo into Fujairah, from where smaller cargoes are re-exported to other locations in the Middle East. In January 2017, *FedCom* and *S&P Global Platts* started publishing weekly inventory data for Fujairah covering all terminals in the Emirate. The aim is to increase transparency and to develop Fujairah further as an oil trading hub for the Middle East. The development goes hand in hand with the publication of new price indices for the region independent of Singapore (*See Box 4.2*). The data showed residual fuel stocks of 8 mb, light distillates at 5 mb and middle distillates at 4 mb at the end of February 2017.

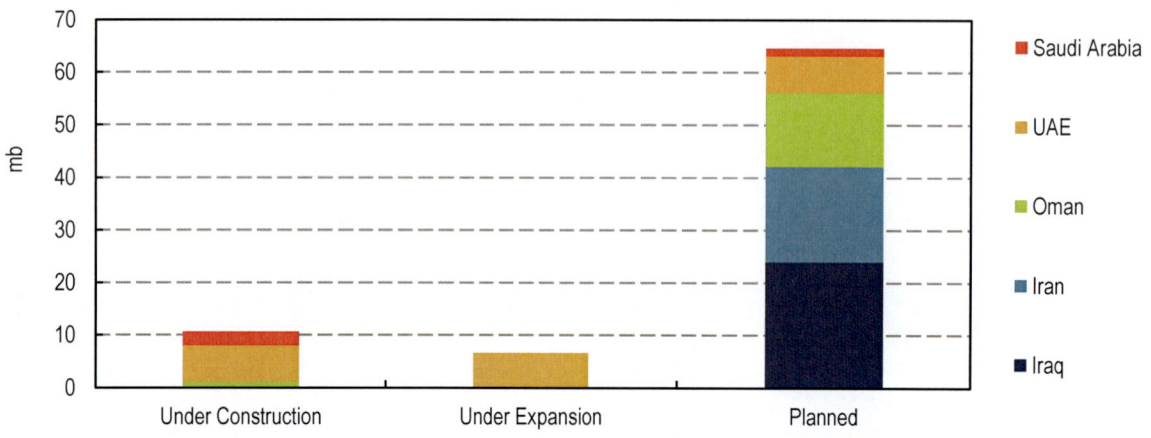

Figure 4.12 Storage capacity under construction, expansion and planned in the Middle East

Sources: TankTerminals.com; IEA.

Oman, situated next to Fujairah, also has 1.1 mb of capacity being built and a further 14 mb planned, including a giant tank farm at Ras Markaz with initial capacity of 10 mb and ambitions to reach 200 mb. Iran and Iraq have both raised their crude oil production greatly over the last few years, increasing the need for additional crude tank capacity to accommodate exports. Lack of ullage (i.e. available tank space) is often blamed for vessel loading delays in Iraq. As such, there is a plan to build 17.5 mb of storage at Al Zubair, in Iraq's south, and a further 3.3 mb in Tuba and 2.9 mb in Fao. Iran plans to build a 10 mb crude storage site on Qeshm Island and an 8.2 mb facility for oil products and chemicals in Asalouyeh.

Africa

Information concerning developments in African inventories remains elusive, with only four countries regularly submitting data to JODI (Algeria, Angola, Nigeria and South Africa), three of which are major crude producers. Africa's second largest consumer, South Africa, stopped publishing stocks data at the end of 2015 and it is unclear if and when it will resume. Over the last few years, developments have focused on East Africa, which has the most open wholesale market on the continent and has seen large gains in consumption. Most investments are now heading to West Africa, which suffers from chronically low storage capacity levels and other infrastructure problems, such as few deep-water ports. Current plans do not match up with forecasts for rising demand, though, meaning that storage issues could arise over the next few years without additional investments.

There are projects to build or expand tank farms in Ghana with the 1 mb BOST Pumpuni Reef terminal and the 0.3 mb Quantum facility in Tema. In Nigeria, which removed some gasoline subsidies in 2016 in an attempt to combat deficits and open up the market, the only project being considered is a 1.3 mb tank farm in Lagos, but it is unclear whether it will go ahead after project operator Oando sold its downstream business to Vitol in 2016. South Africa has 0.7 mb of capacity being built at Burgan Cape, near Cape Town, and a further 29.8 mb planned and at various stages of advancement. In February 2017, *Oiltanking* and *MOGS Ltd* confirmed an 8.8 mb storage project in Saldanha Bay, near Cape Town, connected to a jetty able to handle up to Very Large Crude Carrier (VLCC) tanker sizes. Morocco has plans to build a 1.2 mb terminal at Jorf Lasfar. Equatorial Guinea has plans to build 8 mb of capacity at Bioko Norte, but the project looks to have stalled in 4Q16.

It is estimated that Libya lost 7 mb of crude storage capacity during three separate attacks on the Ras Lanuf and Es Sider terminals during the civil war. While there are few prospects in the short term to rebuild its damaged infrastructure, the later part of our forecast period could be more encouraging. In December 2014, seven tanks out of 19 caught fire in El Sider, leading to a loss of 1.8 mb of capacity. In January 2016, an attack led to the destruction of four tanks in Es Sider and one in Ras Lanuf, totalling around 2.2 mb of capacity. Finally, also in January 2016, a third attack destroyed five tanks at Ras Lanuf, affecting 3 mb of capacity. Both terminals reopened at the end of 2016, but exports have been hampered by the lack of tank space. In Es Sider, between four and five out of 19 storage tanks were operational in January 2017, according to news reports. Work is progressing on three tanks to bring them back into use.

Former Soviet Union

Very little accurate information is available on storage levels in the Former Soviet Union. Significant storage capacity is located at refineries, pipeline junctions, seaborne and rail export terminals with smaller storage facilities located close to production sites and at distribution terminals. Information concerning export terminals is the most widely available. For example, loading programmes for Urals crude and oil products are sent to market participants several weeks in advance. Russia will not be opening any new ports over the medium term; instead, existing terminals will be expanded. Over the 2013-16 period, Primorsk, in Russia's north, converted crude tanks into diesel storage, significantly expanding diesel export capacity from the terminal to 9.8 mb per month.

A 1.9 mb terminal in Novorossiysk was also commissioned at the end of 2016 to handle growing crude flows on the Caspian Pipeline Consortium pipeline. A further 4.8 mb of capacity is under construction or expansion in Russia, with a focus on Black Sea ports such as Novorossiysk, Tuapse and Taman, and the Baltic Sea port of Primorsk. Longer term, there is also a project for a 2.8 mb crude and oil products tank farm in Taman. Exports via neighbours Lithuania and Estonia have been curtailed in the 2013-16 period as Russia favoured flows from its own ports, thereby creating a surplus of tank storage capacity. Transhipments are likely to continue falling over the medium-term.

Latin America

The Latin American storage sector underwent significant changes a few years ago when several refineries closed and were turned into tank farms to facilitate regional crude and product trade. Capacity additions over the next few years will focus on Brazil, where crude production is forecast to increase steeply, and countries situated close to trading routes, such as Panama or the Dutch

Antilles, or where consumption is rising. Crude trade is currently focused on Latin American production, which is sold within the region and exported to North America and Asia. Product trade has also boomed recently due to rising consumption in many countries and a shortage of refining capacity. The US, along with Europe, has exported large amounts of oil products (largely gasoil, but also gasoline and jet fuel) to Latin America as a result.

Data from JODI showed Argentina, Brazil, Chile the Dominican Republic, Ecuador, Jamaica, Nicaragua, Peru and Venezuela regularly publishing figures on oil stocks in the past year, even if sometimes with considerable delays. Since end-2010, oil stocks have increased in Brazil, Chile, Jamaica, Nicaragua, Peru and Venezuela, but have fallen elsewhere. Brazil started building 0.8 mb of tank farms at Ponta Negra in 2016 to service its growing crude production. Crude will be pumped straight from offshore platforms to the terminal, which will be able to handle VLCCs. The project is currently scheduled to finish in 2020 and could one day reach total capacity of 34 mb. There is also a 1.1 mb crude and oil products tank farm being expanded in Puerto Sandino next to Nicaragua's sole refinery, as well as smaller projects in Brazil, Colombia, Haiti and Chile.

> **Box 4.2 Oil price benchmarks move with the times**
>
> *Middle East plays crucial role in oil pricing*
>
> **Figure 4.13 Crude, product exports from five Middle East countries**
>
> Source: JODI.
>
> Record Middle East crude and product output has turned the spotlight on the region's price benchmarks. In 2016, price reporting agency *S&P Global Platts* reinforced its Dubai crude oil reference price by including Qatari medium heavy sour crude Al Shaheen and the UAE's light sour crude Murban. This boosted the amount of physical crude in the Middle East marker, used since the 1980s to price sour crude moving East of Suez, by 1.8 mb/d to 3.6 mb/d. Some 2.4 mb/d is freely traded on the spot market as it does not have destination restrictions, a measure imposed by some producers to limit the resale of their cargoes. The move followed a Chinese buying binge in the summer of 2015, which inflated the price of Dubai and led some industry players to suggest there was insufficient volume to support the benchmark.
>
> The relative lighter quality of Murban against the rest of the Dubai basket, however, made it necessary to calculate each month a compensation paid by the buyer to the seller, known as a quality premium. This measure copies a model used for Ekofisk and Oseberg in the North Sea market since 2013. It means that Murban, with its vast production volume each month, can act more easily as a price cap for the whole Dubai complex when there is strong demand for sour crude.

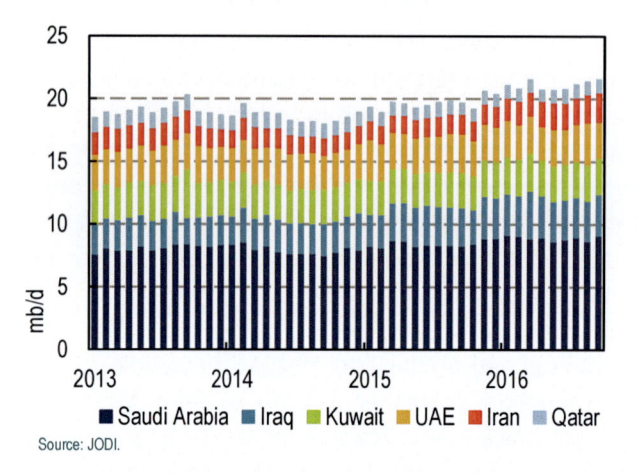

Box 4.2 Oil price benchmarks move with the times (Continued)

In a separate move that is likely to curb price speculation, *Intercontinental Exchange* (*ICE*) proposed position limits for Dubai oil futures of 6,000 lots for May 2017 delivery onwards. Some market participants may be allowed to build larger positions if they can justify it, for example if they are hedging a physical crude cargo. It is unclear at this stage how this will impact physical market liquidity. Dubai is likely to remain the main benchmark for crude delivered East of Suez over the forecast period.

Even with planned OPEC output cuts in 1H17, production from the region is plentiful and generally corresponds to the quality sought by Asian refiners. A separate attempt by *the Shanghai International Energy Exchange* to create a delivered crude futures benchmark for China hit a road-block at the start of 2017 after major traders withdrew from the initiative due to concerns around yuan convertibility and the risks associated with regulation.

Oil product benchmarks are also taking shape in the Middle East as trade volumes rise on the back of new refineries in Saudi Arabia and the UAE and higher consumption in the region. Wholesale oil product prices in the Middle East are usually calculated against Singapore prices plus the cost of freight. But in October 2016, Platts launched independent assessments for gasoline, gasoil, jet fuel and fuel oil in a bid to replace the existing framework. One of the key requirements for oil product benchmarks is storage, and in January 2017, the Emirate of Fujairah in the UAE started publishing data for crude and oil product stocks on a weekly basis in line with existing practices for Amsterdam-Rotterdam-Antwerp (ARA), Houston and Singapore. Further developments in oil products pricing could lead to the development of Middle East oil product derivative contracts, another necessary tool for spot market liquidity.

US crude exports spur search for new pricing

Oil traders have been debating the best pricing basis for US crude exports – traditional benchmarks such as US West Texas Intermediate (WTI), North Sea Brent or an alternative – ever since the lifting of a 40-year export ban at the end of 2015. WTI has traded at a discount to Brent since 2010 due to higher US crude production and pipeline restrictions in the Midwest. The most suitable pricing reference could prove to be WTI for delivery in Houston, which reflects the price of crude flowing from the Permian Basin into the US Gulf Coast hub, or an alternative contract for delivery in Midland, TX. Unlike the original WTI contract basis Cushing, the Houston index covers the cost of transport to the Gulf Coast, enabling a better comparison versus crude traded in the Atlantic Basin.

Field blending with conventional WTI crude and lighter and lower sulphur LTO streams should in theory enable producers to achieve a consistent quality, a key benchmark requirement. Price reporting agency *Argus* said spot trade linked to its WTI Houston index continued to grow in 2H16. And in February, the *Chicago Mercantile Exchange* (CME) launched a financial futures contract settled against this index that can be used for hedging. However, a prospective border tax on crude would boost US prices and likely make exports uneconomic, in effect nipping the fledgling trade in the bud.

North Sea Brent starts shift to import market

Brent, the most widely used spot crude oil benchmark, has started in 2016 a transition towards a delivered market on the expectation that North Sea crude will become less plentiful and Europe more of an importer. The production of the four grades that make up the BFOE complex – Brent, Forties, Oseberg and Ekofisk – stood at 870 kb/d in 2016, equivalent to a little over a third of the spot volume available for trade in the revamped Dubai benchmark and far less than WTI.

Even if output has stabilised recently following investment, it is likely to resume its long-term decline. Additionally, few of the fields due to come online in the North Sea over the next few years are likely to

Box 4.2 Oil price benchmarks move with the times (continued)

qualify as light sweet crude oil and to produce enough oil to offset field depletion elsewhere. Already in 2007, BFOE became sourer following the addition of Buzzard production. Brent has largely become a brand name after

Brent field output slowed to a trickle and Shell announced the imminent closure of Brent Charlie, the last platform attached to the field. Norway's Troll will be added to the BFOE basket from 2018 in a bid to boost loadings back above the symbolic 1 mb/d mark.

It is likely that Troll's relatively high acidity, which disqualified it in the past, will have little impact due to technical advances in refining and the existing practice of blending. The bigger issue, however, is that Troll's volumetric contribution looks insufficient in the longer run. The result is that crudes from outside the North Sea are likely to be considered for addition over the next five to ten years.

The most widely available crudes in Northwest Europe come from Russia (Urals), the Mediterranean (Sahara Blend), the Caspian (CPC Blend, Azeri Light) and West Africa (Qua Iboe, Bonny Light). They vary significantly in specification, are typically delivered on ships of different sizes travelling vast distances and, finally, the volumes reaching Europe change each month. Not all of these crudes will eventually be eligible for inclusion in Brent, but the question of how to compensate buyers and sellers for the various qualities and delivery terms will be central. There is a difference of several dollars per barrel between the lightest and sweetest crudes from West Africa, which typically transact at a premium to Brent, and Urals, which trades at a discount. Moving Brent to a CIF-delivered contract would enable the addition of crudes with varying shipping times to Europe into the benchmark.

Figure 4.14 Differentials to Dated Brent

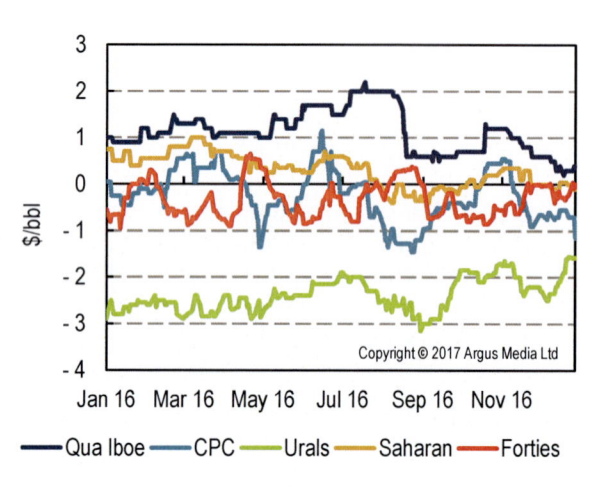

Figure 4.15 BFOE, Troll crude loadings (left), Crude imports into Rotterdam (right)

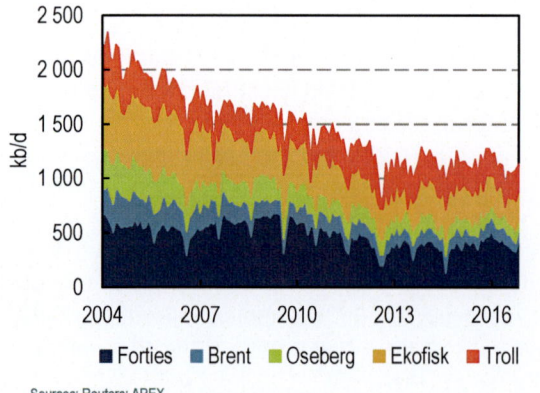

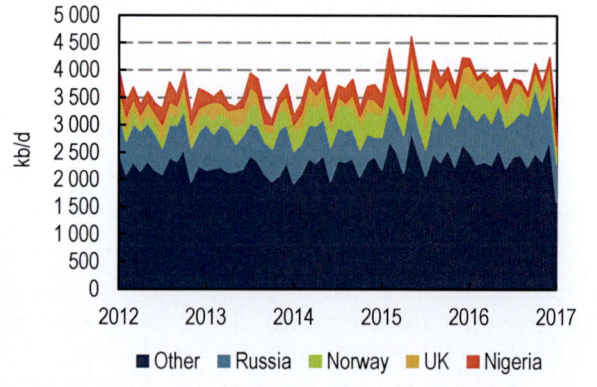

Sources: Reuters; APEX.

5. TABLES

Table 1
WORLD OIL SUPPLY AND DEMAND
(million barrels per day)

	1Q16	2Q16	3Q16	4Q16	2016	1Q17	2Q17	3Q17	4Q17	2017	2018	2019	2020	2021	2022
OECD DEMAND															
Americas	24.5	24.4	25.0	24.6	24.6	24.5	24.4	24.9	24.9	24.6	24.6	24.6	24.5	24.4	24.3
Europe	13.6	13.9	14.4	14.1	14.0	13.8	14.1	14.4	14.0	14.1	14.0	13.9	13.8	13.6	13.5
Asia Oceania	8.5	7.6	7.8	8.4	8.1	8.6	7.6	7.8	8.3	8.1	8.0	8.0	7.9	7.9	7.8
Total OECD	46.7	46.0	47.2	47.1	46.7	47.0	46.0	47.0	47.2	46.8	46.6	46.4	46.2	45.9	45.5
NON-OECD DEMAND															
FSU	4.6	4.6	5.0	5.0	4.8	4.7	4.8	5.1	5.1	4.9	5.0	5.1	5.2	5.3	5.4
Europe	0.7	0.7	0.7	0.7	0.7	0.7	0.7	0.7	0.7	0.7	0.7	0.7	0.8	0.8	0.8
China	11.7	12.1	11.7	12.1	11.9	11.9	12.2	12.3	12.6	12.2	12.6	12.9	13.1	13.4	13.7
Other Asia	13.1	13.1	12.8	13.5	13.1	13.8	13.7	13.4	13.9	13.7	14.3	14.8	15.4	15.9	16.4
Latin America	6.5	6.7	6.8	6.7	6.6	6.5	6.6	6.8	6.8	6.7	6.8	6.9	7.0	7.1	7.2
Middle East	8.0	8.5	8.9	8.4	8.5	8.2	8.6	9.1	8.5	8.6	8.8	9.0	9.2	9.5	9.7
Africa	4.2	4.2	4.1	4.2	4.2	4.4	4.3	4.2	4.4	4.3	4.5	4.6	4.8	5.0	5.1
Total Non-OECD	48.8	49.9	49.9	50.6	49.8	50.0	51.1	51.6	52.0	51.2	52.6	54.1	55.5	56.9	58.3
Total Demand[1]	**95.4**	**95.9**	**97.2**	**97.7**	**96.6**	**97.0**	**97.1**	**98.6**	**99.2**	**98.0**	**99.3**	**100.5**	**101.7**	**102.8**	**103.8**
OECD SUPPLY															
Americas[2]	19.9	19.0	19.3	19.7	19.5	19.6	19.6	19.9	20.0	19.8	20.5	21.1	21.4	21.7	21.8
Europe	3.6	3.4	3.3	3.6	3.5	3.5	3.5	3.2	3.5	3.4	3.4	3.3	3.4	3.5	3.4
Asia Oceania	0.4	0.4	0.4	0.4	0.4	0.4	0.4	0.4	0.4	0.4	0.4	0.5	0.6	0.6	0.5
Total OECD	23.9	22.8	23.1	23.7	23.4	23.5	23.5	23.5	24.0	23.6	24.4	24.9	25.3	25.7	25.8
NON-OECD SUPPLY															
FSU	14.3	14.0	14.0	14.5	14.2	14.4	14.2	14.3	14.5	14.3	14.6	14.6	14.5	14.4	14.3
Europe	0.1	0.1	0.1	0.1	0.1	0.1	0.1	0.1	0.1	0.1	0.1	0.1	0.1	0.1	0.1
China	4.2	4.1	3.9	3.9	4.0	3.9	3.9	3.8	3.8	3.8	3.8	3.8	3.7	3.7	3.7
Other Asia[2]	3.6	3.6	3.5	3.5	3.6	3.5	3.5	3.5	3.5	3.5	3.4	3.3	3.3	3.2	3.2
Latin America[2,4]	4.4	4.4	4.6	4.6	4.5	4.6	4.6	4.7	4.7	4.7	4.8	5.1	5.2	5.3	5.4
Middle East	1.3	1.3	1.3	1.3	1.3	1.2	1.2	1.2	1.2	1.2	1.2	1.2	1.2	1.2	1.2
Africa[2]	2.0	1.9	1.9	2.0	1.9	1.9	1.9	2.0	2.0	2.0	2.0	2.0	2.0	1.9	1.9
Total Non-OECD	29.8	29.4	29.4	29.9	29.6	29.6	29.5	29.7	29.8	29.6	30.0	30.1	30.0	29.9	29.9
Processing Gains[3]	2.3	2.3	2.3	2.3	2.3	2.3	2.3	2.3	2.3	2.3	2.3	2.3	2.4	2.4	2.4
Global Biofuels	1.9	2.5	2.7	2.3	2.3	2.0	2.5	2.8	2.5	2.5	2.6	2.7	2.8	2.8	2.8
Total Non-OPEC Supply[2]	57.9	57.0	57.5	58.2	57.6	57.5	57.7	58.3	58.5	58.0	59.3	60.1	60.4	60.7	60.9
OPEC															
Crude[4]	32.1	32.4	32.8	33.2	32.6										
OPEC NGLs	6.5	6.7	6.8	6.8	6.7	6.7	6.8	6.9	6.9	6.8	6.9	7.0	7.0	7.0	7.0
Total OPEC[2]	38.7	39.0	39.5	40.0	39.3										
Total Supply[4]	96.6	96.0	97.0	98.2	97.0										
Memo items:															
Call on OPEC crude + Stock ch.[5]	31.0	32.3	32.9	32.8	32.2	32.7	32.6	33.4	33.8	33.1	33.0	33.5	34.3	35.1	35.8

1 Measured as deliveries from refineries and primary stocks, comprises inland deliveries, international marine bunkers, refinery fuel, crude for direct burning, oil from non-conventional sources and other sources of supply. Includes Biofuels.
2 Other Asia includes Indonesia throughout. Latin America excludes Ecuador throughout. Africa excludes Angola and Gabon throughout.
  Total Non-OPEC excludes all countries that are currently members of OPEC.
  Total OPEC comprises all countries which are current OPEC members.
3 Net volumetric gains and losses in the refining process and marine transportation losses.
4 Comprises crude oil, condensates, NGLs, oil from non-conventional sources and other sources of supply.
5 Equals the arithmetic difference between total demand minus total non-OPEC supply minus OPEC NGLs.

Table 1a
WORLD OIL SUPPLY AND DEMAND: CHANGES FROM LAST MEDIUM-TERM REPORT
(million barrels per day)

	1Q15	2Q15	3Q15	4Q15	2015	1Q16	2Q16	3Q16	4Q16	2016	2017	2018	2019	2020	2021
OECD DEMAND															
Americas	0.2	0.3	0.3	0.1	0.2	0.1	0.2	0.4	-0.1	0.2	0.2	0.2	0.2	0.2	0.1
Europe	0.0	0.0	0.1	0.2	0.1	0.2	0.3	0.5	0.5	0.4	0.5	0.5	0.5	0.5	0.5
Asia Oceania	-0.1	-0.1	-0.1	-0.1	-0.1	-0.1	0.0	0.0	0.1	0.0	0.1	0.0	0.0	0.1	0.1
Total OECD	0.2	0.3	0.2	0.2	0.2	0.3	0.6	0.9	0.5	0.6	0.7	0.7	0.8	0.8	0.7
NON-OECD DEMAND															
FSU	-0.2	-0.3	-0.2	-0.2	-0.2	0.0	-0.2	-0.1	0.1	0.0	0.0	0.1	0.1	0.1	0.1
Europe	0.0	0.0	0.0	0.0	0.0	0.0	0.0	0.0	0.0	0.0	0.0	0.0	0.0	0.0	0.0
China	0.3	0.3	0.3	0.5	0.4	0.5	0.5	0.1	0.4	0.4	0.3	0.2	0.0	-0.1	-0.2
Other Asia	-0.1	0.0	0.0	0.0	0.0	0.1	0.1	0.0	0.2	0.1	0.2	0.3	0.4	0.5	0.6
Latin America	0.0	0.0	0.0	0.0	0.0	-0.1	-0.1	-0.1	-0.2	-0.1	-0.1	-0.1	-0.1	0.0	0.0
Middle East	0.2	0.2	0.3	0.3	0.3	0.2	0.1	0.0	0.2	0.1	0.1	0.1	0.0	0.0	0.0
Africa	0.0	0.0	0.0	0.0	0.0	-0.1	0.0	0.0	0.0	0.0	-0.1	-0.1	-0.1	0.0	0.0
Total Non-OECD	0.2	0.3	0.3	0.6	0.3	0.6	0.4	-0.1	0.7	0.4	0.4	0.4	0.4	0.5	0.6
Total Demand	**0.3**	**0.5**	**0.6**	**0.7**	**0.6**	**0.9**	**0.9**	**0.7**	**1.2**	**0.9**	**1.1**	**1.1**	**1.1**	**1.3**	**1.3**
OECD SUPPLY															
Americas	0.1	0.0	0.1	0.2	0.1	0.3	-0.3	0.0	0.1	0.0	0.4	0.6	0.5	0.2	-0.1
Europe	0.0	0.0	0.0	0.0	0.0	0.1	0.1	0.2	0.3	0.2	0.1	0.2	0.2	0.2	0.2
Asia Oceania	0.0	0.0	0.0	0.0	0.0	-0.1	-0.1	0.0	-0.1	-0.1	-0.1	-0.2	-0.1	-0.1	-0.1
Total OECD	0.1	0.1	0.1	0.2	0.1	0.3	-0.3	0.1	0.3	0.1	0.4	0.6	0.5	0.3	-0.1
NON-OECD SUPPLY															
FSU	0.0	0.0	0.0	0.1	0.1	0.2	0.1	0.1	0.7	0.3	0.5	0.8	0.8	0.7	0.6
Europe	0.0	0.0	0.0	0.0	0.0	0.0	0.0	0.0	0.0	0.0	0.0	0.0	0.0	0.0	0.0
China	0.0	0.0	0.0	0.0	0.0	-0.1	-0.2	-0.3	-0.4	-0.3	-0.4	-0.4	-0.4	-0.4	-0.4
Other Asia	0.0	0.0	0.0	0.0	0.0	0.1	0.0	0.0	0.0	0.0	-0.1	-0.1	-0.1	-0.1	-0.1
Latin America	0.0	0.0	0.0	0.0	0.0	-0.2	-0.1	0.0	0.0	-0.1	0.0	0.1	0.2	0.2	0.1
Middle East	0.0	0.0	0.0	0.0	0.0	0.0	0.1	0.1	0.1	0.1	0.1	0.1	0.1	0.1	0.1
Africa	0.0	0.0	0.0	0.0	0.0	-0.1	-0.2	-0.1	-0.1	-0.1	-0.1	0.0	0.0	0.0	0.0
Total Non-OECD	0.1	0.1	0.1	0.1	0.1	-0.1	-0.4	-0.3	0.2	-0.2	-0.1	0.4	0.5	0.5	0.4
Processing Gains	0.0	0.0	0.0	0.0	0.0	0.0	0.0	0.0	0.0	0.0	0.0	0.0	0.0	0.0	0.0
Global Biofuels	0.0	0.0	0.0	0.0	0.0	0.0	0.1	-0.1	-0.1	0.0	0.0	0.1	0.1	0.1	0.1
Total Non-OPEC	0.2	0.2	0.1	0.3	0.2	0.3	-0.7	-0.2	0.4	-0.1	0.3	0.9	1.1	0.8	0.3
OPEC															
Crude	0.1	0.0	0.1	0.1	0.1										
OPEC NGLs	-0.1	-0.1	0.0	0.0	-0.1	-0.1	0.0	0.0	0.0	0.0	0.0	0.0	0.0	0.0	0.0
Total OPEC	0.0	0.0	0.1	0.0	0.0										
Total Supply	**0.1**	**0.1**	**0.2**	**0.3**	**0.2**										
Memo items:															
Call on OPEC crude + Stock ch.	0.3	0.4	0.5	0.5	0.4	0.7	1.7	0.9	0.8	1.0	0.8	0.2	0.1	0.5	0.9

Table 2
SUMMARY OF GLOBAL OIL DEMAND

	1Q16	2Q16	3Q16	4Q16	2016	1Q17	2Q17	3Q17	4Q17	2017	2018	2019	2020	2021	2022
	1Q2016	2Q2016	3Q2016	4Q2016	2016	1Q2017	2Q2017	3Q2017	4Q2017	2017	2018	2019	2020	2021	2022
Demand (mb/d)															
Americas	24.5	24.4	25.0	24.6	24.6	24.5	24.4	24.9	24.9	24.4	24.6	24.4	24.5	24.4	24.2
Europe	13.6	13.9	14.4	14.1	14.0	13.8	14.1	14.4	14.0	14.1	14.0	13.9	13.8	13.3	13.5
Asia Oceania	8.5	7.6	7.8	8.4	8.1	8.6	7.6	7.8	8.3	8.0	8.0	8.0	7.9	7.9	7.8
Total OECD	46.7	46.0	47.2	47.1	46.7	47.0	46.0	47.0	47.2	46.8	46.6	46.4	46.2	45.9	45.5
Asia	24.8	25.2	24.5	25.6	25.0	25.6	25.9	25.6	26.5	25.9	26.8	27.7	28.5	29.3	30.1
Middle East	8.0	8.5	8.9	8.4	8.5	8.2	8.6	9.1	8.5	8.6	8.8	9.0	9.2	9.5	9.7
Latin America	6.5	6.7	6.8	6.7	6.6	6.5	6.6	6.8	6.8	6.7	6.8	6.9	7.0	7.1	7.2
FSU	4.6	4.6	5.0	5.0	4.8	4.7	4.8	5.1	5.1	4.9	5.0	5.1	5.2	5.3	5.4
Africa	4.2	4.2	4.1	4.2	4.2	4.4	4.3	4.2	4.4	4.3	4.5	4.6	4.8	5.0	5.1
Europe	0.7	0.7	0.7	0.7	0.7	0.7	0.7	0.7	0.7	0.7	0.7	0.7	0.8	0.8	0.8
Total Non-OECD	48.8	49.9	49.9	50.6	49.8	50.0	51.1	51.6	52.0	51.2	52.6	54.1	55.5	56.9	58.3
World	**95.4**	**95.9**	**97.2**	**97.7**	**96.6**	**97.0**	**97.1**	**98.6**	**99.2**	**98.0**	**99.3**	**100.5**	**101.7**	**102.8**	**103.8**
of which:															
US50	*19.4*	*19.4*	*19.9*	*19.6*	*19.6*	*19.5*	*19.4*	*19.8*	*19.8*	*19.6*	*19.6*	*19.6*	*19.5*	*19.4*	*19.3*
Euro5	*8.1*	*8.2*	*8.4*	*8.3*	*8.2*	*8.2*	*8.2*	*8.2*	*8.2*	*8.2*	*8.1*	*8.1*	*7.9*	*7.8*	*7.7*
China	*11.7*	*12.1*	*11.7*	*12.1*	*11.9*	*11.9*	*12.2*	*12.3*	*12.6*	*12.2*	*12.6*	*12.9*	*13.1*	*13.4*	*13.7*
Japan	*4.4*	*3.7*	*3.7*	*4.2*	*4.0*	*4.4*	*3.5*	*3.6*	*4.1*	*3.9*	*3.8*	*3.8*	*3.7*	*3.7*	*3.6*
India	*4.4*	*4.3*	*4.0*	*4.4*	*4.3*	*4.6*	*4.6*	*4.3*	*4.6*	*4.5*	*4.8*	*5.1*	*5.3*	*5.6*	*5.9*
Russia	*3.6*	*3.4*	*3.8*	*3.8*	*3.6*	*3.5*	*3.7*	*3.9*	*3.8*	*3.7*	*3.8*	*3.9*	*3.9*	*3.9*	*4.0*
Brazil	*3.0*	*3.1*	*3.1*	*3.1*	*3.1*	*3.0*	*3.0*	*3.1*	*3.2*	*3.1*	*3.1*	*3.2*	*3.2*	*3.2*	*3.3*
Saudi Arabia	*2.9*	*3.3*	*3.5*	*3.1*	*3.2*	*2.9*	*3.3*	*3.6*	*3.2*	*3.2*	*3.3*	*3.3*	*3.3*	*3.4*	*3.4*
Korea	*2.6*	*2.5*	*2.5*	*2.7*	*2.6*	*2.7*	*2.6*	*2.6*	*2.7*	*2.7*	*2.7*	*2.7*	*2.7*	*2.7*	*2.7*
Canada	*2.4*	*2.4*	*2.5*	*2.4*	*2.4*	*2.4*	*2.4*	*2.5*	*2.4*	*2.4*	*2.4*	*2.4*	*2.4*	*2.3*	*2.3*
Mexico	*2.0*	*1.9*	*1.9*	*2.0*	*2.0*	*1.9*	*1.9*	*1.9*	*2.0*	*1.9*	*1.9*	*1.9*	*1.9*	*1.9*	*2.0*
Iran	*2.0*	*1.9*	*1.9*	*2.0*	*2.0*	*2.1*	*2.0*	*2.0*	*2.0*	*2.0*	*2.1*	*2.2*	*2.2*	*2.3*	*2.3*
Total	*66.6*	*66.2*	*67.1*	*67.5*	*66.8*	*67.1*	*66.8*	*68.0*	*68.6*	*67.6*	*68.2*	*68.8*	*69.3*	*69.7*	*70.1*
% of World	*69.7*	*69.1*	*69.0*	*69.1*	*69.2*	*69.2*	*68.8*	*69.0*	*69.1*	*69.0*	*68.7*	*68.4*	*68.2*	*67.8*	*67.5*
Annual Change (% per annum)															
Americas[1]	0.1	-0.1	0.1	0.2	0.1	0.0	-0.2	-0.6	1.2	-0.9	0.9	-0.9	0.4	-0.4	-0.8
Europe[2]	1.4	2.6	1.6	2.8	2.1	1.5	1.1	-0.3	-0.8	0.4	-0.4	-0.7	-1.0	-3.5	1.2
Asia Oceania[3]	-1.5	0.9	1.0	2.2	0.6	0.8	-1.1	-0.2	-0.7	-1.1	0.0	-0.6	-0.5	-0.6	-0.6
Total OECD	0.2	0.9	0.7	1.3	0.8	0.6	0.1	-0.4	0.3	0.1	-0.3	-0.4	-0.5	-0.7	-0.8
Asia	4.9	4.3	2.7	4.5	4.1	3.4	2.9	4.6	3.6	3.6	3.4	3.2	3.0	2.8	2.8
Middle East	1.6	-0.3	-0.1	0.2	0.3	2.5	1.0	2.3	1.5	1.8	2.2	2.4	2.4	3.0	2.0
Latin America	-2.3	-1.6	-1.1	-2.1	-1.8	-0.1	-0.5	0.0	2.1	0.4	1.3	1.5	1.5	1.6	1.7
FSU	6.3	-0.8	3.0	6.1	3.6	0.1	5.1	3.9	0.7	2.4	2.2	1.7	1.5	1.5	1.4
Africa	1.8	3.8	3.4	2.8	2.9	4.7	2.7	2.4	2.9	3.2	3.6	3.7	3.6	3.5	3.3
Europe	3.4	5.1	2.2	3.0	3.4	3.0	0.7	2.0	2.5	2.0	2.7	2.3	2.1	2.1	1.9
Total Non-OECD	3.2	2.2	1.7	2.9	2.5	2.6	2.3	3.3	2.7	2.7	2.8	2.7	2.6	2.6	2.4
World	**1.7**	**1.6**	**1.2**	**2.1**	**1.7**	**1.6**	**1.2**	**1.5**	**1.5**	**1.5**	**1.4**	**1.3**	**1.1**	**1.1**	**1.0**
Annual Change (mb/d)															
Americas	0.0	0.0	0.0	0.1	0.0	0.0	0.0	-0.1	0.3	-0.2	0.2	-0.2	0.1	-0.1	-0.2
Europe	0.2	0.4	0.2	0.4	0.3	0.2	0.2	0.0	-0.1	0.0	-0.1	-0.1	-0.1	-0.5	0.2
Asia Oceania	-0.1	0.1	0.1	0.2	0.0	0.1	-0.1	0.0	-0.1	-0.1	0.0	0.0	0.0	-0.1	-0.1
Total OECD	0.1	0.4	0.3	0.6	0.4	0.3	0.0	-0.2	0.1	0.1	-0.2	-0.2	-0.2	-0.3	-0.3
Asia	1.2	1.0	0.6	1.1	1.0	0.8	0.7	1.1	0.9	0.9	0.9	0.9	0.8	0.8	0.8
Middle East	0.1	0.0	0.0	0.0	0.0	0.2	0.1	0.2	0.1	0.2	0.2	0.2	0.2	0.3	0.2
Latin America	-0.2	-0.1	-0.1	-0.1	-0.1	0.0	0.0	0.0	0.1	0.0	0.1	0.1	0.1	0.1	0.1
FSU	0.3	0.0	0.1	0.3	0.2	0.0	0.2	0.2	0.0	0.1	0.1	0.1	0.1	0.1	0.1
Africa	0.1	0.2	0.1	0.1	0.1	0.2	0.1	0.1	0.1	0.1	0.2	0.2	0.2	0.2	0.2
Europe	0.0	0.0	0.0	0.0	0.0	0.0	0.0	0.0	0.0	0.0	0.0	0.0	0.0	0.0	0.0
Total Non-OECD	1.5	1.1	0.8	1.4	1.2	1.2	1.1	1.6	1.4	1.4	1.4	1.4	1.4	1.5	1.4
World	**1.6**	**1.5**	**1.2**	**2.0**	**1.6**	**1.5**	**1.2**	**1.4**	**1.5**	**1.4**	**1.3**	**1.2**	**1.2**	**1.2**	**1.0**
Revisions to Oil Demand from Last Medium Term Report (mb/d)															
Americas	0.1	0.2	0.4	-0.1	0.2	0.2	0.2	0.2	0.1	0.2	0.2	0.2	0.2	0.1	
Europe	0.2	0.3	0.5	0.5	0.4	0.5	0.5	0.5	0.5	0.5	0.5	0.5	0.5	0.5	
Asia Oceania	-0.1	0.0	0.0	0.1	0.0	0.1	0.1	0.1	0.1	0.1	0.0	0.0	0.1	0.1	
Total OECD	0.3	0.6	0.9	0.5	0.6	0.7	0.7	0.7	0.7	0.7	0.7	0.8	0.8	0.7	
Asia	0.7	0.6	0.1	0.7	0.5	0.4	0.5	0.5	0.5	0.5	0.4	0.4	0.4	0.4	
Middle East	0.2	0.1	0.0	0.2	0.1	0.2	0.1	0.1	0.2	0.1	0.1	0.0	0.0	0.0	
Latin America	-0.1	-0.1	-0.1	-0.2	-0.1	-0.1	-0.1	-0.1	-0.1	-0.1	-0.1	-0.1	0.0	0.0	
FSU	0.0	-0.2	-0.1	0.1	0.0	0.0	0.0	0.0	0.0	0.0	0.1	0.1	0.1	0.1	
Africa	-0.1	0.0	0.0	0.0	0.0	-0.1	-0.1	-0.1	-0.1	-0.1	-0.1	-0.1	0.0	0.0	
Europe	0.0	0.0	0.0	0.0	0.0	0.0	0.0	0.0	0.0	0.0	0.0	0.0	0.0	0.0	
Total Non-OECD	0.6	0.4	-0.1	0.7	0.4	0.4	0.3	0.3	0.4	0.4	0.4	0.4	0.5	0.6	
World	**0.9**	**0.9**	**0.7**	**1.2**	**0.9**	**1.2**	**1.1**	**1.0**	**1.1**	**1.1**	**1.1**	**1.1**	**1.3**	**1.3**	
Revisions to Oil Demand Growth from Last Medium Term Report (mb/d)															
World	0.8	0.6	0.2	1.1	0.8	0.8	0.1	0.2	0.0	0.2	0.0	0.0	-0.1	0.1	

* France, Germany, Italy, Spain and UK

Table 3
WORLD OIL PRODUCTION
(million barrels per day)

	1Q16	2Q16	3Q16	4Q16	2016	1Q17	2Q17	3Q17	4Q17	2017	2018	2019	2020	2021	2022
OPEC															
Crude Oil															
Saudi Arabia	10.19	10.32	10.61	10.55	10.42										
Iran	3.14	3.59	3.67	3.79	3.55										
Iraq	4.30	4.30	4.43	4.62	4.41										
UAE	2.87	2.98	3.12	3.13	3.03										
Kuwait	2.89	2.86	2.92	2.86	2.88										
Neutral Zone	0.00	0.00	0.00	0.00	0.00										
Qatar	0.66	0.66	0.64	0.64	0.65										
Angola	1.76	1.74	1.72	1.61	1.71										
Gabon	0.23	0.23	0.23	0.22	0.23										
Nigeria	1.69	1.47	1.25	1.46	1.47										
Libya	0.36	0.32	0.31	0.57	0.39										
Algeria	1.10	1.09	1.13	1.12	1.11										
Ecuador	0.54	0.55	0.55	0.54	0.55										
Venezuela	2.39	2.26	2.19	2.12	2.24										
Total Crude Oil	32.13	32.36	32.77	33.23	32.63										
Total NGLs[1]	6.55	6.66	6.77	6.77	6.69	6.72	6.79	6.89	6.90	6.83	6.93	6.96	6.99	7.03	7.03
Total OPEC[2]	38.68	39.02	39.54	40.00	39.31										
NON-OPEC[3]															
OECD															
Americas	19.89	18.96	19.32	19.65	19.46	19.56	19.57	19.88	20.03	19.76	20.47	21.06	21.36	21.67	21.83
United States	12.73	12.61	12.29	12.52	12.54	12.60	12.89	12.97	13.18	12.91	13.49	13.91	14.09	14.21	14.19
Mexico	2.54	2.49	2.46	2.37	2.46	2.30	2.26	2.22	2.20	2.24	2.20	2.20	2.23	2.29	2.38
Canada	4.61	3.86	4.57	4.76	4.45	4.66	4.42	4.68	4.66	4.60	4.78	4.95	5.04	5.18	5.27
Chile	0.01	0.00	0.01	0.01	0.01	0.00	0.00	0.00	0.00	0.00	0.00	0.00	0.00	0.00	0.00
Europe	3.63	3.43	3.33	3.63	3.50	3.55	3.46	3.24	3.52	3.44	3.45	3.34	3.36	3.48	3.45
UK	1.08	1.04	0.96	0.98	1.01	1.00	0.98	0.89	0.98	0.96	1.07	1.07	1.03	1.00	0.98
Norway	2.04	1.93	1.90	2.12	2.00	2.02	1.97	1.84	2.03	1.96	1.88	1.81	1.89	2.04	2.05
Others	0.51	0.45	0.47	0.53	0.49	0.52	0.52	0.51	0.50	0.51	0.49	0.46	0.44	0.43	0.42
Asia Oceania	0.43	0.41	0.45	0.43	0.43	0.43	0.43	0.42	0.43	0.43	0.45	0.53	0.56	0.55	0.53
Australia	0.36	0.34	0.37	0.35	0.35	0.36	0.36	0.35	0.36	0.36	0.38	0.47	0.50	0.49	0.47
Others	0.08	0.08	0.08	0.07	0.08	0.07	0.07	0.07	0.07	0.07	0.07	0.06	0.06	0.06	0.06
Total OECD	23.95	22.80	23.10	23.70	23.39	23.54	23.46	23.54	23.98	23.63	24.36	24.93	25.28	25.70	25.81
NON-OECD															
Former USSR	14.26	14.04	13.99	14.51	14.20	14.38	14.25	14.31	14.46	14.35	14.56	14.57	14.49	14.39	14.34
Russia	11.30	11.21	11.27	11.58	11.34	11.43	11.28	11.33	11.47	11.38	11.45	11.44	11.40	11.39	11.31
Others	0.00	0.00	0.00	0.00	0.00	0.00	0.00	0.00	0.00	0.00	0.00	0.00	0.00	0.00	0.00
Asia[2]	7.84	7.64	7.49	7.46	7.61	7.39	7.33	7.29	7.24	7.31	7.25	7.09	7.01	6.97	6.90
China	4.19	4.06	3.95	3.93	4.03	3.90	3.86	3.82	3.78	3.84	3.84	3.76	3.72	3.74	3.74
Malaysia	0.73	0.71	0.70	0.70	0.71	0.69	0.69	0.70	0.71	0.70	0.69	0.66	0.65	0.64	0.64
India	0.85	0.85	0.85	0.84	0.85	0.84	0.83	0.83	0.83	0.83	0.82	0.82	0.82	0.82	0.78
Indonesia	0.88	0.88	0.88	0.88	0.88	0.87	0.87	0.86	0.86	0.87	0.84	0.82	0.80	0.78	0.75
Others	1.19	1.15	1.11	1.11	1.14	1.08	1.08	1.07	1.06	1.07	1.06	1.03	1.02	1.00	0.98
Europe	0.14	0.14	0.14	0.13	0.14	0.13	0.13	0.13	0.13	0.13	0.12	0.11	0.11	0.10	0.10
Latin America[2]	4.36	4.45	4.56	4.60	4.49	4.62	4.64	4.70	4.67	4.66	4.84	5.14	5.22	5.28	5.43
Brazil	2.40	2.55	2.73	2.77	2.61	2.80	2.81	2.88	2.86	2.84	3.05	3.38	3.49	3.57	3.69
Argentina	0.62	0.61	0.61	0.61	0.61	0.60	0.60	0.60	0.60	0.60	0.60	0.59	0.59	0.59	0.58
Colombia	0.96	0.91	0.85	0.85	0.89	0.84	0.85	0.85	0.84	0.85	0.83	0.80	0.77	0.74	0.72
Others	0.38	0.38	0.38	0.37	0.38	0.37	0.37	0.37	0.36	0.37	0.37	0.37	0.37	0.39	0.43
Middle East[2]	1.25	1.25	1.27	1.27	1.26	1.22	1.20	1.24	1.24	1.23	1.23	1.22	1.21	1.21	1.25
Oman	1.01	1.01	1.02	1.01	1.01	0.96	0.94	0.98	0.98	0.96	0.97	0.96	0.95	0.94	0.92
Syria	0.03	0.03	0.03	0.02	0.03	0.02	0.02	0.02	0.02	0.02	0.02	0.02	0.02	0.04	0.06
Yemen	0.01	0.01	0.02	0.03	0.02	0.03	0.03	0.03	0.03	0.03	0.02	0.02	0.02	0.03	0.05
Others	0.21	0.21	0.21	0.21	0.21	0.21	0.21	0.21	0.22	0.21	0.22	0.22	0.22	0.21	0.21
Africa	1.98	1.87	1.95	1.97	1.94	1.91	1.94	2.00	2.03	1.97	2.04	2.00	1.96	1.89	1.86
Egypt	0.70	0.70	0.69	0.67	0.69	0.67	0.66	0.65	0.65	0.66	0.63	0.61	0.58	0.56	0.54
Equatorial Guinea	0.29	0.28	0.28	0.28	0.28	0.29	0.28	0.28	0.27	0.28	0.26	0.23	0.21	0.20	0.18
Sudan	0.09	0.07	0.09	0.08	0.08	0.09	0.09	0.09	0.08	0.09	0.08	0.08	0.07	0.07	0.06
Others	0.90	0.82	0.90	0.93	0.89	0.87	0.91	0.98	1.02	0.94	1.06	1.09	1.09	1.07	1.08
Total Non-OECD	29.82	29.40	29.40	29.95	29.64	29.65	29.49	29.66	29.76	29.64	30.03	30.13	29.99	29.86	29.88
Processing Gains[4]	2.27	2.27	2.27	2.27	2.27	2.29	2.29	2.29	2.29	2.29	2.32	2.35	2.38	2.41	2.44
Global Biofuels	1.89	2.53	2.69	2.27	2.35	2.03	2.47	2.82	2.48	2.45	2.59	2.67	2.76	2.76	2.79
TOTAL NON-OPEC[2]	57.93	57.00	57.45	58.19	57.64	57.51	57.71	58.32	58.52	58.02	59.31	60.08	60.40	60.72	60.92
TOTAL SUPPLY	96.61	96.03	96.99	98.19	96.96										

1 Includes condensates reported by OPEC countries, oil from non-conventional sources, e.g. Venezuelan Orimulsion (but not Orinoco extra-heavy oil), and non-oil inputs to Saudi Arabian MTBE. Orimulsion production reportedly ceased from January 2007.
2 Total OPEC comprises all countries which are current OPEC members.
   Total Non-OPEC excludes all countries that are current members of OPEC.
   Latin America excludes Ecuador throughout. Africa excludes Angola and Gabon throughout. Asia excludes Indonesia throughout.
3 Comprises crude oil, condensates, NGLs and oil from non-conventional sources.
4 Net volumetric gains and losses in refining and marine transportation losses.

Table 3a
SELECTED NON-OPEC UPSTREAM PROJECT START-UPS

Country	Project	Peak Capacity (kbd)	Start Year	Country	Project	Peak Capacity (kbd)	Start Year
OECD Americas				UK	Mariner	55	2018
USA	Coalacanth	24	2016	UK	Cragganmore	20	2019
USA	Gunflint/Freedom	30	2016	UK	Cheviot	20	2020
USA	Heidelberg	80	2016	**OECD Asia Oceania**			
USA	Julia	30	2016	Australia	Wheatstone	30	2017
USA	Kodiak	20	2016	Australia	Prelude	30	2018
USA	Point Thomas	10	2016	Australia	Ichthys	130	2018
USA	Stones	50	2016	Australia	Greater Enfield	40	2020
USA	Thunder Horse	75	2016	**FSU**			
USA	Big Foot	75	2018	Russia	Vladimir Filanovsky	120	2016
USA	Stampede	80	2018	Russia	East Messoyakhskoe	100	2016
USA	Constellation (Hopkins)	15	2019	Russia	Trebs and Titov	100	2016
USA	Appomattox	175	2020	Russia	Novoportovskoye	100	2016
USA	Mad Dog Phase 2	140	2021	Russia	Taas-Yuriakh	100	2017
Canada	Christina Lake Ph F (Cenovus)	50	2016	Russia	Suzunskoye	90	2016
Canada	Foster Creek Ph G	30	2016	Russia	Yamal Mega project	100	2019
Canada	Horizon ph 2B	45	2016	Azerbaijan	Shah-Deniz 2	65	2018
Canada	Mackay River ph 1	35	2017	Kazakhstan	Kashagan phase 1a (restart)	375	2016
Canada	Hangingstone (Japan Canada Oil Sands	20	2017	Kazakhstan	Tengizchevroil FGP	260	2022
Canada	Fort Hills ph 1	160	2017	**Asia**			
Canada	Horizon ph 3	80	2017	China	Peng-Lai 19-3	80	2018
Canada	Hebron	150	2017	China	Weizhou -4	50	2020
Canada	Jackfish expansion	20	2018	India	Mumbai High	50	2018
Canada	Christina Lake Ph G	50	2019	India	B-127	15	2017
Canada	Pike 1A	35	2019	India	Manik	20	2021
Canada	Kirby North	40	2020	India	Barmer Hill	25	2018
Canada	Pike 1B	35	2020	Malaysia	Malikai	60	2016
Canada	Suncor - Meadow Creek East ph 1	40	2020	**Latin America**			
Canada	Mackay River ph 3	40	2021	Brazil	Atlanta EPS	45	2016
Canada	Mackay River ph 4	35	2022	Brazil	Cidade de Caraguatatuba (Lapa)	100	2016
Canada	Suncor - Meadow Creek East ph 2	40	2022	Brazil	Cidade de Marica (Lula Alto)	150	2016
OECD Europe				Brazil	Cidade de Saquarema (Lula Central)	150	2016
Denmark	Solsort	15	2022	Brazil	P-66 (Lula Sul)	150	2017
Denmark	Hibonite	15	2022	Brazil	Tartaruga Verde/Tartaruga Mestica	150	2017
Norway	Goliat	90	2016	Brazil	P-67 (Lula Norte)	150	2017
Norway	Ivar Aasen	55	2016	Brazil	Libra pilot	45	2018
Norway	Gina Krog	65	2017	Brazil	P-68 (Lula Ext. Sul)	150	2018
Norway	Martin Linge	40	2018	Brazil	Libra ph 1	180	2020
Norway	Kristin	40	2019	Brazil	Buzios Phase 1-5	750	2018-20
Norway	Trestakk	20	2019	Brazil	Marlim redevelopment	100	2021
Norway	Njord	50	2020	Brazil	Sepia	180	2021
Norway	Johan Sverdrup ph 1	440	2020	Brazil	Berbigao/Sururu (Iara)	140	2022
Norway	Oda	35	2020	Guyana	Liza	100	2020
UK	Monarb redevelopment	25	2016	**Africa**			
UK	Solan	20	2016	Congo	Nene Marine	35	2016
UK	Schiehallion (Quad 204)	120	2017	Congo	Moho North	100	2017
UK	Catcher	45	2017	Congo	Litchendjili	10	2017
UK	Clair Ridge	120	2017	Ghana	Tweneboa-Enyera-Ntomme	80	2016
UK	Kraken	50	2017	Ghana	OTCP	30	2018
UK	Western Isles	30	2017	Uganda	Albert Basin (Kingfisher)	60	2021

Table 3b
Selected OPEC upstream project start-ups

Country	Project	Peak Capacity (kbd)	Start Year
Crude Oil Projects			
Angola	Mafumeira Sul	150	2016
Angola	East Hub Development	80	2017
Angola	Kaombo	230	2017
Angola	Malange	50	2021
Ecuador	ITT (Ishpingo-Tambococha-Tiputini)	160	2016
Iran	North Azadegan (Phase 1)	75	2016
Iran	Yadavaran (Phase 1)	115	2016
Kuwait	Ratqa	270	2018
Nigeria	Bonga NW	45	2016
Nigeria	Erha North 2	50	2016
Nigeria	Etim/Asasa	60	2016
Nigeria	Egina	220	2017
Nigeria	Uge	80	2020
Nigeria	Zabazaba/Etan	120	2022
Nigeria	Bonga SW & Aparo	150	2022
Saudi	Shaybah Expansion	250	2016
Saudi	Khurais Expansion	300	2018
UAE	Nasr	65	2018
UAE	Sarb	100	2018
UAE	Umm Lulu	105	2018

Country	Project	Peak Capacity (kbd)	Start Year
NGL & Condensate Projects			
Angola	Mafumeira Sul Phase 2--Block 0	10	2016
Iran	South Pars 15 & 16	30	2016
Iran	South Pars 15-16 (condensate)	75	2016
Iran	South Pars 19 (condensate)	75	2016
Qatar	Barzan condensate	50	2016
Saudi	Hasbah (Wasit)	30	2016
Saudi	Shaybah NGL (non-associated)	275	2016

Table 3c
Non-OPEC supply - MTOMR and WEO definitions
(million barrels per day)

	Calculation	2006	2011	2016	2017	2018	2019	2020	2021	2022
Medium Term Oil Market Report definitions										
NON-OPEC SUPPLY		50.1	52.3	57.6	58.0	59.3	60.1	60.4	60.7	60.9
Processing gains		2.0	2.1	2.3	2.3	2.3	2.3	2.4	2.4	2.4
Global biofuels		0.8	1.8	2.3	2.5	2.6	2.7	2.8	2.8	2.8
NON-OPEC PRODUCTION (excl. processing gains and biofuels)	1	47.3	48.3	53.0	53.3	54.4	55.1	55.3	55.6	55.7
Crude	2	41.4	41.8	45.0	45.0	45.8	46.3	46.3	46.5	46.5
of which: Condensate	3	2.2	2.4	2.9	3.0	3.1	3.3	3.4	3.5	3.4
Tight oil	4	0.0	1.1	4.3	4.5	5.0	5.4	5.6	5.8	5.8
Un-upgraded bitumen	5	0.5	0.8	1.5	1.6	1.8	1.9	2.0	2.1	2.2
NGLs	6	4.7	5.2	6.6	6.8	7.1	7.2	7.4	7.5	7.6
Syncrude (Canada)	7	0.6	0.9	0.9	1.0	1.1	1.1	1.1	1.1	1.1
CTL, GTL, kerogen oil and additives[1]	8	0.5	0.5	0.4	0.4	0.4	0.5	0.5	0.5	0.5
World Energy Outlook definitions										
NON-OPEC PRODUCTION (excl. processing gains and biofuels)	=1	47.3	48.3	53.0	53.3	54.4	55.1	55.3	55.6	55.7
Conventional		45.6	45.1	45.8	45.7	46.1	46.2	46.1	46.0	46.0
Crude oil	=2-3-4-5	38.7	37.5	36.3	35.9	35.9	35.7	35.3	35.1	35.0
Natural gas liquids (total)	=3+6	6.9	7.6	9.5	9.8	10.2	10.5	10.8	10.9	11.0
Unconventional		1.2	2.7	6.8	7.1	7.8	8.3	8.7	9.0	9.1
EHOB (incl. syncrude)[2]	=5+7	1.1	1.6	2.4	2.6	2.8	2.9	3.0	3.2	3.3
Tight oil	=4	0.0	1.1	4.3	4.5	5.0	5.4	5.6	5.8	5.8
CTL, GTL, kerogen oil and additives[1]	=8	0.5	0.5	0.4	0.4	0.4	0.5	0.5	0.5	0.5

1 CTL = coal to liquids; GTL = gas to liquids.
2 Extra-heavy oil and bitumen

Table 4

WORLD REFINERY CAPACITY ADDITIONS
(thousand barrels per day)

	2016	2017	2018	2019	2020	2021	2022	Total
Refining Capacity Additions and Expansions[1]								
OECD Americas	105	40	193					233
OECD Europe	-268		200					200
OECD Asia Oceania	-143	-132						-132
FSU	46	35	138	60	30			263
Non-OECD Europe								
China	70	560	60	260	420	600	320	2,220
Other Asia	-220	460		182	250	470	252	1,614
Latin America		40			33			73
Middle East	156	170	88	520	317	633	177	1,905
Africa	30	30		60	30		530	650
Total World	-224	1,203	679	1,082	1,080	1,703	1,279	7,026
Upgrading Capacity Additions[2]								
OECD Americas	127		55					55
OECD Europe	20		128					128
OECD Asia Oceania								
FSU	254	240	375	176	95			886
Non-OECD Europe	40							
China	45	410	182	34		430	94	1,150
Other Asia	185		31	80			45	156
Latin America				29		133		162
Middle East	147	-41		221	41	215	180	617
Africa		57	20	75				152
Total World	819	666	791	615	136	778	319	3,305
Desulphurisation Capacity Additions[3]								
OECD Americas		35						35
OECD Europe	-170		114					114
OECD Asia Oceania								
FSU	73	97	98					195
Non-OECD Europe								
China	152	425	296	60		492	180	1,453
Other Asia	18	90	10	209			50	359
Latin America	48			64		74		138
Middle East	140	60	107	425	122	811		1,525
Africa	95	42	45					87
Total World	356	750	670	757	122	1,376	230	3,905

1 Comprises new refinery projects or expansions to existing facilities including condensate splitter additions. Assumes zero capacity creep.
2 Comprises gross capacity additions to coking, hydrocracking, residue hydrocracking, visbreaking, FCC or RFCC capacity.
3 Comprises additions to hydrotreating and hydrodesulphurisation capacity.

Table 4a
WORLD REFINERY CAPACITY ADDITIONS:
Changes from Last Medium-Term Report
(thousand barrels per day)

	2015	2016	2017	2018	2019	2020	2021	Total
Refining Capacity Additions and Expansions[1]								
OECD Americas	-34	-296	-200	93	-40			-443
OECD Europe		-10		-14				-24
OECD Asia Oceania	20	175	-155					21
FSU	132		-105	88	60	30		73
Non-OECD Europe	-6							
China	-74	-257	-70	-210	-180	120	400	-197
Other Asia	90	-145	190	-260	-10	-214	370	-69
Latin America	13		40	-205	-33	-7	-280	-485
Middle East	-29	-150	118	38	-185	-136	-122	-437
Africa			30	-106	-60	-500		-636
Total World	112	-682	-152	-576	-448	-707	368	-2,197
Upgrading Capacity Additions[2]								
OECD Americas								
OECD Europe								
OECD Asia Oceania								
FSU								
Non-OECD Europe								
China								
Other Asia		-33						-33
Latin America			-163	-85				-248
Middle East						-108	108	
Africa					25			25
Total World		-33	-163	-85	25	-108	108	-256
Desulphurisation Capacity Additions[3]								
OECD Americas								
OECD Europe								
OECD Asia Oceania								
FSU								
Non-OECD Europe								
China								
Other Asia		-84	90					6
Latin America			-40	-80				-120
Middle East		-60	60			-72	72	
Africa								
Total World		-144	110	-80		-72	72	-114

1 Comprises new refinery projects or expansions to existing facilities including condensate splitter additions. Assumes zero capacity creep.
2 Comprises stand-alone additions to coking, hydrocracking or FCC capacity. Excludes upgrading additions counted under 'Refinery Capacity Additions and Expansions' category.
3 Comprises stand-alone additions to hydrotreating and hydrodesulphurisation capacity. Excludes desulphurisation additions counted under 'Refinery Capacity Additions and Expansions' category.

Table 4b
SELECTED REFINERY CRUDE DISTILATION PROJECT LIST

Country	Project	Capacity (kbd)[1]	Start Year	Country	Project	Capacity (kbd)[1]	Start Year
OECD Americas				*China*			
Canada	North West Redwater Partnership - Edmonton	80	2018	China	Rongsheng Petrochemical - Zhoushan island	400	2021
United States	Targa Resources - Corpus Christi	35	2018	China	Shenghong Petrochemical - Lianyungang	320	2022
United States	Meridian Resources - Davis, North Dakota	27	2018	China	PetroChina - Kunming	260	2017
United States	Calument Montana Refining - Great Falls	20	2017	China	CNOOC - Huizhou	200	2017
United States	ExxonMobil - Beaumont	20	2017	China	PetroChina - Jieyang	200	2021
United States	Valero - St. Charles	20	2018	China	Sinopec - Shanghai Gaoqiao	140	2019
United States	Flint Hills Resources - Corpus Christi	16	2018	China	Ningbo Daxie - Ningbo Zhejiang	120	2020
United States	Valero - Port Arthur	15	2018	China	CNGC - Huajin, Lianoning	120	2019
OECD Europe				China	PetroChina - Renqiu, Hebei	100	2017
Turkey	Socar - Aliaga	200	2018	China	Sinopec - Jingmen	100	2020
OECD Asia Oceania				China	Sinochem - Quanzhou	60	2018
Japan	Fuji Oil - Sodegaura	-13	2017	China	Sinopec - Zhanjiang, Guangdong	200	2020
Japan	Showa Shell - various	-34	2017	*India*			
Japan	Idemitsu Kosan - Ichihara	-50	2017	India	Indian Oil Co. Ltd. - Panipat	200	2021
Japan	Cosmo Oil - Yokkoaichi	-63	2017	india	BPCL - Visakhapatnam	150	2021
Japan	Tonen General - various	-72	2017	India	BPCL - Kochi, Ambalamugal	120	2017
South Korea	HyunDai Oil Refinery - Seosan	100	2017	India	Indian Oil Co. Ltd. - Koyali, Gujarat	86	2019
Middle East				India	Indian Oil Co. Ltd. - Barauni	60	2021
Bahrain	Bahrain Petroleum Co. - Sitra	355	2020	India	HPCL - Mahul, Mumbai	60	2019
Bahrain	Bahrain Petroleum Co. - Sitra	-262	2021	India	Indian Oil Co. Ltd. - Mathura	60	2021
Iran	National Iranian Oil Co. - Abadan	195	2020	India	HPCL/MITTAL (HMEL) - Bhatinda	44	2017
Iran	National Iranian Oil Co. - Persian Gulf Star Refinery	120	2019	India	BPCL - Mumbai	40	2022
Iran	National Iranian Oil Co. - Persian Gulf Star Refinery	112	2017	India	BPCL - Bina	36	2019
Iran	National Iranian Oil Co. - Persian Gulf Star Refinery	112	2017	*Other Asia*			
Iran	National Iranian Oil Co. - Siraf	60	2022	Brunei	Zhejiang Hengyi Petrochemicals - Pulau Muara Besar	160	2022
Iran	National Iranian Oil Co. - Abadan	-233	2020	China, Taiwan	Chinese Petroleum Corp. - Ta-Lin	150	2017
Iraq	INOC - Karbala	140	2022	China, Taiwan	Chinese Petroleum Corp. - Ta-Lin	46	2017
Iraq	Qaiwan - Bazian	50	2021	China, Taiwan	Chinese Petroleum Corp. - Ta-Lin	-100	2017
Kuwait	Kuwait National Petroleum Co. - Shuaiba	-186	2017	Indonesia	Pertamina - Balikpapan, Kalimantan	100	2020
Kuwait	Kuwait National Petroleum Co. - Al-Zour	615	2021	Indonesia	Pertamina/Saudi Aramco - Cilacap, Central Java	52	2022
Kuwait	Kuwait National Petroleum Co. - Mina Abdulla	200	2018	Malaysia	Petronas - RAPID	150	2020
Kuwait	Kuwait National Petroleum Co. - Mina al-Ahmadi	-112	2018	Viet Nam	PetroVietnam/KPC/Idemitsu Kosan - Nghi Son	200	2017
Oman	Oman Refinery Co. - Duqm	230	2021	*FSU*			
Oman	Oman Refinery Co. - Sohar	82	2017	Azerbaijan	SOCAR - Heydar Aliev	30	2020
Saudi Arabia	Saudi Aramco - Jizan	400	2019	Belarus	Naftan - Novopolotsk	35	2017
Saudi Arabia	Saudi Aramco - Rabigh 2	50	2017	Kazakhstan	Kazmunigas - Pavlodar	20	2018
Saudi Arabia	Saudi Aramco - Jeddah	-88	2022	Kazakhstan	Kazmunigaz/PetroChina - Chimkent	15	2018
United Arab	ENOC - Jebel Ali	65	2022	Kazakhstan	Kazmunigas - Atyrau	10	2018
Africa				Russia	Mari El refinery - Mari Republic	63	2018
Cameroon	SONARA - Cape Limboh Limbe	30	2017	Russia	Yayski - Irkutsk	60	2019
Egypt	MIDOR - Alexandria	60	2019	Russia	Antipinsky Refinery - Antipinsky	30	2018
Nigeria	Dangote Oil Refining Company - Lagos	500	2022	*Non-OECD Americas*			
Uganda	Total/Tullow/CNOOC - Albertine Graben	30	2020	Argentina	Bridas - Campana	40	2017
Uganda	Total/Tullow/CNOOC - Albertine Graben	30	2022	Peru	Petroperu SA - Talara	33	2020

Table 5
World Ethanol Production[1]
(thousand barrels per day)

	2015	2016	2017	2018	2019	2020	2021	2022
OECD North America	996	1,019	1,027	1,034	1,039	1,044	1,045	1,045
United States	966	991	998	1,003	1,008	1,013	1,013	1,013
Canada	29	28	28	28	27	27	26	26
OECD Europe	88	81	94	107	110	115	99	94
Austria	5	4	4	4	4	4	3	3
Belgium	6	7	7	8	8	8	7	7
France	17	15	17	18	19	20	16	16
Germany	16	16	17	17	17	17	16	15
Italy	0	0	0	1	1	1	1	1
Netherlands	6	2	5	7	7	8	6	6
Poland	4	3	4	4	5	5	4	3
Spain	8	6	8	9	9	9	8	6
UK	9	8	11	14	15	16	13	13
OECD Pacific	4	5	5	8	9	9	9	9
Australia	4	4	4	6	7	7	7	7
Total OECD	**1,089**	**1,105**	**1,126**	**1,148**	**1,157**	**1,168**	**1,153**	**1,147**
FSU	3	3	3	4	4	4	4	4
Non-OECD Europe	1	1	1	2	2	2	2	2
China	45	49	56	59	62	65	66	67
Other Asia	41	49	50	68	76	85	91	91
India	13	19	18	25	29	32	36	36
Indonesia	1	1	1	1	1	1	1	1
Malaysia	0	0	0	0	0	0	0	0
Philippines	3	4	5	5	5	5	6	6
Singapore	1	1	1	1	1	1	1	1
Thailand	20	21	22	30	34	39	41	41
Latin America	552	519	536	568	588	616	642	670
Argentina	14	14	15	17	18	19	19	19
Brazil	516	469	499	526	544	572	596	624
Colombia	8	8	9	9	9	10	10	10
Middle East	1	1	1	1	1	1	1	1
Africa	4	4	5	6	9	10	11	11
Total Non-OECD	**648**	**625**	**652**	**708**	**741**	**783**	**817**	**847**
Total World	**1,737**	**1,730**	**1,778**	**1,856**	**1,899**	**1,951**	**1,970**	**1,994**

1 Volumetric production; to convert to energy adjusted production, ethanol is assumed to have 2/3 energy content of conventional gasoline.

Table 5a
World Biodiesel Production
(thousand barrels per day)

	2015	2016	2017	2018	2019	2020	2021	2022
OECD North America	88	105	112	122	129	134	135	136
United States	83	98	104	114	120	124	124	126
Canada	5	6	8	8	9	10	10	10
OECD Europe	228	227	237	254	258	268	234	232
Austria	4	5	5	6	6	6	6	6
Belgium	5	7	7	8	8	9	8	7
France	46	41	44	45	45	45	42	40
Germany	57	50	52	58	58	62	52	52
Italy	9	11	13	14	14	15	12	12
Netherlands	32	31	31	33	34	35	29	29
Poland	17	16	15	17	17	18	15	15
Spain	22	25	26	27	28	28	23	22
UK	3	3	5	6	7	8	8	8
OECD Pacific	11	12	12	12	12	13	13	13
Australia	3	1	1	1	1	3	3	3
Total OECD	327	344	361	388	399	416	382	381
FSU	3	3	3	3	3	3	3	3
Non-OECD Europe	3	3	3	4	5	5	3	3
China	16	19	22	23	25	28	29	29
Other Asia	92	114	138	162	173	188	198	203
India	3	3	3	5	5	7	8	10
Indonesia	29	50	68	87	94	102	108	111
Malaysia	17	15	18	20	22	23	23	24
Philippines	3	3	3	4	4	9	9	9
Singapore	18	18	17	18	18	18	18	18
Thailand	21	23	28	29	29	30	30	30
Latin America	119	133	143	154	162	168	169	172
Argentina	35	51	51	56	60	60	60	60
Brazil	67	66	77	82	85	91	92	93
Colombia	10	9	9	10	10	11	11	12
Middle East	0	0	1	1	1	1	1	1
Africa	2	3	3	4	4	5	5	5
Total Non-OECD	235	275	313	352	374	398	409	416
Total World	562	618	674	741	773	814	791	797

Online bookshop

www.iea.org/books

PDF versions at 20% discount

E-mail: books@iea.org

International Energy Agency
iea
Secure Sustainable Together

- Global Gas Security series
- Energy Policies Beyond IEA Countries series
- Energy Statistics series
- Energy Technology Perspectives series
- Gas
- Coal
- Oil
- Renewable Energy
- World Energy Outlook series
- Energy Efficiency Market Report
- Energy Policies of IEA Countries series
- World Energy Investment series
- Medium-Term Market Reports series

This publication reflects the views of the IEA Secretariat but does not necessarily reflect those of individual IEA member countries. The IEA makes no representation or warranty, express or implied, in respect of the publication's contents (including its completeness or accuracy) and shall not be responsible for any use of, or reliance on, the publication.

Unless otherwise indicated, all material presented in figures and tables is derived from IEA data and analysis.

This document, as well as any data and any map included herein are without prejudice to the status of or sovereignty over any territory, to the delimitation of international frontiers and boundaries and to the name of any territory, city or area.

IEA Publications,
International Energy Agency
Website: www.iea.org
Contact information: www.iea.org/aboutus/contactus
Typeset in France and Printed in France by IEA, Mars 2017
Cover design: IEA. Photo credits: © Shutterstock, Inc : Pumatokoh.

IEA/OECD possible corrigenda on: www.oecd.org/about/publishing/corrigenda.htm

The paper used has been produced respecting
PEFC's ecological, social and ethical standards